Items should be ret
shown below. Item
borrowers may b
telephone. To r
barcode label
This can be
Renew onl'
Fines cha
incurred
charged

Leab

Dι
Bail

r

WAR AND REVOLUTION
IN THE WEST OF IRELAND

Dr Conor McNamara has written extensively about the history of the Irish revolution and rural society. He was previously a winner of the National Library of Ireland, History Fellowship (2009) and was awarded the 1916 Scholar in Residence at NUI Galway (2015–17). He was a Moore Institute, NUI Galway, Visiting Fellow (2017) and this is his fourth publication.

WAR AND REVOLUTION IN THE WEST OF IRELAND

GALWAY, 1913–22

Conor McNamara

IRISH ACADEMIC PRESS

First published in 2018 by
Irish Academic Press
10 George's Street
Newbridge
Co. Kildare
Ireland
www.iap.ie

9781785371608 (Paper)
9781785371592 (Cloth)
9781788550192 (Kindle)
9781788550208 (Epub)
9781788550215 (PDF)

British Library Cataloguing in Publication Data
An entry can be found on request

Library of Congress Cataloging in Publication Data
An entry can be found on request

Interior design by www.jminfotechindia.com
Typeset in Adobe Garamond 11/14 pt

Cover design by www.phoenix-graphicdesign.com
Cover/jacket front: Members of the Irish Volunteers and RIC outside Athenry
RIC barracks in advance of the handover of the building to the Volunteers, 1922.
Courtesy Sean Cleary, Athenry, Co. Galway.
Cover/jacket back: Body of Volunteer Pat Loughnane, murdered by Crown Forces,
Shanaglish, Co. Galway, November 1920.
Courtesy Hardiman Library, NUIG.

Printed and bound by TJ International Ltd, Padstow, Cornwall

Contents

Acknowledgements

I relied upon the support of a large number of scholars, friends and researchers in the writing of this book. Cormac Ó Comhraí read an early draft and gave valuable feedback. Tony Varley was as supportive as ever with his knowledge of the complexities of land issues in the West. Carla King supervised the original doctoral thesis from which this study emerged and I am most grateful for her support. Tom Desmond Senior was an inspirational mentor in the Manuscripts Department of the National Library. Miriam Moffitt was most generous with her research on the Protestant experience of revolution. Martin O'Donoghue read sections of the manuscript and provided valuable insights into the period during our time in Galway. I am most grateful to Mary Harris, History Department, NUI Galway, for giving me a wonderful opportunity at the University. Dan Carey, Moore Institute, NUI Galway, has been most encouraging and supportive of my work throughout my time at the Moore Institute. Likewise, Martha Shaughnessy and Chloe Michaels Graham, Moore Institute, and John Cox, Aisling Keane, Niall McSweeney and Barry Houlihan of the Hardiman Library have been most helpful. Marie Mannion, Heritage Officer, Galway County Council, has been exceptional in promoting public history in the West. Éamonn Gilligan and Gerry Cloonan, Craughwell; Brian Quinn, Gabe Cronnelly and Séan Cleary, Athenry; Luke Callinan, Galway and too many others to mention, have given me the benefit of their knowledge of the characters and events described in this book. All the team at Irish Academic Press, including Conor Graham, Myles McCionnaith, Ciara Connelly and Fiona Dunne have been fantastic to work with. I am very grateful to the Moore Institute, NUI Galway for awarding me a Visiting Scholar Award in late 2017 which allowed me to finish this project. My greatest thanks is due to John Cunningham, History Department, NUI Galway, for his encouragement and support. I am grateful to Jackie and Matthew Meagher, New York, and Gerard Meagher and everyone at The Old Town, Manhattan, for their wonderful support over the last number of years. I would like to thank my wife Meredith for her unstinting belief in this project. I am most thankful to my parents, Dermot and Helen, for instilling in all of us an enduring interest in Irish history.

Conor McNamara
Athenry, Co. Galway
February 2018

List of Tables

INTRODUCTION

'The Gnarled and Stony Clods of Townland's Tip': Galway in 1913

This study explores social and political change in Galway from 1913 to 1922 and examines how rural communities mediated the unprecedented upheaval of the revolutionary period. The period that has become known as the Irish revolution was traditionally perceived as an heroic phase in the Irish nation's historic quest for national self-determination, culminating in the withdrawal of the Crown Forces and the victory of the revolutionary forces of the Republic. The struggle for independence was fought within a climate of insecurity and fear, however, and the uncertainty that the rise of militant nationalism engendered, fuelled political antagonism between an older, more respectable generation of nationalists and an impatient generation of young revolutionaries.

The under-articulated fault lines of rural society were frequently obscured in national political discourse by the unchallenged hegemony of the Irish Parliamentary Party (IPP) and the distaste for sectional politics which the desire for nationalist solidarity inculcated. Political culture in Galway – as elsewhere in Ireland – was characterised by factionalism and the intensity of local political rivalries. For many nationalists, the rise of militant republicanism represented the primordial forces of anarchy and bloodshed, and rural communities were required to choose between the old and respectable, and the new, the young and the unknown. This study examines the uncertainty the republican campaign generated among ordinary nationalists which frequently manifested itself across generational cleavages between younger republicans and older generations of nationalists, an economic chasm between the rural poor and strong farmers and landowners, a political gulf between the urban world of the small town and its rural environs, and a sectarian rift between the small Protestant community and the Catholic majority.

The principal issues permeating scholarly investigation into the Irish revolution concern the extent to which ordinary people's social and political aspirations evolved and the degree to which they found expression in the respective campaigns of the Irish Volunteers and Sinn Féin. The evolution of the struggle reflected the broader complexities of Irish society and the advance of violent nationalism defies a linear, national meta-narrative. A comprehensive study of events within diverse communities reveals many surprising and frequently awkward conclusions, which in retrospect, could not have been accommodated in the domain of conventional local history.

Political revolution fuelled a violent and traumatic period of turmoil and the social solidarity required by the leadership of nationalist Ireland partially obscured the complexity of a society characterised by divergent political traditions. To gain an appreciation of the formative dynamics of the Irish revolution, an analysis of the complex evolution of public opinion across diverse regions and communities is necessary. A coherent understanding of the nuances of local communities, events and personalities must be integrated into any survey of national transformations. A uniformity of experience of political upheaval across disparate regions cannot be assumed in a society where an intensely local sense of identity saw national events interpreted through distinctly local prisms of identity and allegiance. A failure to grasp the complex spectrum of regional distinctiveness reinforces an assumed meta-narrative, strengthening an imagined national narrative.

While nationalist political discourse before the rise of the Volunteers appeared fundamentally consensual, respectable and deferential, this apparent consensus concealed a complexity of allegiance and diversity of political tradition that found full expression in the rough and tumble of local politics. On a national level, malcontents on the nationalist fringe could be dismissed as deviant or insignificant within the culture of political complacency which the imminent arrival of Home Rule sustained. To extrapolate consensus between political elites into a similar political complacency at a local level, however, represents a failure to acknowledge the complex spectrum of political traditions that existed within Irish nationalism.

Counties Galway and Clare were exceptional in the opening decades of the twentieth century for the amount of violence over land. Initially, this book examines the nature and evolution of land agitation in the years prior to the emergence of militant republicanism. Only through a thorough examination of the capacity of agrarian groups to organise, agitate and mobilise at the beginning of this period can the later waves of agrarianism, facilitated by the rise of militant republicanism, be contextualised.

Pivotal developments that transformed nationalist Ireland were witnessed in 1914, invigorating the tradition of physical force and ultimately destroying the IPP. One of the many unforeseen casualties of the conflict, John Redmond's party was ultimately a victim of its support for the British War effort. This study undertakes to examine the impact of the First World War, recruitment to the military, the political culture of the IPP and the evolution of the Irish Volunteers in the period before the 1916 Rising.

Within this context, the remarkable events of Easter Week 1916 in Galway are examined. In the historiography of Easter Week, events outside Dublin have, until recently, received scant attention and most standard works on the topic have focused solely on the capital. The national aspect of the 1916 Rising has been neglected to the detriment of a full appreciation of the aims of the Rebellion's planners. A close analysis of events in Galway, where the enigmatic Liam Mellows was Volunteer organiser, illustrates the potential for popular mobilisation that existed outside the capital. The consequences for the three hundred men deported from the county in the aftermath of the Rebellion and for Liam Mellows, in particular, were significant.

In Galway as elsewhere, Sinn Féin decisively defeated the IPP in the 1918 General Election and their success was driven by a series of political and economic factors, of which, the War was the formative catalyst. The veteran leaders of Galway's political establishment faced a younger, more energetic cadre of opponents, many of whom had been incarcerated for their political beliefs. The political and economic developments that facilitated the rise of Sinn Féin and the Volunteers before the outbreak of the War of Independence are the next factors considered.

The Independence struggle in Galway was characterised by a campaign of attrition by the Volunteers against the Royal Irish Constabulary (RIC), and by the Crown Forces against the civilian population in general, including members of the Volunteers. In terms of the regional distribution of republican activity, a key theme of the literature has been the disparate regional variations between active and non-active areas. A spatial differentiation in terms of violence emerged in Galway as the Volunteers in the north of the county, along with those in the western districts of Connemara, carried out the bulk of attacks on the Crown Forces while the towns, and parts of the east of the county remained relatively unaffected by violence. In considering this, the factors that contributed to the emergence of active republican areas and the evolution of guerrilla warfare are explored.

Following on from this, the book examines the impact of the Crown Forces in Galway and the experience of local communities in the face of unprecedented violence. The conduct of the Crown Forces in Galway matches that of some of the most active areas in Ireland, in terms of the extreme nature of the violence perpetrated on civilians and republicans alike. In Galway, the violence of the police outweighed the threat the Volunteers represented, and a sustained republican campaign proved problematic. The reckless behaviour of the Crown Forces played a formative role in conditioning the response of both the Volunteers and the wider community to the independence struggle.

The experience of the southern Protestant community during the years 1918–22 was undoubtedly negative and accelerated the pre-existing trend of migration of Irish Protestants to Britain and further afield. In this respect, Donald L. Horowitz has noted that in periods of political upheaval, ethnic tension is often at the root of violence that results in killings, appropriation of resources and the flight of large numbers of people.[1] The experience of the Protestant community in Galway during the revolution and the degree to which hostility towards the minority community surfaced during the period are the last issues to be explored. Few European states in the modern era have been impervious to ethnic conflict; however, even in divided societies, communal conflict cannot be reduced to the common denominator of ethnic or religious ties and there are always a range of issues at play including class resentment and historical grievance.

'Ireland's Fighting Story'

Popular perceptions of the independence struggle were influenced in the early decades of the Free State by the publication of combatants' accounts that focused on what author Desmond Ryan termed 'the spirit of the struggle for Independence at the height of its glory, with all the incalculable fire of 1916 behind it and a rose misted future before it'.[2] Accounts of the exploits of republican leaders such as Dan Breen and Tom Barry displayed similar motifs with a common emphasis on the dangers faced by the Volunteers, the heroism of their sacrifice, the cowardice of the Crown Forces and the magnanimity of a united nationalist people.[3] The paradigm of 'Ireland's Fighting Story' could rejuvenate the questionable record of areas that had remained relatively dormant during the conflict as combatants sought retrospectively to defend their revolutionary credentials in print.[4]

The historical re-interpretation of the era that began in the 1960s was preceded by writers with first-hand experience of the revolution who had fundamentally questioned many popularly held assumptions. While these works tended towards hagiography, there are many valuable insights to be found in combatants' accounts and Peadar O'Donnell, Liam Mellows and Ernie O'Malley, in particular, left detailed accounts of seminal events, that despite garnering popular appeal, present nuanced analyses of the period.[5] Based on their own experiences, these writers questioned seminal nationalist assumptions regarding the degree of popular support for the Volunteers, the character of the republican leadership and the evolution of Sinn Féin. Conscious of the role of social class during the revolution, O'Donnell believed the movement exploited the rural poor, 'as the tyrannical aspects of the [British] conquest were declared outside the scope of the struggle'.[6] Likewise, Mellows wrote, 'Sinn Féin, while nominally, a nationalist party was, in fact, a bourgeois party.'[7] Ernie O'Malley was later to write bitterly of the lack of popular support for the republican cause, noting, 'There is no idea of honour, an indefinite sense of playing the game, no real courage and not sufficient bulldog grit.'[8]

The academic assessment of the Irish revolution evolved considerably in the 1960s with the publication of a number of important reinterpretations.[9] Historians such as F.X. Martin, William Irwin Thompson and F.S.L. Lyons questioned the degree to which interpretations of the period had been influenced by retrospective romanticism and the inherent necessities of nation building. The so-called revisionist approach sought to detach, as it was perceived, historical myths from reality, irrespective of nationalist sensitivities. The emerging historical orthodoxy fundamentally questioned the *a priori* assumptions surrounding the period with the reputations, abilities and rationale of the republican leadership subjected to unprecedented historical scrutiny. Thereafter, historians became less deferential, immeasurably more sceptical and fundamentally more dispassionate.

Ernest Rumpf and Anthony Hepburn's pioneering study *Nationalism and Socialism in Twentieth Century Ireland* represented a landmark in the academic investigation of the distribution of revolutionary violence.[10] Rather than analysing Irish nationalism in terms of its own rhetoric, they stressed the diversity of variables: geographic, agricultural, economic and cultural which accounted for the emergence and pattern of revolutionary violence. While some of their conclusions have since been challenged, Rumpf and Hepburn's approach, along with the bulk of their findings, have had a profound influence on later historians.

The influence of this new historical approach, combined with the pioneering methodology of Rumpf and Hepburn, is most evident in the work of historian, David Fitzpatrick. Fitzpatrick's seminal article, 'The Geography of Irish Nationalism', expanded the statistical analysis pioneered by Rumpf to examine three major manifestations of nationalism: violence, voting and participation in political organisations.[11] Employing a range of statistical data including, judicial statistics, election results and the Crime Special Branch statistics of the RIC, Fitzpatrick provided a more thorough analysis of the variety of republican activity than had previously been produced. He later employed his statistical approach and scepticism of the existing historiography to produce a major account of the revolution in a single county. *Politics and Irish Life 1913–1921: Provincial Experience of War and Revolution* examined the revolution in County Clare and was the first major analysis to challenge the common assumption that the rise of militant nationalism represented a fundamental and radical break with the constitutional tradition of the IPP and its local organisation, the United Irish League.[12] Fitzpatrick highlighted the profound continuity between the manipulation of social discontent and the romantic attachment to violent radicalism by the IPP and the complementary tactics of the 'new' revolutionaries.

The 'so-called revolution' thesis influenced a new generation of historians who emphasised the emasculation of radical social forces within the militant tradition that was most apparent in the revolutionaries' commitment to property values and their conservative stance on social reform.[13] Fitzpatrick's study emphasised the profoundly local nature of the revolutionary experience and his conclusion that only detailed local studies can establish the complex realities of the revolution was taken up by a number of younger historians. Peter Hart in Cork, Michael Farry in Sligo, Marie Coleman in Longford, John O'Callaghan in Limerick and Joost Augusteijn in a range of counties have all examined the nature of political and social upheaval during the period.[14] In recent years, Four Courts Press has launched an ambitious scheme to produce a case study of the revolution in each Irish county. The proliferation of regional studies of the revolution has been complemented by the recent publication of a range of thematic studies which have reconfigured the Irish experience of the First World War as central to a comprehensive understanding of the evolution of Irish nationalism.[15] An unprecedented popular interest in the experience of Irish soldiers who fought for Britain and the experience of ex-servicemen in Ireland has been mirrored by the realisation that an historical understanding of the experience of the Protestant minority in the South of Ireland is a crucial component in developing a comprehensive analysis of the nature of the revolution. Peter Hart's assessment of the experience of Protestants in Cork has generated much controversy but the legacy of his work lies in making the experience of the minority communities a subject of close historical scrutiny.

Despite the body of academic work published over the last two decades, Fitzpatrick's conclusions about the links between separatism and social change merit re-examination in the context of the varying degrees of support for political violence that existed in different regions. Political change can only be comprehensively analysed within the local *milieu* of conflicting voices, contested interpretations and disparate expectations through which political change and social unrest were mediated. To study patterns of upheaval and change in isolation or simply as components of larger forces of change is to underestimate the true complexity of Irish nationalism. Fitzpatrick's conclusions regarding the degree of continuity between the IPP and Sinn Féin has attracted both supporters and detractors and he has subsequently been critical of historians 'hankering after lost opportunities for social revolution'.[16] Fergus Campbell challenged Fitzpatrick's analysis of continuity and change by examining the intersection between political and agrarian conflict in County Galway.[17] Campbell emphasised the key influence of the radical tradition as being of paramount importance in shaping events and public opinion, as opposed to the elitism of the constitutional traditions of the IPP. Campbell's pioneering work on Galway has been instrumental in highlighting the primacy of land hunger as a salient catalyst for political change.

County Galway in 1913

The west of Ireland where the Irish Volunteers were founded in 1913 was a conservative society where hardship and the daily struggle to provide food and clothing dominated most families' lives. As a single county, Galway provides a compelling case study of the period as the cultural, linguistic and economic diversity within the county contributed to a remarkably complex social structure. Galway was an overwhelmingly rural society and the vast majority of people were either directly or indirectly reliant on agriculture for their livelihoods. The apparent uniformity of country life, however, concealed deeply divergent cultural and economic realities. Galway, west of Lough Corrib, comprised an extreme physical landscape of mountains, lakes and bog. Clifden, an English-speaking market town, was the only town in west Galway, with the majority of people surviving in conditions of abject poverty in small coastal communities scattered along the shores of Galway Bay. The vast majority of the county's Irish speakers lived in west Galway and in 1911, 7,811 people still spoke no English at all.[18] The largest villages in west Galway, Spiddal, Carraroe, Rosmuc, Roundstone and Oughterard relied on remittances from America to supplement meagre incomes from fishing and subsistence farming. The uniqueness of these communities and their exceptional cultural, environmental and economic realities were wholly distinct from the social and economic realities in the east of the county.

While travellers to the west coast marvelled at the immense natural wonders of the region, the prevalence of dire poverty that haunted Connemara had barely eased during the decades that preceded independence. Sinn Féin member, Patrick Moylett, recalled that in north Connemara, 'the horrifying scenes of desolation and death of the famine years were not quite half a life time past and their marks were still visible on the living. They were etched deep on the minds and hearts of the people and sculpted on their features.'[19] A government committee investigating economic conditions was informed in 1907 that parish committees of the Congested Districts Board were 'gradually destroying the once all prevalent custom of keeping horses, pigs and cattle in dwelling houses but poor sanitation remained a health problem'.[20] A witness to the committee 'did not think Spiddal exceptionally unhealthy as regards manure heaps, but perhaps it was in as far as houses were huddled together, making sanitation and cleanliness difficult. The district had rather a bad name but typhus had always come from Galway.'[21] The same report described the people of Letterfrack as living 'in a state of desolation'[22] while at Oughterard 'the barest necessities of life could, in many instances, not be obtained from land alone and the people were largely dependent on help from friends in America'.[23] The drain of the young through emigration decimated western communities, as one witnessed testified, 'the able bodied emigrating, the weak and sickly remaining'.[24] In 1907, children in the Carna district regularly came to school without food for their midday meal, not eating from their breakfast until five o'clock in the evening, as 'there was little milk in the district and many of the children had none during the winter'.[25] 'The feeding of school children would enable them to learn better,' the government was told, but was problematic as 'it touched their pride'.[26] 'Shopkeepers took advantage of the general poverty,' the committee was informed, 'and it was they who filled the bench and the public boards and they who were able to compel their debtors to vote for them.'[27] Many large landowners resisted notions of social progress and landlord Henry Burke declared, 'If the labouring classes were raised by means of education and grants of houses and plots of ground, it would be at the expense of the industrious farmer ... one class could not be raised without lowering another by artificial means.'[28] A remarkable number of people still lived on the many islands scattered off the Connemara coast.[29] In 1911, there were 2,679 people living on the Aran Islands, Gorumna Island sustained 1,540 people, with 801 living on Lettermore and 460 on Lettermullen. Off the north Connemara coast, Inishbofin sustained a population of 691 people, with 110 living on nearby Inishshark. Pressure for land saw islands in Lough Corrib sustaining small communities including eleven houses on Inchiquin Island and ten on Inishmacatreer.

For many people in east Galway, the west of the county remained an impenetrable and far-off place of which they knew little. Disinterest and a general lack of comprehension of social conditions on the west coast manifested itself in the conspicuous absence of sustained coverage in Galway newspapers of the dire poverty that characterised the western seaboard. An important connection between the two districts came from the pervasiveness of *spailpín* workers as a source of cheap agricultural labour for farmers in the east. *Spailpín* labourers made their way from Connemara to hiring fairs in towns such as Athenry and Loughrea to be hired as seasonal farm workers at harvest time. They slept in outhouses and barns and collected their pittance after backbreaking toil. The legacy of the *spailpín* system lay in the humiliation that the hiring fair represented to western communities where the young dreamed of Boston and New York and escape from servitude. In his short story 'The Year 1912', Máirtín Ó Cadhain wrote of the seminal importance of emigration to the people of Connemara, 'a race whose guardian angel was the American trunk, whose guiding star was the exile ship, whose Red Sea was the Atlantic'.[30]

East Galway is popularly conceived of in terms of north and south, with an imaginary frontier stretching from Galway town to Ballinasloe and the banks of the Shannon. Galway town remained the 'capital' of the west despite its waning economic fortunes over previous centuries and by the turn of the century, as John Cunningham has noted 'Galway entered the 20th century at a low ebb, its population falling, its economy declining, its buildings collapsing. The "Citie of the Tribes" was no longer officially a city and its so-called tribes, with their fortunes and influence, were thoroughly dispersed.'[31] The town was not without its charms, however, as an American visitor wrote in 1913:

> We found the streets crowded, next morning, with the most picturesque people we had seen anywhere in Ireland, for it was Saturday and so market day, and the country-folk had gathered in from many miles around. The men were for the most part buttoned up in cutaways of stiff frieze, nearly as hard and unyielding as iron; and the women, almost without exception, wore bright red skirts, made of fuzzy homespun flannel, which they had themselves woven from wool dyed with crimson.[32]

Galway town contained the county's only industries with the urban poor finding employment in the docks, the fertiliser factory, McDonogh's timber mills and in the town's relatively large commercial sector. The town's merchants retained grand notions of the importance of their city and a self-consciously cosmopolitan elite composed of a coterie of merchant families held sway in civic life. The extraordinary figure of Mártín Mór McDonogh dominated commerce and public life, as Cunningham notes, 'Gruff, overbearing and arrogant, Mártín Mór dominated the town's economic life, and directed its civic affairs through his membership of the Urban Council, of the Harbour Board, of the Galway Race Committee. He was very much the public face of the town.'[33]

The people of the Claddagh, a small Irish- and English-speaking village 'down west' of the town centre, continued to enjoy ancestral rights to fish along the Galway coast and the Claddagh fleet and the fish market at the Spanish Arch contributed to the often raucous atmosphere in the town. A quintessential garrison town, Renmore Barracks was the home of the Connaught Rangers and the officer class mixed with the town's social elite, adding a martial air to the pretensions of commercial society. While the docks were an important centre for the economy, they had declined in importance as a major port and in 1913, only 168 vessels arrived at Galway docks, a significantly smaller number than the ports of Limerick (549 vessels) or Sligo (483 vessels).[34] Saturday was the town's busy day with street traders, publicans and 'spirit dealers' dependent on the trade of country people coming to market.[35]

As outlined in Table 1, Irish speakers were concentrated in the west of the county and the nature of the cleavage between the English-speaking east and the Irish- and English-speaking west is apparent, with 4,375 speakers of Irish only in the Oughterard district of west Galway, compared to a mere eight in the urban district of Ballinasloe. In the ten years before the 1911 census, the population of speakers of Irish only in the county dropped by almost a quarter from 9,443 to 7,811. The decline of the language in west Galway had been ongoing for many decades and was vividly recalled in Máirtín Ó Cadhain's short story, 'The Gnarled And Stony Clods Of Townland's Tip' where the elderly Peits ponders the 'unbearable burden of having to spend what was left of his days among a generation of people who were alien to him and his traditional style. He understood in the depths of his old and lucid love that he was the last and late survivor of his people.'[36]

Popular perceptions of the west in the early twentieth century were heavily influenced by the accomplishments of the Celtic revival and the endeavours of Anglo-Irish figures such as Galway landowners, Edward Martyn and Lady Gregory. Their championing of the dignity of the rural poor influenced writers such as Synge and Yeats who idealised the west coast in their early work. For an authentic portrayal of the west during this period, however, the literary works of Máirtín Ó Cadhain lay bare the dark ambiguities, seething resentments and petty humiliations of rural life. Stripping rural society of its magical residue and replacing the myths and idealisations of cosmopolitan artists with a gritty,

TABLE 1

Speakers of Irish only, and Irish and English, Co. Galway, 1901/1911

County District	Irish Only 1901	Irish Only 1911	Irish and English, 1901	Irish and English, 1911
Ballinasloe urban	8	17	480	759
Galway urban	69	56	5,744	4,892
Ballinasloe rural	Nil	Nil	1,262	1,114
Clifden	1,162	834	12,656	10,912
Galway rural	2,874	2,220	16,219	15,709
Glenamaddy	94	46	10,295	8,775
Gort	55	21	7,193	5,816
Loughrea	40	20	7,281	6,206
Mountbellew	34	14	7,671	6,541
Oughterard	4,711	4,375	9,580	10,022
Portumna	Nil	Nil	586	795
Tuam	395	208	20,461	19,171
Total	9,442	7,811	99,428	90,712

Source: Table XXXVII showing the number of persons who spoke Irish only and Irish and English in each county district in the county of Galway: *Census Returns for Ireland, 1911, Showing Area, Houses, and Population; also the Ages, Civil or Conjugal Condition, Occupations, Birthplaces, Religions, and Education of the People, Province of Connaught*, p. 224, H.C., 1913 (Cd. 6052, 6052-I, 6052-II, 6052-III, 6052-IV, 6052-V), cxvii, p. 1.

uncompromising realism, Ó Cadhain knew first-hand the ways of the village and the drudgery of servitude. In the short story, 'The Road to Brightcity', Ó Cadhain provided a haunting portrayal of the hardship of rural life for Brid, the wife of a small farmer in south Connemara:

> There were dark ideas slinking at the edge of her mind, and bitterness to sting her feelings, but to her conscious mind the drag and drudgery of life never seemed anything to grumble at. Even Mike the shop – it never occurred to her that he should be complained of and penalised for putting three different prices on the one article according to whether a body was badly in need of credit, or a safe bet, or able to pay on the dot.[37]

Galway ranked near the top of all standard economic indicators of poverty in 1911 and with very limited economic prospects at home, emigration and seasonal migration remained crucial to the rural economy. In 1911, 2,614 people were designated as paupers and 1,311 received relief in ten workhouses, with 1,313 receiving outdoor relief.[38] These grim institutions retained their fearful reputations and the shame of admission was reserved for the utterly destitute and incapable. The Royal Commission on Congestion in Ireland noted the poverty that rural tenants continued to suffer in east Galway and the precariousness of their existence:

> The Tuam rural tenantry was in great poverty, labour was scarce and many people eked out an existence cutting turf from bogs and selling it in the town. They were industrious but under present conditions, it seemed mockery to exhort them to self-help ... In three or four cases there was gombeenism with 100 per cent but was less flourishing than formerly.[39]

Most rural people bought the essential commodities they could not produce in the local shop that often functioned simultaneously as a grocer, butcher, public house and undertaker.[40] Items were usually paid on credit with bills settled after stock or crops were sold. Indebtedness to the shopkeeper haunted many families and in the most serious cases, unpaid bills could result in land being forfeited. The shame of such a catastrophe was the most painful of fates a family could suffer and it was not unknown for an unscrupulous shopkeeper to exhaust a small farmer's finances in order to claim a piece of land. The economic ties between shopkeepers and farmers and the system of indebtedness was one of the main reasons why shopkeepers were barred from sitting on the parish committees of the Congested Districts Board, a government body set up to alleviate poverty in the West of Ireland in 1891. The chairman of a local committee in Connemara explained:

> The shopkeeper might favour his own customer in the selection [of grants] and grants from the Parish Committee for improvements, which the tenant would otherwise have paid for himself might set free an otherwise unattainable sum for the payment of the shopkeeper ... The shopkeeper might have a collusive interest in where he got his materials.[41]

As indicated in Table 2, the population of Galway dropped steadily in every census from 1871 with a total population of 182,224 in 1911 representing a drop of 5 per cent over the previous ten years. In the ten years between 1905 and 1914, the average number of emigrants from Ireland per year was 30,073.[42] Emigration acted as a crucial economic pressure valve, releasing parents from the financial burden of their children and holding out the prospect of a better

TABLE 2
Population decline, Galway, 1871–1911

Year	Inhabited Houses	Population	Population Decrease	Percentage Decrease
1871	45,564	248,458	23,020	8.48 %
1881	42,954	242,005	6,453	2.60 %
1891	39,366	214,712	27,293	11.28 %
1901	36,223	192,549	22,163	10.32 %
1911	34,945	182,224	10,325	5.36 %

Source: Table II: Comparative View of Houses and Population of the County of Galway as Constituted at each of the ten Censuses: *Census Returns for Ireland, 1911* …

life for the young. From 1901 to 1911, 26,464 people emigrated from Galway, representing a significant drop on the 36,820 who had emigrated over the previous ten years.[43]

Migratory labour provided vital income for many rural families with roughly three quarters of the 8,687 migratory labourers enumerated in Ireland in 1915 leaving Connacht for work in Britain.[44] These figures under-represent the extent of migratory labour and the enumerators themselves believed their data represented approximately 60 per cent of the entire total. Of the eight Poor Law districts with the highest ratios of migratory employment, seven were in Connacht (Swinford, Westport, Belmullet, Castlebar, Claremorris, Castlereagh and Glenamaddy). Of the 7,354 seasonal migrants who were enumerated in 1915, only 1,578 were farmers with the vast majority being the sons of labourers and tenants. In 1913, 71 per cent of these men went to England and Wales, with 24 per cent going to Scotland.[45]

In 1915, the weekly wages of agricultural labourers in Connacht, who did not have accommodation provided or who did not receive allowances of any kind, ranged from 13 to 16 shillings for ploughmen, 13 to 15 shillings for herdsmen, 11 to 13 shillings for labourers and 7 to 10 shillings for boys.[46] These rates were slightly behind the average rates paid elsewhere in the country but many agricultural workers were paid partly in cash with allowances such as food, fuel, access to land, housing and board, making precise comparisons problematic. The sale of turf supplemented meagre incomes for many, particularly in south Connemara. A visitor to Galway in 1907 wrote of his encounter with a group of turf cutters in Connemara:

TABLE 3
Emigration from Connacht, May 1851–December 1910

	Population	Males	Females	Total
Galway	248,816	107,930	119,615	227,545
Leitrim	91,756	40,611	41,941	82,552
Mayo	239,664	86,536	107,725	194,261
Roscommon	136,865	55,008	58,388	113,396
Sligo	110,431	39,570	44,248	83,818
Total	827,532	329,655	371,917	701,572

Source: Table III – Emigration statistics For Ireland for the Year 1910: *Report and Tables Showing the Number, Ages, Conjugal Conditions, and Destinations of the Emigrants from Each County and Province in Ireland during the Year 1910; also the Occupations of the Emigrants, and the Number of Emigrants who Left Each Port in Each Month of the Year* H.C., 1911 (Cd. 5607).

The vast level stretches of the bog extended as far as the eye could see in every direction. Nothing but black mounds and coarse grass, with now and then a stunted scrub of grass covered hillock could be seen. In all parts of this vast stretch of waste land, where millions of square yards of peat lay open for the gathering, men, women and children were at work cutting the brick shaped masses and carrying them off to be dried. Many could be seen moving the piles and re-stacking the blackish brown blocks, which after drying, resembled decaying wood.[47]

Ballinasloe, Loughrea and Athenry were the largest towns in south Galway, with Tuam, the only relatively large town in the north of the county. The town of Ballinasloe was described by a witness to the Royal Commission on Congestion in Ireland in 1907 as possessing streets where 'labourers were huddled together in filthy slums'.[48] The witness believed the high level of admissions to the county asylum situated in the town was primarily due to emigration as 'the flower of the population having emigrated, those weak in body and mind were left behind'.[49] Claiming four-fifths of the houses occupied by labourers were unfit for human habitation, a local priest concluded, 'these abodes are an insult to God and they degrade men and women made to His image and likeness, herded together in these wretched dens to the level of brutes'.[50] In Loughrea, labourers' cottages were described by a member of the Rural District Council in 1914 as 'a living disgrace … situated in the midst of a smiling and peaceful landscape, these abodes of men are in dull and gloomy contrast'.[51]

In communities with few social amenities, taking part in societies of a sporting, civic or political nature offered social outlets for ordinary people. The sheer variety of clubs testified to the social value of such groups. In towns such as Loughrea and Ballinasloe, choral and amateur dramatic societies thrived, along with branches of the Town Tenants' League, the Ancient Order of Hibernians, the United Irish League, the Gaelic League, Sinn Féin and the Land and Labour Association. Fraternities such as the Loughrea Trade and Labour Society, the Athenry Labourers' Society, the Irish Grocers and Vintners' Assistants' Association, the Galway Grocers' Association, the Ballinasloe Workingmen's Association and the Galway Artisans' and Labourers' Housing Association proliferated.

While most rural people were traditionally circumspect about interacting with the RIC, and the poor continued to view the force as they always had – as something of a menace – to have a son become a constable remained an aspiration ranking behind having a priest or a teacher in the family. With the professions confined to the bourgeoisie, the military provided a livelihood for the working poor, many of whom had no option but to join their local regiment or face a lifetime of economic desperation. While ordinary people delighted in poking fun at the pretence and 'shoneenism' inherent in the upper tiers of the Crown Forces, in towns such as Ballinasloe, the barracks was one of the few avenues of employment for whole generations.

Social life, as far as it existed for the poor, was sometimes boisterous. Faction fighting at fairs, festivals and GAA matches, in particular – while much less common than during the previous century – remained a feature of rural life. A trial of a group of Galway men for riot and unlawful assembly was changed to Dublin in May 1912 after the County Inspector of the Royal Irish Constabulary (RIC) stated in court that an impartial trial was not possible in the county due to the undue sympathy of Galway jurors.[52] Disputes over land between neighbouring families could rapidly escalate into gun attacks between rival factions and the practice of shooting into the windows of houses at night with shotguns was endemic in certain districts. In December 1912, a Dublin judge proclaimed 'the district of Athenry is a disgrace to Ireland. Day after day, night after night, and week after week, heaps of outrages were being committed there and not one offender was being made amenable to justice.'[53] The quick recourse to violence to settle personal disputes was exacerbated by the tolerance of excessive alcohol consumption that was a feature of communal occasions, including funerals, wakes, fairs and pattern days. It is this complex and diverse community that will be discussed over the coming chapters and how the unprecedented social and political upheaval of the Irish revolution was mediated.

CHAPTER 1

A Tradition of Violence: Agrarian Agitation, 1910–18

This chapter examines land agitation in Galway before the rise of republican militancy and the extent to which elaborate communal and associational structures existed through which the rural poor exerted considerable influence over their social and economic 'betters'. As Tony Varley has shown, the cessation of land redistribution by the Congested Districts Board (CDB) for the duration of the First World War contributed to the economic desperation of the rural poor and 'the war impinged greatly on how hard, and by what means, western nationalists were prepared to press for redistributive land reform'.[1] Fergus Campbell has highlighted the formative influence of land hunger among the rural poor on the subsequent development and character of the republican movement in County Galway and the transformative role of land agitations.[2] It is instructive, therefore, to examine the scale, nature and evolution of land agitation in the years prior to the widespread emergence of militant republicanism.

A common theme of the literature on peasant societies is the dislocation that rural communities experience with the advance of agricultural commercialisation that undermines traditional institutions including bonds between peasants and their economic masters.[3] The period covered in this study should have been one of opportunity for the rural poor, many of whom had reason to hope that they would benefit from an acceleration in land division, yet, the suspension of land redistribution during the War heightened the sense of disappointment and desperation among small farmers, just as steadily rising prices increased the profits of middling farmers. This contributed to an acute sense of alienation from and disaffection with the machinations of the state, principally the Estate's Commission and the CDB, both of which were charged with redistributing estates of land, and the sense of moral outrage felt by many communities was summed up by the refrain of western agitators – the road for the bullock and the land for the people!

In terms of the development of Sinn Féin in rural districts of east Galway, Campbell has asserted that, 'far from being established on the basis of the "Home Rule tradition", Sinn Féin emerged from the radical agrarian and republican political culture of [Thomas] Kenny's secret society'.[4] While the Irish Republican Brotherhood (IRB) and agrarian secret societies were separate and distinct phenomena, Campbell's research has demonstrated how the IRB was closely involved in land agitation in Galway for many years. The police described the main area of IRB influence at this time as, 'all along the Railway line right up to Tuam and for a few miles on each side of the line. Then again in Galway, just touching places along the line to Clifden and fairly active at Leenane and Letterfrack.'[5] Campbell has stated that the 'Galway Secret Society' owed its origins to an offshoot of the violent revolutionary movement, The Invincibles, started in Galway in 1881 and was blamed by police for a number of agrarian murders in the county in the 1880s.[6] Under blacksmith Thomas Kenny from the village of Craughwell, the society grew to have a presence throughout the county and its influence became considerable. The society's main aim was the redistribution of grazing land among the rural poor and this represented a continuum in the centrality of agrarian secret society influence in Galway from the land struggle in the nineteenth century through to the struggle for independence in the twentieth. Through all manner of intimidation, including attacks on property and animals, assault and even murder, the society exercised a great deal of control in east Galway, particularly in the hinterland between Athenry, Craughwell and Loughrea.

The defining feature of agriculture in Connacht has always been the scarcity of economically viable land and the 1903 and 1909 Land Acts did not address the prevalence of uneconomic holdings among the rural poor.[7] The new legislation did little to further the creation of an economically viable class of small farmers in very impoverished districts because the amount of good land available for distribution was so small and the number of tenants so numerous. The sheer impossibility of satisfying so many land-hungry tenants in areas where land was poor heightened the desperation of potential claimants and fuelled the violence that characterised agrarian disputes.[8] As Varley has noted, resolving the inherent blight of rural poverty could not be resolved by large-scale land redistribution as the abundance of uneconomic farms combined with the predominance of poor land meant that despite the vast process of land redistribution which the state had embarked upon, the potential benefits would always be heavily constricted in the west.[9]

Counties Galway and Clare were exceptional in the opening decades of the twentieth century for the degree of violence over land. The *Connacht Tribune* declared in an editorial in March 1915:

The second main factor [after drunkenness] that leads to unrest in the County is the delay in the agrarian settlement of certain districts. Unfortunately this leads to evils by no means directly connected with the land problem, for there is no disguising the fact that instances have occurred where reckless irresponsible men have made so-called agrarian emancipation the cloak for acts of outrage that bring disgrace and shame upon the whole community. Men of this class are a distinct danger to the country and can in no way serve the high purpose they protest to advocate. Their spurious patriotism, behind which they shelter personal motives, is by no means new.[10]

Land redistribution

Galway was remarkable for the volume of land transferred from large landowners to small tenants under consecutive land acts. In terms of the amount of land transferred by the state under the 1903 and 1909 Land Acts, Galway ranks a clear first, when any number of categories is considered. Under the 1903 Land Act, 166,507 acres of land was transferred in the county to small tenants from November 1903 to March 1918.[11] This figure equates to just under the entire amount transferred in the province of Munster (169,988) or the amount transferred in all of Ulster and Leinster combined (90,138 and 80,774 acres respectively). In terms of allotments of untenanted land, i.e., grassland previously given over to the grazing of sheep and cattle, the figures are even more remarkable with a total of £731,071 advanced by the

TABLE 4
Summary of Land Acts in Ireland, 1870–96

Acts	Holdings	Acreage	Purchase Money
Act of 1870	877	52,906	859,522
Act of 1881	731	30,657	355,594
Acts of 1885–88	25, 367	942,625	10,162,834
Acts of 1891–96	46, 834	1,482,749	13,401,226
Total	73,809	2,508,937	24,779,176

Source: Summary of proceedings for sales of holdings under earlier land purchase acts, 1870–1896: *Irish Land Acts, 1903–09: Report of the Estates Commissioners for the Year from 1st April, 1917, to 31st March, 1918, and for the Period from 1st November, 1903, to 31st March, 1918, with Appendix*, p. iv, H.C., 1919 (Cmd.; 29), xxiv, p. 137.

state under the combined 1903 and 1909 Land Acts up to March 1918.[12] In County Roscommon, where the next highest amount of money was allocated, the government invested £118,188 and in no other county was more than £100,000 allotted, with Galway dwarfing counties like Clare by a figure of roughly ten to one.[13]

The ongoing fracturing of social class facilitated by land redistribution coalesced with the rise of the shopkeeper/grazier as a social and economic force and the displacement of landlords from the upper tiers of the economic structure.[14] The land issue became reconfigured as a sizable rural proletariat, who were unable to take advantage of successive land acts, were exploited by the emergence of a new class of graziers who increasingly replaced landlords as the main targets for agitation by the rural poor.[15] Graziers were farmers who owned, or more often leased, large grassland farms or 'ranches', stocking them with cattle and sheep. This agrarian class had the capital to outbid smaller farmers for available land under the predominant eleven-month lease system and the rural poor blamed graziers for denying them access to land – creating a society, the poor frequently claimed – in which bullocks were valued over people. Many of the old Galway gentry families, such as the Mahons of Ahascragh, who sold their estates to the state over the previous decades, had retained enough land to become graziers and these farms were often leased to other large farmers.

Fundamental structural changes to the rural economy had been ongoing since the early nineteenth century and a relentless decline in crop acreage in the west testified to a formative switch from tillage farming to pastoral farming among landowners of all sizes. Crop acreage in Connacht decreased by 65 per cent from 1851 to 1914, representing a decrease of 235,128 acres given over to the grazing of sheep and cattle.[16] Pastoral farming was less labour intensive, provided little seasonal employment and was historically resented by the rural poor with clearances and the displacement of the role of the agricultural labourer seen as a function of the unstoppable advance of grazerism. The relentless rise in the amount of land under hay across the country since the Famine, with an increase in 1,059,776 acres between 1851 and 1914, is testimony to the unstoppable dominance of grassland farming.[17] The preference for sheep and cattle over tillage was not confined to strong farmers and the emergence of a formative class of sturdy smallholders in Galway is attested to by the small but significant growth in agricultural credit associations.[18]

While lacking dialectical sophistication, social and economic tension between broadly defined social groups remained a formative feature of a rural society increasingly defined by the ranks of the class of sturdy smallholders

TABLE 5
Land holdings in Connacht, 1914

	>1 acre	1–5 acres	5–15 acres	15–30 acres	30–50 acres	50–100 acres	100–200 acres	200–500 acres	Over 500 acres
Galway	2,350	2,942	9,658	8,990	4,518	2,353	865	465	273
Leitrim	929	513	4,082	4,974	1,847	761	189	46	14
Mayo	2,171	2,684	13,697	10,430	3,110	1,575	590	423	214
Roscommon	1,482	1,313	6,892	6,425	2,063	888	379	202	58
Sligo	1,156	1,116	4,899	4,409	1,572	736	274	135	38
Total	8,088	8,568	39,228	35,228	13,110	6,313	2,297	1,271	597

Source: Table showing the number of occupiers resident in each county and province in the year 1914: *Agricultural Statistics, With Detailed Report, For Ireland*, p. 9., H.C., 1916 (Cd.; 8266), xxxii, p. 621.

who had replaced large landowners as the dominant social group in the rural economy.[19] There were almost 17,000 households living off less than five acres of land in Connacht in 1914 with 40,110 families surviving on farms of between five and fifteen acres and 35,695 families occupying farms of between fifteen and thirty acres.[20] As Table 5 indicates, at the bottom of rural society in Galway in 1914 were a sizable minority of farmers/labourers occupying 2,350 plots of less than one acre of land and 2,942 plots consisting of less than five acres. These landholders supplemented their incomes with seasonal work, casual labour and remittances. The most numerous class of land holdings in the county constituted the ranks of the small farmers and plots consisting of between 5 and 15 acres totaling 9,658 farms, with plots of between 15 and 30 acres comprising 8,990 farms. Middling and strong farmers constituted a significant social group with 4,518 plots of between 20 and 50 acres and 2,353 plots of between 50 and 100 acres. Large farms or 'ranches' occupied a formative economic position with 865 farms of between 100 and 200 acres; there were an additional 465 farmers who occupied farms of between 200 and 500 acres. A minority of landholders held farms of a vastly greater scale with 273 landowners occupying farms of over 500 acres, testifying to the continuing saliency of landlordism.

For the rural poor, the eleven-month land lease was synonymous with the increasing marginalisation of the agricultural labourer. As the regulations in the government's land acts only applied to leases of one year or more, eleven-month leases were excluded from government stipulations. Occupiers leasing under the eleven-month system could be evicted without notice and did not gain formal tenancy of their farms, thus, a spiral of economic marginalisation based on access to land led to an increasing concentration of economically valuable grassland in the hands of the relatively small number of farmers. The system was most prominent in counties Roscommon, Galway and Clare, and in parts of the midlands, including Kildare and Westmeath. In 1915, Meath had the most land rented under the eleven-month system nationwide with 73,038 acres, with Galway a close second with 72,801 acres.[21] Crucially, Meath did not have as high a number of smallholders as Galway and agrarian violence was not a significant feature. Better comparisons with similar sized counties like Mayo with 30,449 acres and Tipperary with 20,146 acres highlight the dominance of the grazing system in Galway where over twice that amount of land was leased under eleven-month leases.[22]

Historically, the prevalence of this system, which excluded thousands of small tenants from access to land, had been a major source of turmoil and violence. Localised campaigns against individual graziers were a recurring phenomenon in the opening decades of the century and frequently involved considerable violence, including intimidation, the maiming of beasts and people, burnings and shootings.[23] The failure to develop a precise classification of what was contemporaneously labelled by the authorities as 'outrage', without analysing the nature, form and causes of these disturbances has obscured the complexity of the phenomena. As both Campbell and Terence Dooley have shown, rather than viewing agrarian agitation as the opportunism of a greedy peasantry, these manifestations of crisis among the rural poor involved a level of crude sophistication which cannot be dismissed as mere 'unrest'.[24]

Galway, Clare and Roscommon consistently featured in police statistics as the most violent centres of agrarian agitation. In terms of crimes against property from 1908 to 1912, Galway ranked second nationally, behind Clare, once the major metropolitan centres of Dublin and Belfast are excluded.[25] When the exact type of offence is contextualised, the remarkable level of a particular kind of violence in the county becomes apparent. In 1914, Galway ranked first nationally for convictions for 'intimidation by threatening letter' with seventy convictions, with Mayo, the second highest, having a mere eighteen convictions.[26] In terms of malicious injury to property, Galway ranked second behind Belfast with sixteen convictions, while in terms of convictions for 'assaulting dwelling houses by firing shots into them', Galway ranked first nationally with nineteen of the forty-five convictions nationwide. These types of crimes were associated with agrarian agitation and should not be extrapolated into an extraordinary propensity for 'ordinary violence' in the county, as for other crimes such as larceny, drunkenness and riot, the figures for Galway are unremarkable.

Men imprisoned for their role in agrarian disputes were frequently treated as heroes upon their release. After being released from custody in Galway jail for a riot at an anti-grazier demonstration near Clifden, land agitator, P.J. Wallace told a crowd of supporters, 'all the CDB succeeded in doing was looking after and giving jobs to broken down military colonels and land agents and sending ladies around to teach people how to cook eggs, paying more attention to bulls, boars and rams than poor people'.[27] William O'Malley, MP for Connemara, had been a trenchant critic of the CDB. In November 1914, as the new members of the Board were being considered for their five-year term, O'Malley wrote to the CDB requesting that a Galway member be appointed. Decrying the difficulties faced by tenants in what it described as the 'agricultural slums' of Galway, the *Connacht Tribune* echoed O'Malley's sentiments, complaining that western tenants were 'too often made pawns of purely experimental measures by the Board'.[28]

To understand changes in popular collective action in Western Europe over the last three centuries, historian Charles Tilly analysed the effect on collective violence of major structural transformations such as urbanisation and industrialisation.[29] The social organisation of groups contending for power in western European countries changed over the nineteenth century and the nature and targets of their goals altered accordingly. There was a decline in collective violence by small communal groups, either struggling for power with one another or trying to resist the centralisation of power in nation states, in favour of a transition to collective violence that erupts as broadly based interest groups, organised associationally, within the structures of the political parties and voluntary associations, seeking to influence the state and make claims to rights not previously enjoyed. In Connacht, collectivities composed of the rural poor traditionally sought to 'regain' access to land popularly perceived to have been theirs prior to the Cromwellian confiscations of the seventeenth century. In the imagination of the rural poor, 'grazierism' and landlordism had no legitimacy and the agrarian agitators were righting an historical injustice perpetrated on their ancestors.

Writing about the Irish Land War of 1879–82, Samuel Clark applied Tilly's model to rural unrest in nineteenth-century Ireland.[30] He concluded that collective action had begun to change significantly in Ireland during the nineteenth century. Active collectivities had become less local and more often national in their scope, less often re-active and more often pro-active in their aims, and less communal and more often associational, in their organisational basis and structure. The oath-bound agrarian combinations and feuding factions of the pre-Famine period tended to be highly localised, but as the century progressed, there was a noticeable transition away from this type of inherently local collective action to broader national collective action involving national movements such as the Fenians, the Land League and the United Irish League.[31]

Numerous examples of all three categories of collective action identified by Tilly – associational, communal and competitive – were active in Galway during the years immediately preceding the rise of militant nationalism. Small campaigns, which were communal in character, were based on bonds of extended kinship within small districts. Larger agitations that were associational in character were prominent in the hinterland between Ballinasloe, Loughrea and Portumna, and were organised within the structures of the United Irish League. The vast Ashtown, Clanricarde and Clonbrock estates were divided into numerous dispersed portions in the north and east of the county and were the focus of complex and concerted campaigns by tenants for a number of decades. The Irish Parliamentary Party (IPP) supported these campaigns with priests and MPs providing crucial support. Feuds between small farmers and tenants, which had their origins in competing interpretations of rights and entitlements to land, constituted a significant source of violence. In the period 1913–16, feuds between organised factions took place at Boyhill and Graige Abbey, near Athenry; in Lackagh village in the parish of Turloughmore; around the village of Craughwell; and in the Riverville and Bookeen districts that previously comprised the large Dunsandle estate. These feuds over how land was to be divided or had already been divided to the dissatisfaction of local parties frequently involved sustained violence, aggravated by the abundance of local knowledge about the whereabouts of potential targets in inherently 'neighbourly' disputes.

'Thoroughly organised and quite unscrupulous': communal agitations

Communal collectivities composed of groups of small tenants bound together by intimate bonds of family and townland frequently sprang up on landed estates in frustration at landowners' refusal to sell their land to the CDB for division. In a parish such as Athenry, numerous communal agitations were simultaneously active, with small groups of tenants targeting different landlords in their respective vicinities. The bounds of communal collectivities did not generally extend beyond neighbouring townlands and there is scant evidence of co-operation between agitators involved in separate disputes. During the early years of the revolution in Galway, several communal agitations were active in the Athenry district with long-running agitations at Moorpark, Tiaquin and Colemanstown.[32] The police noted the tension in the district in the summer of 1914: 'land hunger is very keen around Athenry and the forces of disorder there are thoroughly organised and quite unscrupulous'.[33] As Fergus Campbell has highlighted, these agitations often had the support of local IRB members and an overlap in terms of membership existed with the authorities noting in February 1915: 'these secret societies around Athenry and Loughrea, if not actually IRB circles, are believed to be under the control of that organisation and work in connection with the Estates Commissioners and the UIL [United Irish League] in furthering agitation.'[34]

The violence employed by communal collectivities involved a considerable degree of crude sophistication and as conflicts between tenants and landowners escalated, an intensification in the level of pressure employed by tenants followed recognisable patterns. Communal agitations generally commenced with a formal delegation of tenants to the landowner. The intense 'smallness' of the groups was a common feature, as too large a number of competing claims for inclusion in any subsequent division became inherently problematic. When landowners refused to concede to their tenants wishes and give up their land to the relevant state board for division, an escalation of coercion, often lasting many years, frequently commenced. Campaigns by tenants often commenced with the invoking of a boycott of the landowner, extending to his workmen, his family and any merchants or tradesmen who interacted with them. When local communities commenced agitations, the UIL frequently offered moral support. James Vallely of the Letterfrack UIL explained the position of his party in relation to a boycotted landowner at Tullycross: 'Graziers were surely something they were all striving to be rid of, but certainly a grabber was a still more loathsome creature. He was something to be despised and shunned by all decent and respectable people. Thank God Connemara would soon be rid of all grabbers and graziers and the members of the branch should feel proud that they were involved in such work.'[35] Boycotts were generally adhered to by the wider rural community and were powerful instruments of communal coercion. Landowner Walter Joyce told a meeting of landowners in Galway in 1914 that because of a boycott by tenants of his estate, 'I have lost my labourers and have great difficulty in working a farm of over 1,400 acres for the last four years. I have to go a distance of nine miles to draw coal and it takes a large force of police to protect me. When I go to mass, I and my family have to be protected by forty policemen.'[36]

As campaigns wore on, cattle and sheep drives involving the scattering of a landowner's stock represented an escalation in hostilities, with drives often forming festive occasions with large crowds, 'rough music' and fife and drum bands cheering the drivers on. Repeated cattle drives inevitably provoked the police into establishing a permanent police presence on boycotted farms which made open confrontation between agitators and landowners more difficult. While wider associational collectivities usually refrained from more extreme violence, smaller communal collectivities frequently escalated their campaigns at this point with threatening letters, the digging of graves outside homes, arson and assaults on farm workers forming part of a pattern of intimidation. The knocking of stone walls, the spiking of meadows, the gouging of animals and the arson of outhouses or farm equipment was frequently resorted to as such disputes wore on.

Communal campaigns were facilitated by the police's inability to secure criminal convictions in cases of agrarian violence and at the Galway assizes in March 1908, the police secured only two of the twenty-six cases brought for conviction.[37] In extreme cases, gun attacks on landowners and farm workers represented the most serious phase in tenant campaigns. A long running communal agitation was active in Athenry against landowner Frank Shawe-Taylor of Moorpark, which lasted seven years and culminated in Shawe-Taylor's murder in March 1920. In March 1913, a tenants' deputation requested a meeting with Shawe-Taylor to 'convey the strength of feeling' among the tenants of the district that he surrender his farm of untenanted grazing land to the CDB.[38] He allegedly consented to give up 249 acres of the farm, but this offer proved unacceptable to the tenants who were resolute that the whole farm be sold. The police noted, 'the people feel it wasn't really a genuine offer, but made for the purpose of trying to fool them, hence his unpopularity'.[39]

Shawe-Taylor's determination to resist the demands of the tenants led to repeated threats against him and weeks after the initial deputation he was placed under constant police protection.[40] As no local would work on the estate, farm workers from the Property Defense Association had to be brought in from the north of Ireland and police were forced to keep track of all changes of personnel on the farm. The agitators' threats were not idle rhetoric and in April 1914, a malicious fire destroyed an extensive collection of out-houses and farm equipment.[41] The subsequent claim for compensation, for what local people claimed was an accidental fire, heightened ill feeling and in June, he sought £600 compensation at Tuam quarter sessions. The court was told that a man who sold him oats had his house burned down and his brother's home fired into.[42] In March 1915, a herd on the farm was brutally assaulted and a man subsequently sentenced to six months in Galway jail for the attack.[43] The judge noted the defendant would have got twelve months but for a character reference provided by the Royal Irish Constabulary (RIC) sergeant in Athenry.[44] The willingness of a police officer to stand as character witness for a defendant in an assault case in which the victim sustained brain damage was indicative of the local RIC's sympathy in the case. Four months later, another workman from the estate was viciously beaten while attending a hurling match in Athenry, being struck about the head by a group of men with hurls.[45]

With increased police surveillance, the agitation at Moorpark died down for some time; however, Shawe-Taylor continued to be boycotted for a further seven years. In the ensuing period, the community rigidly observed the boycott and the Shawe-Taylor family remained protected by a constant police escort. The land at Moorpark could only be farmed with the assistance of the Property Defence Association with workmen living within the confines of the property protected by a permanent police hut. The boycott was punctuated by sporadic acts of violence and the grim determination of the community left the family in no doubt about their isolation and vulnerability. The agitation came to a conclusion with the killing of Shawe-Taylor on 2 March 1920; the shooting took place amidst a resurgent campaign of agrarian violence.

'Standing menaces to the peace': associational campaigns

There were three major associational land agitations active in Galway at the commencement of the First World War, directed against three of the county's largest landowners: the Marquis of Clanricarde, who held a vast estate in the district between Loughrea and Portumna in south east Galway; Lord Ashtown of Woodlawn, whose estate was situated in the Kilconnell district between Loughrea and Ballinasloe; and Lord Clonbrock of Ahascragh, whose estate was in the Ballinasloe hinterland. All three agitations were supported by the UIL, the clergy and local MPs and involved significant levels of intimidation, cattle driving and sporadic battles with the police.

As well as hunger for land, the tenants' campaigns were fuelled by elements of religious and political resentment. In 1901, Ashtown fired his Catholic workmen replacing them with Scottish planters who were subsequently targeted by a boycott by the local herdmens' association and the UIL.[46] Likewise in 1903, there were sixty-four Scottish and northern planters in possession of amalgamated plots on the Clanricarde estate from which Catholic tenants had been evicted between 1886 and 1914.[47] All of the three landowners were advanced unionists and Clonbrock was a leading officer in the County

Galway Unionist Association and the Irish Landowners Convention. Ashtown held views of the most extreme kind, producing his own loyalist news-sheet, *Grievances From Ireland*; he acted as President of the fringe group, the Imperial Loyalist Federation.[48]

Herbert George de Burgh, the second Marquis of Clanricarde, succeeded to the title of the third Earl of Clanricarde in April 1874. Clanricarde was a figure of hatred in Galway, where his vast estate of 52,000 acres was scattered across 128 separate plots.[49] *The Times* of London famously described him as 'a danger to society', for his campaign of evictions in the winter of 1886 that led to the imprisonment of approximately 160 people.[50] Clanricarde never actually set foot on his family estate in Galway but his name remained infamous after the notorious Woodford evictions.[51] In April 1914, the *Connacht Tribune*, under the banner, 'Two Snapshots of the Loneliest Landlord Peer of the Realm', published 'sensational shots of the man behind the mask', proclaiming: 'The studies are as remarkable as they are pathetic, although throughout Ireland, little sympathy will be felt … Still standing aloof, defiant, possessing not even the relenting powers of the pharaohs of old. He has driven a coach and horses through all laws, human and Divine.'[52] Upon his death in April of 1916, the *Irish Independent* contended that Clanricarde was, 'probably, the most hated man in Ireland, and friendless, even amongst his own class':[53] 'Clanricarde was almost the last of his race, the race of absentee landlords, whose neglect of their duties produced much of the misery of Ireland and the distraction of England in the last two centuries.'[54] The *Connacht Tribune*, in a lengthy and unforgiving death notice stated, 'Today, the people remain to inherit his acres, another sits on the throne from which he has been called to higher account and glory no longer guards Clanricarde's grave.'[55]

While the Clanricarde estate comprised a vast patchwork of farms scattered across the south and east of County Galway, there were four major portions of the estate which were perceived as distinct units. The Woodford and Derrybrien portions of the estate lay on the slopes and uplands of the Slieve Aughty Mountains and consisted of very poor agricultural land – being mostly scrubland, bog, wood and mountain. The Portumna and Loughrea portions of the estate, while of mixed quality, generally contained better agricultural farms and comprised a mixture of good and wet grassland, suitable for the grazing of cattle and sheep. Over half of the overall estate was made up of holdings not exceeding a valuation of £7 and many were held in intermixed plots with tenants' holdings consisting of detached patches scattered among other farms.[56]

The tenants' struggle that began on the estate in the winter of 1886 lasted several decades and Clanricarde's infamy contributed to political demands by the IPP for legislative reforms that gave new compulsory powers of purchase to the state in 1909.[57] In total, 186 tenants on the estate were evicted for non-payment of rent with 120 eventually reinstated in their old holdings or given new holdings; 66 of the evicted tenants were never re-instated.[58] The estate was the scene of a prolonged and bitter campaign of boycott and intimidation involving numerous bombings, several murders and continuous low-level warfare against the police, process servers, Clanricarde's workmen and agents and the 'Clanricarde planters', who had taken possession of most of the 254 farms from which tenants had been evicted.[59]

The tenants' campaign centred around the northern planters who had been brought in to replace the evicted tenants and occupied enlarged holdings. Along with the Property Defence Association's workmen, they were the subject of a widespread boycott and were unable to purchase any farm materials or food stuffs in the surrounding towns of Ballinasloe, Loughrea and Portumna. The planters were unable to farm their land effectively as they could not hire labour and shopkeepers would not serve them and only the assistance of 'emergency men' and the protection of the police prevented more drastic measures being taken against them.

Contempt for the planters was echoed by Galway's MPs. In anticipation of legislation designed to address the issue of evicted tenants in 1904, Galway MP John Roche told the House of Commons that the government's treatment of small tenants in south east Galway was reminiscent of, 'what might be expected from a three card trick man on a race course'.[60] With regard to the evicted tenants, he claimed, 'there would never be a settlement of the land question in Ireland until they were re-instated in their old homes and that there would never be peace in the country until the question of the evicted tenants was settled to the satisfaction of all concerned'.[61] The grazing lands on the Clanricarde estate, from which the tenants had been evicted, was in the hands of 'planters', he told the house, 'many of whom had never paid a penny of rent, although houses had been built for them at considerable expense. There ought to be no difficulty in getting rid of those people and in bringing about a settlement of the evicted tenants question.'[62] While statements made under parliamentary privilege in the House of Commons need to be viewed with some circumspection, Roche stated:

> During the past twenty years, more than half the number of planters upon the Clanricarde estate, after enjoying holdings made up of nine or ten holdings grouped together, had walked away without paying a penny of rent. One of these planters, a gentleman named Flower, got nine of these

holdings, and a house was built for him on that farm costing about £400. He stopped there for about three or four years and during that time, not one four footed beast of any sort or description did he put upon the land. Mr. Flower paid no rent, and when he was pressed for it, being unable to pay, he thought the best thing to do was to clear out.[63]

Under the terms of the Wyndham Land Act of 1903, tenants or their representatives who had been evicted over the previous twenty-five years were eligible to apply to purchase their original holdings. If they could not successfully regain their old farms, they were eligible for inclusion in the division of alternative estates, generally in the same locality from which they had been evicted. Despite these procedures, there were several problems that the evicted tenants from the Clanricarde estate faced. The allotment of Clanricarde evictees to plots of land on neighbouring estates was problematic due to the number of cases involved. Evicted tenants were resented by neighbouring tenants; they feared that evicted tenants from neighbouring districts would be favoured above sitting tenants, whilst sitting tenants expected that they would be prioritised in any land division. Martin Finnerty, a local UIL leader in south Galway, admitted before the Royal Commission on Congestion in 1908 that there had been a scheme proposed to bring evicted tenants from the Clanricarde estate onto an estate near Woodford, but 'to say the least, the feeling would not be one of welcome', as 'the feeling in the locality is that farmers' sons should be first'.[64]

The problems faced by evicted tenants were addressed by the 1907 Evicted Tenants Act that gave the Estates Commissioners compulsory powers to acquire land for evicted tenants. However, compulsory purchase was limited and tenanted land, lands subject to land purchase annuities, or demesne land could not be included in any compulsory purchase.[65] These clauses, if sufficiently exploited by a determined landlord provided adequate loopholes to prevent the state from purchasing portions of estates by compulsion. Following the passage of the Evicted Tenants Act, Clanricarde endeavoured to prevent the application of the powers to the estate. As the Act passed into law, his agent summoned a meeting of the planters on the estate with the object of trying to get them to pledge that they would resist any legislation that might be introduced. Several planters told his agent Edward Shaw-Tener that they were 'in fact delighted with the legislation' and 'would be very glad to take compensation and clear out'.[66] Shawe-Tener attempted to get the planters to sign a written pledge to resist any change in their status and when this failed, he attempted to split up the 3,938 acres of untenanted land by planting new tenants across the estate so that there would technically be no untenanted land and thus, the estate would be exempt from government legislation.[67] By 1908, following the successful passage of the Act, the remaining planters on the estate were reported to be protesting against the delay in compensating them caused by Clanricarde's legal appeals.[68]

The Clanricarde estate was among a number of properties that were the intended targets of the compulsory purchase clause of the government's 1909 legislation which provided limited compulsory powers of purchase for the first time. The Portumna branch of the Clanricarde tenants wrote to the CDB in February 1910; the letter was accompanied by a memorial signed by 448 tenants, requesting that the compulsory powers of the 1909 Act be put into effect with immediate effect. In December, the CDB authorised its members to take all necessary steps to initiate proceedings for purchase and in 1912, sent a final offer of £269,115 to Clanricarde's representatives. They received no co-operation from the marquis who unsuccessfully appealed the decision in the House of Lords with the court of appeal eventually fixing the final price at £228,000.[69] In December 1914, the House of Commons unanimously dismissed, without costs, a final appeal by Clanricarde against the sale. Following the purchase of the estate, 'the unfortunate mystic, hated by his own class in Ireland' was, the *Connacht Tribune* claimed:

> A standing menace to the peace with 52,000 acres including the town of Loughrea and other villages that he has never visited. Between 1879 and 1883, 239 families were evicted, and his agent Joyce even went to court to clear his name of the stigma. At a time when nearly all the landlords of Galway were endeavouring to do their duty to the people, Clanricarde was issuing processes and ejectments and preparing the way hard and fast for another campaign.[70]

Clanricarde's agent Edward Shaw-Tener spent the year in advance of the outcome of the appeal to the House of Lords, pursuing back rents and going to the courts for notices of eviction against tenants across south Galway.[71] The issue of outstanding rents was inherently problematic and in September 1915, the police noted, 'A certain amount of tension exists at present amongst the tenants on the Portumna portion of the Clanricarde estate. They have in the last few days been called upon by the CDB to pay one year's rent, due last May. They consider this a hardship as they expected they would not have to pay any rent until the purchase annuities.'[72]

The impending division of a large estate frequently generated a new phase of organisation within communities as the potential for conflict between tenants over competing entitlements began to loom. The decision of the House of Lords was greeted with jubilation in east Galway where the tenants had been organised on the basis of their local UIL cumainn, as well as the much larger, 'Loughrea Clanricarde Tenants Committee' and the 'Portumna Clanricarde Tenants Committee'. January 1915 saw a new phase of organisation as new tenants' committees were formed within the districts of Portumna, Killimore, Eyrecourt and Laurencetown prior to the CDB beginning the process of division.[73] Outstanding issues included the status of town tenants in relation to the distribution, the position of evicted tenants and their eligibility for inclusion in the division, and conversely, the status of the planters who had taken evicted farms on the estate. A group of tenants had been withholding rent in anticipation of a successful outcome for the CDB in the courts, and at Derrybrien, a combination withholding rent were placed under notice of eviction; the agitation subsequently collapsing when the majority of tenants decided to settle.[74]

While the agitation on the Clanricarde estate demonstrated the potential longevity of such agrarian campaigns, the agitation on the Clonbrock estate illustrates the inherent complexities involved in agitations on large estates encompassing numerous disparate districts and communities. Such agitations inevitably involved a range of separate distinct conflicts against individual graziers who rented land from the landlord on different parts of the estate. These complex campaigns were often pursued with different levels of commitment by separate groups of tenants, and the level of co-operation between various groups across large estates varied.

In 1914, the Clonbrock tenants in east Galway refused to accept their landlord's initial offer of sale to the CDB and were determined not to settle until the landlord had been stripped of all his land and the graziers who rented from him forced into giving up their leases.[75] Throughout the campaigns, tenants refused to accept any offers short of their full demands and were prepared to maintain their campaigns over a number of years rather than opt for a quick settlement. The complexities of these campaigns necessitated enormous organisational work, as portions of the estate were spread across many districts, with numerous graziers leasing farms of varying size and quality. Full co-ordination between tenant groups could not be guaranteed and the complexity of organising a united campaign in such circumstances militated against a cohesive estate-wide campaign. The complex web of farms, graziers and tenants involved highlights the convoluted nature of such campaigns and in February 1914, an Estate Commissioners meeting of tenants on the Clonbrock estate at Kilconnell was attended by delegates from the districts of Fohenagh,

Ahascragh, Kilrickle, Mullagh, Killure, Quansboro and Cappataggle.[76] At the Quansboro estate in Mullagh, a large meeting was attended by ninety-nine tenants to discuss the terms of sale of grassland farms in the Abbeygormican and Gurtymadden districts; these consisted of five non-resident grass farms leased by a number of different graziers. The Mullagh UIL leaders advised tenants not to sign any agreement until they got all the grassland on the estate and the tenants unanimously agreed to a united policy.[77]

Later that month, a grazing farm at Abbeygormican had all its stock driven off and police arrested twenty-five men who were subsequently charged with riot and returned for trial.[78] The arrest of the Abbeygormican cattle drivers did not deter the agitators and the following month at Lonmore near New Inn, stock was driven off the grassland farm of Joseph Colohan with a second drive taking place at Toormore in March leading to the arrest of five men.[79] Colohan was one of the biggest graziers in the east of the county with large grazing farms at Ballyeighter, Killure, Toormore and Bellvue, and later in the month, his stock was driven at Bellvue with ten men bound to the peace.[80] The agitation on the Clonbrock estate spread to nearby farms, and in April, fifty men armed with sticks drove sheep off the grazing farm of Thomas Finn at Poppyhill, situated eight miles from Loughrea.[81] As the men involved in the dispute were brought in chains to Galway jail, a party of 170 Irish Volunteers lined the railway platform to cheer them and jeer at the police. In June, the Poppyhill portion of the estate was given over to the agitators on their own terms while the agitation on adjoining lands continued. In August shots were fired into the home of a grazier who was holding a farm of 185 acres at Poppyhill. He had previously surrendered fifty acres to the agitators in 1914 but the tenants were holding out for the entire farm and the Lonmore farm at New Inn and the Abbeygormican grazing farm at Gurtymadden remained under constant police protection.[82]

January 1915 saw a significant victory for the tenants as Colohan had his police protection lifted after surrendering his farm to the CDB, and in April, the Seagriff portion of the estate was sold to the CDB, 'signalling another major victory for the local people'.[83] The final victory for the tenants was announced in November 1915 when the Estates Commissioners acquired 900 acres of grazing land on the Clonbrock estate at Aughrim.[84] The Toormore farm of 115 acres occupied by Joseph Colohan, which was driven several times during the previous four years, was included in the division with Colohan allotted a farm of 130 acres in lieu.[85]

The complexities of the agitation on the Clonbrock estate demonstrates the range of groups, districts and tactics involved in tenant campaigns on very large estates constituting a complex array of localised disputes against different graziers on dispersed farms. Some graziers were more determined than others and by applying pressure to the most vulnerable and varying their tactics where necessary, tenants could successfully intimidate graziers into giving up their tenancies, while ensuring that farmers were discouraged from taking leases on newly vacated farms. A successful agitation on one estate could also spread into neighbouring districts. Following the success of the Clonbrock agitation, a public meeting held in July 1915 saw several hundred tenants vow to embark on a similar agitation on the Lawrence and Pollock estate, until, the meeting declared, the landlord and the grazier, 'were driven from their midst'.[86]

'Worse than the blacks of darkest Africa': neighbourly disputes

Violent feuds between tenants over land were characterised by the readiness of organised factions, often bound together by ties of extended kinship, to resort to extreme violence in disputes with their neighbours. Competitive agitations can be classified into two categories: disputes within localities in advance of a division of land by the state where one or more parties was perceived by others as making an unfair claim for inclusion in a division; and disputes between parties following a division of land to the dissatisfaction of one or more parties who believed they had been treated unfairly.[87]

The Dunsandle estate had been the seat of the Daly family located between Loughrea, Athenry and Craughwell. The Dalys had been the dominant political faction in the county during the late eighteenth and early nineteenth century, but with the social and political transformation of Ireland in the latter half of the century, the family's influence had waned.[88] Following the death of William Daly, the Dunsandle estate was sold to the Estates Commissioners with large portions of Riverville and Bookeen district divided among the tenants.[89] Discontent over the manner in which the estate was divided led to a bitter and lengthy feud between organised factions bonded by kinship and a shared conviction they had been discriminated against by the Estates Committee who were alleged to have favoured members of their own extended families in the allocation of land. Between 1913 and 1919, seven of the ten-man Dunsandle Grazing Land Committee were wounded in gun attacks, while during the same period, seven former members of the Kilconieron and Killimordaly Estates Committee, plus two of their supporters, remained under constant police protection.[90] That so many people in such a small area were accompanied by a constant police patrol and that even these drastic measures failed to prevent attacks attests to the level of violence an unsatisfactory division of land could provoke.

The nature of the division process favoured by the Estates Commissioners differed from that of the CDB and the Dunsandle dispute highlights the inherent flaws in the workings of the Estates Committees whose unsatisfactory handling of the division of estates contributed to feuding. In divisions carried out by the Estates Commissioners, 'impartial' farmers were selected to sit on committees that decided on the allocation of plots based on the criteria of need and ability. As previously discussed, in the Athenry region, the police alleged that secret societies worked hand in hand with both the UIL and the Estate Committees, favouring local organised factions in their allocations of land. Serious problems frequently arose when the deliberations of committees were perceived to be unfair or impartial, and due to the nature of the committee system, violent discontent inevitably arose between neighbouring families.

The police concurred with the view that the division at Dunsandle was unjust and noted that violence, 'is likely to continue until there is a proper division of the lands by the Estates Commissioners or the CDB'.[91] The sheer volume of violent incidents connected with the dispute illustrates the passions provoked by hunger for land between longstanding neighbours. When violent disputes arose, the poor were more vulnerable to the violence of their neighbours than strong farmers; as for tenants who travelled bye-ways on foot or by cart, the eyes of their neighbours were rarely averted and jealousies and resentments could explode at any time.

A dispute similar to the Dunsandle feud existed on the Pollock estate on the Galway–Roscommon border near the village of Creggs; it demonstrated that the clergy were not exempt from the ire of the rural poor when a division of land was deemed unsatisfactory by members of the community. Friction arose in the area after a division of the Pollock estate at Skehard with tenants divided into two factions, one under the Parish Priest Canon Geraghty and one under the farmer William Naughton.[92] The latter group believed the parish priest had been improperly favoured in the distribution made by the Estates Committee with both sides resorting to violence and intimidation against members of the opposing faction.[93] As in the Dunsandle dispute, the fairness of the division was questionable, with the Canon managing to lease 300 acres of land from the estate, prompting the Glenamaddy Board of Guardians to call for an inquiry into the sale.[94] The police concurred with this view noting, 'three large farmers who purchased their holdings on this property some years ago have been requested to surrender portions of their lands for division among the local people. The priest pretended he wanted to keep the land to re-divide it but kept it for himself.'[95]

Outrage at the division led to repeated drives of the Canon's stock and in May 1914, 300 men and women accompanied by a fife and drum band drove cattle as far as Glenamaddy.[96] Constant police protection became necessary to protect the farm and twelve men were subsequently prosecuted for riot.[97] Following the incident, a meeting of Skehard tenants was held at Kilbegnet chapel where the Canon explained to an assembled crowd that he only agreed to take the land in order that it might then be divided up among the local poor but, 'in order to live in peace and concord, and God knows I desire both from the debts of my soul, I have agreed to leave the settlement of this unfortunate misunderstanding to the tenant's solicitor and to mine'.[98] Pending the division, Canon Geraghty continued to assert his legal ownership of the land and his entitlement to set the farm to grazing and the situation remained tense until the CDB repossessed the priest's farm later in the year.[99]

While violence against members of the clergy was rare, jealousy over land could provoke violence against the most vulnerable by relatives and neighbours. In March 1915, the house of John Kelly, an 80-year-old farmer from the Ballinderreen district in south Galway was attacked with gunfire.[100] Nine shots were fired into the cottage and Kelly died from his wounds. The estate on which he lived was in the process of being divided by the CDB and he had previously surrendered twenty-three acres, obtaining six acres from the CDB in return. The police noted, 'It was probably thought that he still held the twenty-six acres or someone coveted the six he received in exchange.'[101] Three men were remanded in Galway jail for trial; however, the police believed, 'there is a difficulty in getting evidence, as even the relatives of the deceased may be described as hostile'.[102] A week after the murder, the Bishop of Galway Dr Thomas O'Dea addressed a public letter to Father Walsh of Ballinderreen to be read out at all masses in the parish. Anticipating a lack of co-operation with the police, the Bishop condemned the perpetrators as:

> Outlaws worse than the blacks of darkest Africa. If any of your people know the perpetrators of this shocking crime, they should at once hand in their names to the police and give evidence against them in court. I repeat that I hold your parish responsible until they show that they are Christians by protesting publicly the horror that they feel at such an outrage perpetrated in their midst.[103]

A similar case only a month later bore parallels to the murder of John Kelly with widespread intimidation and the violation of taboos on the use of violence against the vulnerable. At Loughgeorge, in the parish of Claregalway, the house of Mrs Fox, a widow with a large family of young children, was fired into and her 13-year-old son wounded.[104] Mrs Fox had been in financial difficulties following the death of her husband and was in danger of having to sell her small plot of land. To relieve the situation, it was arranged that the eldest of the Fox daughters would marry a neighbouring farmer who agreed to provide financially for the family with the small farm constituting a dowry. According to the police, the arrangement 'did not suit the views of certain neighbours who expected, through her difficulties, to eventually secure the lands for themselves'.[105] Mrs Fox had earlier received a series of threatening letters and a local farmer with thirty acres was arrested and charged with the shooting. The arrested man was a cousin of Mrs Fox's late husband and had hoped to come into possession of the farm after the death of his cousin. During the trial, a neighbour who had initially claimed to have seen the accused fleeing the scene gave evasive answers to evidence and retracted his initial statements. The case subsequently rested on circumstantial evidence including Mrs Fox's son's testimony that he had recognised his cousin as the gunman on the night he was shot. Following the withdrawal of the key witness, the accused was released due to lack of evidence.

Power and the poor

In the years preceding the rise of militant republicanism, a tradition of violence and an alternative moral code existed in the rural countryside; it represented sophisticated and longstanding mechanisms through which the seemingly powerless exerted influence over landowners. Far from being anarchic, isolated or random, the rituals of violence employed by collectivities of the poor reflected the long traditions and coda of land agitation and reflected the widespread contempt for petty landlordism. The rural poor in the west of Ireland faced two separate and distinct economic phenomena in relation to land: the dominance of the grazing system that excluded the poor from renting grassland farms in areas where land was profitable, exacerbated by the inadequacy of plots distributed among tenants in areas where land was economically unviable. The widespread sympathy for agitators among the community, the difficulty in prosecuting those involved and the violent disdain for large landowners among the rural poor can be understood in this context.

The saliency of land hunger and the ability of the rural poor to sustain lengthy campaigns of intimidation was an enduring feature of rural society in Galway in the early years of the revolution. Both the rural UIL and the inherently respectable leadership of the IPP provided political and practical support to the groups involved despite the prevalence of agrarian violence and widespread coercion. The prevalence of agrarian violence before the rise of the republican movement, the elaborate and clandestine nature of tenant organisation and the passions that land hunger unleashed were symptomatic of a rural society in which particular forms of violence were tolerated and even admired.

In the Galway countryside, violence worked but the factors that compelled collectivities to reject integration with wider national associations and choose clandestine modes of organisation were complex, multiple and ultimately unclear. The temptation to view agrarian violence as irrational or anarchic is too simplistic and in the context of transitional peasant communities worldwide, the modes of resistance used by the rural poor represented rational survival mechanisms employed by communities that found themselves excluded from the capitalist market for land.[106] These agrarian campaigns conformed to the modes of reaction to economic crisis and exploitation observed in other contemporary transitional peasant societies as the rural poor found themselves excluded once land became a commoditised resource rather than a right.[107] The forms of association, violence and moral justification used by collectivities formed part of an historical continuum of agrarianism and the ferocity, persistence and widespread nature of violent agitations constituted the historical residue of more primitive economic conditions.

CHAPTER 2

Rural Society and the Outbreak of War, 1914–16

War, the most terrible war the world has ever known has burst upon us with swift and startling suddenness. Even as we write telegraphists are sending us the news that the North Sea has closed its waters over the heads of thousands of the first hapless victims. The contemplation of what may follow paralyses the mind: but the duty of the hour is to keep the mind sane, the head cool, and to be prepared for eventualities.[1]

Connacht Tribune editorial on the outbreak of the First World War

While the rural community was largely supportive of the British War effort during the First World War, this support was comparatively passive and recruitment in the west of Ireland was the lowest in the British Isles. The War had a profound effect on rural society and with rising prices for produce, the sons of middling and strong farmers benefitted from the booming economy and had little incentive to join the urban poor in their early rush to reap the financial rewards of enlistment in the great military adventure their social betters promoted. While the War boosted the prospect of a better wage for the labour of the rural poor, the rising cost of foodstuffs and other necessities pushed many into enlisting as a means of augmenting their families' meagre wages. For the urban poor, the recruitment propaganda of the early War years promised an alluring alternative to the tedium of the lanes, the labourer's cottage and the public house. It was a vision of War that soon proved to be a brutal deception.

Local government was devolved in 1898 and the establishment of town councils and rural and urban district councils swept away the last vestiges of landlord involvement in civil administration. For most people, involvement in politics meant membership of their local United Irish League (UIL) branch.

The UIL was the grassroots organisation of the IPP and was founded in 1898 with the motto 'the land for the people'. Issues such as striking the annual rates for property owners, the building of labourers' cottages and public sanitation occupied the energies of local bodies, incubating democracy at a grassroots level. Involvement in constituency issues varied between MPs but many representatives saw their primary function as legislating at Westminster with local issues often left to party activists. Local politics was often boisterous, frequently characterised by the intensity of local rivalries and political meetings were covered in detail by partisan newspaper editors.

Pivotal developments were witnessed in 1914 that transformed politics in Ireland, invigorated the physical force tradition and destroyed the IPP. The outbreak of conflict in 1914, coupled with the militant resistance of northern unionists to the Home Rule Bill created conditions in which militant movements gained a hitherto unthinkable popular credibility. The War years saw the erosion of support for the IPP among an increasingly sceptical population. Galway's five MPs were personally committed to the War effort and like their leader, John Redmond, assumed the War would be brief and that Catholic Ireland's participation would nullify Edward Carson's enthusiastic warmongering. Their contempt for the erstwhile local rivals in Sinn Féin stemmed not from any aversion to republicanism but a deep-rooted sense that the rise of Sinn Féin reflected the rank ingratitude of a younger generation of rural smallholders who had benefited from successive land reform acts wrought by the IPP whose leadership and analysis they now had the temerity to challenge. A generational and class dimension to the political struggle within nationalism was central to political discourse from the outset.

The outbreak of the First World War was to have fundamental repercussions for Irish society; however, despite the upheaval about to be wrought by the conflict, there was little to indicate the imminent demise of the nationalist political establishment in Galway until the latter end of the War. The political culture of the IPP at the beginning of the revolutionary era has been characterised by Michael Wheatley as eminently respectable, conservative and profoundly un-revolutionary, with activists concerned with distinctly local political issues.[2] The dominance of the UIL was unchallenged and consequently, party structures became increasingly dormant and the movement's apparent lack of vigour became a source of concern for the national leadership in 1915.

While the UIL constituted a broad organisation encompassing diverse political traditions, two distinct political cultures were apparent in Galway. Unlike the rural UIL – as discussed in the previous chapter – which tended to focus on the central issue of land reform, the political culture of Galway's towns tended to be conservative, socially respectable and vociferously pro-War. Urban elites in Galway City, such as leading 'public men', Philip O'Donnell and Máirtín Mór McDonogh or Loughrea's Member of Parliament, William Duffy, tended to come from mercantile or professional backgrounds. While Galway's local newspaper editors were staunch supporters of the UIL, the domination of towns by conservative merchant families provoked the East Galway Democrat to accuse the local branch of the UIL of being dominated by merchants who entered politics to stymie the provision of labourers' cottages for the working poor.[3] While support for the War waned dramatically from mid-1916 onwards, the towns did not develop a strong republican organisation at any point.[4] Popular hostility to Sinn Féin and the Volunteers remained profound across social classes throughout the period and was to be a notable feature of War of Independence. Captain of the Galway brigade of the Irish Volunteers Larry Lardiner later recalled, 'there were some towns at this time, notably Galway City and Loughrea, where it was impossible to do anything for the Volunteers, the inhabitants were so hostile and the number of Volunteers in these places was small. Ballinasloe might be added to the above.'[5] Likewise, Volunteer John Hosty of Galway town told the Bureau of Military History:

> The finest body of fifth columnists in Ireland were in Galway town. The remainder of the County, especially around Castlegar area, was pretty good and could always be relied on for any help required. They were a deterrent factor against the likelihood of any of us here in town getting a bashing. You could always call on them if necessary and, did the other side know it, not half.[6]

'The auld stock': the War and the Irish Parliamentary Party

The lack of a serious electoral challenge to the IPP in Galway can retrospectively be identified as an obvious factor in the party's inability to fend off the Sinn Féin challenge when the latter comprehensively defeated the party in the General Election of 1918. Without the benefit of hindsight, however, there seemed to be little for the IPP to be alarmed about during the early years of the War. Complacency characterised the 1914 local elections and in Galway town, eighteen of the sitting candidates were re-elected.[7] With no Sinn Féin representatives standing, two labour candidates were elected with the UIL taking the remaining seats.

There were five parliamentary constituencies in the county until the General Election of December 1918 when the county's electoral boundaries were re-drawn and Galway town lost its borough status, leaving the constituencies of Galway north, south, east and the newly enlarged Galway west constituency. In 1914, Stephen Gwynn was the only MP of the five Galway representatives that had ever beaten a nationalist opponent in an election in the county (he defeated landowner, John Shawe-Taylor in a by-election in 1906). In the 1910 General Election, four of the five victorious candidates were returned unopposed with Gwynn defeating an independent unionist from Bradford, J.L. Wanklyn.[8] In the preceding General Election in 1906, only six candidates competed for the five available seats in the county, with north Galway being the only contested constituency.[9] Absenteeism was no barrier to political representation and only two of the county's five MPs – James Cosgrave of Eyrecourt and William Duffy of Loughrea – actually lived in Galway.

The history of the Galway town borough illustrates the political complacency of the IPP and the disconnection this fostered with the wider electorate. The borough had not been represented by a native Galwegian since the unionist, Martin Morris, later Lord Killanin, was returned in a by-election in 1901. Gwynn's two predecessors were both unlikely representatives: Charles Ramsey Devlin, who later became a Member of Parliament in his native Canada, was returned in a by-election in 1903; this had come about due to charges of high treason brought against incumbent, Arthur Alfred Lynch, an Australian anti-imperialist.[10]

William O'Malley was MP for West Galway and was born in Ballyconnelly on Connemara's north western shore; he first claimed the west Galway seat as an anti-Parnell MP in 1895.[11] O'Malley was returned unopposed in five consecutive elections between 1895 and 1910. He moved to England in his late teens to attend the Hammersmith Training College for Teachers but spent his working life as a journalist in London, Brighton and Hove, becoming manager of *The Star* and later writing for *The Sun*.[12] He married Mary O'Connor, sister of prominent nationalist MP T.P. O'Connor, and their only son, William, was killed in action in France in 1917. A director of the *Connacht Tribune* newspaper to which he contributed a weekly article, *Letter from Westminster*, O'Malley wrote in English, rather than Irish, the first language of a large number of those he represented in parliament. O'Malley was, for all intents and purposes, an absentee representative for Connemara. His main political gripe was the Congested Districts Board (CDB) and its perceived inefficiency was the subject of sustained criticism. While he was genuinely echoing the feelings of his constituents on this matter, O'Malley's anger may also have been influenced by his disappointment at not having been selected as a representative of the Board when its trustees were selected for their seven-year term in 1915.

Absenteeism nurtured an obvious form of dislocation among representatives from the realities of their constituents' daily concerns, something that would be brutally exposed during the 1918 General Election. William O'Malley crucially underestimated the strength of local feeling in a celebrated agrarian dispute over grazing land at Tullycross, near Clifden in 1915.[13] His initial condemnation of the Letterfrack UIL was evidence of how aloof he had become from popular sentiment. His failure to support the tenants provoked a stinging rebuke from UIL representatives, who forced him to travel to Clifden to explain his remarks; once there he hastily visited his incarcerated constituents.[14] Following his defeat in the 1918 General Election he retired to Athlone, where he spent many of his remaining years defending the record of the IPP in his self-serving biography.[15]

While the 'auld stock' of Galway politics peppered their political rhetoric with frequent references to the land fights of the late nineteenth century, their personal investment in the recruitment effort was profoundly held. William O'Malley and his colleagues were personally and politically committed to the War effort and those who gathered in town squares to hear recruitment speeches were left in no doubt that Ireland was at War and Galway was on the front line. While on a recruitment drive on the Aran Islands in February 1916, O'Malley proclaimed:

> Notwithstanding what they might be told by certain people, they must realise that this was Ireland's war as much as it was England's, for if England went down before the Germans, Ireland would undoubtedly go down too. Ireland's future depended on the part she played in this world war and those who told the people – he did not care who they were – that young Irishmen should stay at home and that the war was no concern of theirs, were men who were prepared to see Ireland governed by the barbarous Huns, and had no true conception of the great and far-reaching issues involved in the war.[16]

Stephen Gwynn, MP for Galway town borough, was a quintessential Anglo-Irish gentleman, constituting an uncharacteristically cosmopolitan figure in the somewhat dour political scene in Galway town. The son of a Church of Ireland clergyman and a grandson on his mother's side of the nineteenth-century nationalist, William Smith O'Brien, Gwynn entered nationalist politics in 1906 when, after a decision that was not universally popular in Galway, he was imposed on the local party organisation.[17] Gwynn grew up in Dublin and Donegal within a unionist landowning social milieu and studied literature at Oxford, publishing on an array of Irish topics including history, novels and literary criticism. In 1911, he was asked by John Redmond to write *The Case for Home Rule*, in which he espoused Ireland's claim for self-governance:

> The demand for Home Rule means no less and no more than this: Ireland asks for an Irish Parliament, with an executive responsible to it, to deal with purely Irish affairs, subject to Imperial supremacy.

> In other words, we ask that laws relating to Ireland alone shall be made by a popularly elected assembly sitting in Ireland, having leisure to deal with the necessities of the case, and possessing first-hand knowledge of them: and that responsibility for the administration of Ireland shall be confided to a Ministry chosen by Ireland, and going out of office when Irish public sentiment demands a change.[18]

Converted to moderate nationalism during the Boer War, Gwynn became associated with the Gaelic League until 1909 and sent his son Denis to attend Patrick Pearse's school, St Enda's in Rathfarnham. Gwynn later described canvassing for election in Galway as 'a disgusting job' and his successful election for the borough as a 'comic saga'.[19] Like his fellow Galway MPs, Hazelton and O'Malley, Gwynn did not live in his constituency, being more at home in London's political and literary circles.

Upon the outbreak of the War, Gwynn was very active in the recruitment campaign and regularly appeared on public platforms across the west of Ireland. He was rewarded by being made the western representative on the government's Recruitment Board and was one of only five Irish MPs to enlist, serving as a lieutenant with the 6th battalion, Connaught Rangers, eventually being made a *chevalier* of the *Legion d'honneur* in July 1917.

As always in Irish politics, behind the candidates stood the real political movers, in Gwynn's case, the indomitable Máirtín Mór McDonogh. Originally from humble peasant stock, McDonogh's father dragged his family out of poverty in south Connemara by working as a middleman for local landlords.[20] By marrying wisely and investing in land and cattle, he laid the foundation for his son's business empire. McDonogh & Sons consisted of a large fertiliser factory, general stores and numerous commercial ventures and McDonogh was the primary employer and businessman in Galway town, as well as being chairman of the urban district council, among numerous other bodies. In

1929, he was ruthlessly parodied in Liam O'Flaherty's banned novel, *The House of Gold*, with O'Flaherty contending, 'In every little town in Ireland, you will find a man like Ramon Mór, a grabber, who makes his money by worse usury than Shylock ever practiced.'[21]

McDonogh's monopoly in business allowed him to dominate commerce in Galway town and in 1911, he formed the Galway Employers' Federation to counter the establishment of a fledgling union of dock workers. The emergence of organised labour in the town dated back to August 1911 with the inaugural meeting to found the Galway Workers' and General Labourers' Union (GWGLU).[22] William O'Halloran became the full-time secretary of the union and 150 members enrolled at a preliminary meeting in the Racquet Court Theatre.[23] In a year of turmoil for dock workers across Ireland, 600 Galway dock workers walked out of work at the end of March 1913 in protest at the Employers Federations' refusal to agree new pay rates and conditions.[24] The strike spread to other trades and police reinforcements were drafted to deal with any potential defiance. In April, scab labour from Liverpool provided by the Shipping Federation appeared on the dockside.[25] The strike lasted five weeks and was settled following negotiations with the employers making modest concessions. The episode epitomised the contempt held for notions of social progress and the plight of the urban poor in Ireland's rural towns amongst a prominent coterie of leading merchants, many of whom were allied to the IPP and regarded as staunch nationalists.

Few were safe when McDonogh's ire was raised. At a recruitment rally in Eyre Square, he ridiculed a group of agricultural labourers waiting to be hired nearby:

> I'll hire you and I will give you more pay than you will get from the farmers. Why do ye not go? Perhaps ye were thinking that on the lands that ye were going to there would be no German bullets, well, ye will be in as much danger on the bogs from God's lightening as on the battlefield from German bullets.[26]

McDonogh's ridicule of those who failed to heed the call to enlist mirrored that of the wider establishment; noting the poor recruitment figures in Galway, Judge Boyd commented at the summer assizes in 1915, 'If men were men, and do not fear to encounter their enemy, what I would like to see in County Galway is a little more manly spirit to come forward to the defence of the Realm.'[27] For leading public men such as McDonogh, Galway's duty in the

War was clear, as Jackie Uí Chionna has explained, 'McDonogh was 54 when war broke out, and, as a committed home ruler, as he saw it, his duty was clear. His commitment to the war was absolute.'[28]

The visit of the Lord Lieutenant Lord Wimborne provides a snapshot of Galway's political allegiances in January 1916. With the main streets bedecked in red, white and blue, the procession of dignitaries was received by a guard of honour from the Craughwell Company of the Redmondite National Volunteers and paraded under royal standards with union jack flags decorating Eyre Square.[29] With a banner proclaiming, 'One Life, One Navy, One Throne' holding pride of place, Wimborne was officially welcomed at a reception attended by an exhaustive list of prominent citizens.[30] There was no discord surrounding the visit and the occasion represented an immense boost to the local UIL. As ever, Thomas Kenny, editor of the *Connacht Tribune*, was on hand to record the tenor of events and the tone of its coverage left readers in no doubt of the majesty of the occasion:

> The event made a curious appeal to the public and for some weeks, strenuously, for some days, all classes of the community contributed intelligent effort and hearty goodwill toward making it a success, whatever their private leanings. Is there something in the people of Galway that easily disposes them to a deferential recognition of the claims of high authority and glittering prerogative?[31]

While Stephen Gwynn represented a self-consciously cosmopolitan approach to national politics, Loughrea's own William Duffy represented an infinitely more local style of representation. As MP for south Galway since 1900, he controlled a large political organisation from his base in the town where his family ran a substantial grocery business. Through trusted local lieutenants, Duffy's organisation dominated civic bodies and ensured that when the Volunteer movement split in September 1914, all but a handful from the town stayed loyal to John Redmond. After the split, National Volunteer parades were generally held in Loughrea and organised by Duffy, often in direct response to Irish Volunteer parades in Athenry. As we shall see, when the Gaelic Athletic Association (GAA) in the county split along political lines, the new Redmondite, National Gaelic Athletic Association, held its meetings in Loughrea, and were chaired by UIL councilor Martin Ward, while the original county board of the GAA, which was dominated by the Irish Republican Brotherhood (IRB), continued to hold meetings in Athenry. Such local rivalries were commonplace and pursued with zeal on the battlefield of the local GAA fields.

Rather than constituting fundamentally separate and distinct traditions, parliamentary and extra-parliamentary agitation was frequently intertwined. To bolster popular support, militant and quasi-separatist language was frequently employed by IPP representatives. William Duffy was imprisoned during the Plan of Campaign of 1886–7 and loudly and repeatedly proclaimed his connection to the violence of the period as a badge of honour. Remarkably, Duffy secured a farm from the CDB in the Closetoken area in 1915 when an estate was redistributed by the local branch of the UIL. As the local MP, he personally handled the transfer of the land on behalf of the tenants and his acquisition of the farm was resented by local tenants. Duffy's farm was attacked and stone walls knocked down in a series of night raids in 1915.[32] He remained unrepentant, however, claiming he only came into possession of the farm after the needs of local tenants were satisfied. Volunteer Patrick Coy later recalled, 'He [Duffy] had a big following in the town composed of a mixture of the well-to-do and the stone and bottle throwing element. The latter were mainly ex-British soldiers and their families.'[33] Duffy was one of the few IPP members to be successfully elected as both an MP and a TD and he was returned to Dáil Éireann for the Irish Centre Party in 1927.[34]

'Honest' James Cosgrave, MP for South Galway, won his seat in east Galway in a 1914 by-election caused by the death of the sitting MP John Roche. Roche was a tenant farmer from the Clanricarde estate and a revered local figure, having been jailed for his activities during the Plan of Campaign in 1886.[35] He in turn, had been preceded by Land Leaguer and Fenian Matt Harris, who had been a close associate of Michael Davitt and the founder of the Ballinasloe Tenants' Defence Association. For many years Cosgrave was at the head of the tenants' campaign in south-east Galway to have the estate of the Marquis of Clanricarde purchased by the CDB, the same campaign his predecessors had fought and the defining political issue in the countryside between Portumna and Loughrea. A native of Eyrecourt, Cosgrave appeared on platforms for several generations addressing tenants' meetings and acting as secretary to the Portumna Clanricarde Tenants Association. He was vocal in the campaign for the release of tenants arrested after a riot in Loughrea in May 1914, during which cattle drivers fought a pitched battle with police.[36] In October 1918, Cosgrave was still battling the military, police and landowners and along with two local priests, he faced down a force of military and police that arrived to clear stock from a 200-acre ranch that tenants were occupying with their cattle.[37] Along with William Duffy, Cosgrave was very active in recruitment campaigns and this may have undone much of his hard-earned popularity. His decision not to stand in the 1918 General Election was a major blow to the party, leaving a void that could not be filled. The organisation was unable to persuade any candidate to stand, leaving Liam Mellows to take the seat unopposed for Sinn Féin.[38]

MP for north Galway Richard Hazleton was educated at Blackrock College in his native south Dublin and was first elected in Galway in a by-election in 1906. A moderate nationalist, he was prone to ending political speeches by asking for a rendition of 'God Save the King', much to the intense irritation of his colleagues.[39] He spent an inordinate part of his tenure defending his reputation and livelihood through the law courts.[40] He did not confine his political interests to Galway and was permanently based in south Dublin. Returned in Galway again in 1910, he also stood unsuccessfully in the North Louth constituency, where he was defeated by T.M. Healy by just over one hundred votes. Following the result, Healy managed to petition Hazleton for his costs, and in the process, tried to force him to retire his seat due to his bankruptcy.[41] A claim for £2,000 in costs was made and Healy and his followers started proceedings in the English courts with the objective of making Hazleton bankrupt, and therefore unable to continue as an MP. In anticipation of the court's findings, Hazleton retired his seat in Galway in June 1914. The courts subsequently overturned the original bankruptcy decision, which had forced the by-election in the first place. Hazleton once again secured the support of the Party and was automatically re-elected unopposed.

Hazleton involved himself less in his constituency as his financial and legal problems mounted and he was not as prominent in the local recruitment campaign as his colleagues. As one of the key organisers of the Party's strategy for the 1918 General Election, he stood unsuccessfully in Louth, losing by 255 votes to J.J. O'Kelly of Sinn Féin. Embittered by the collapse of the Party, he emigrated to England shortly afterwards and spent the remainder of his life in London.

War and recruitment

With Galway's nationalist newspaper editors championing the exploits of Irish regiments at the front and local political leaders haranguing crowds from platforms up and down the county, the reticence of the rural poor to join the War effort was notable. Throughout the War, the farming community was singled out by recruiters and politicians alike for their relative reticence to join the War effort. James Craig offered a succinct explanation in Parliament for

Irish farmers' reticence: 'If you have two farmers, one of whom goes and the other remains, the feeling in the breast of the farmer who goes out to fight is that his neighbour and competitor is having it all his own way, and that he is undergoing great trial and suffering in order that his neighbour may reap all the benefits when the War is over.'[42] The recruiting board estimated that in August 1915, there were 416,409 men of military age in Ireland, 252,000 of whom worked in agriculture. Noting the chasm in recruiting figures between the urban and rural poor, the authorities blamed the economic boom in agriculture for farmers' sons reluctance to join the military.[43] Concluding that recruits from urban centres had reached maximum capacity, the authorities concluded in January 1916:

> It will be evident that the smaller class of those outside the industry of agriculture, from which in the main the recruits have up to the present been drawn, is not in a position to provide an additional large contingent of recruits, although further support may be expected from the commercial and shop assistant classes, or from those engaged in occupations in which their services can be replaced by women.[44]

Irishmen joined the military for a variety of personal, political and economic reasons.[45] The appeal to patriotism espoused by political leaders and recuitment propaganda targeting farmers may have had a formative influence during the early months of the War; however, economic necessity was the most significant factor. The Inspector General of the Royal Irish Constabulary (RIC) noted the popular mood in rural Ireland in August:

> All classes displayed a strong patriotic and anti-German feeling and joined irrespective of creed and politics in giving a hearty send off to the reservists when they left to join the colours. Popular feeling is undoubtedly in sympathy with Great Britain and hostile to Germany. Sinn Feiners, and other extremists, are here and there making efforts to stir up anti-British feeling by the dissemination of seditious literature, setting forth that 'Ireland has no quarrel with Germany', 'England's difficulty is Ireland's opportunity', etc., which must do a certain amount of harm; but it has not yet affected the public mind to any serious extent. There is a general dread of German invasion.[46]

The vibrancy of Galway's local newspapers was remarkable with four politically partisan papers produced weekly: two in Galway town and one in Tuam and

Ballinasloe respectively – all of which were vehemently opposed to Sinn Féin and the Irish Volunteers throughout the period (bar a brief period between late 1917 and September 1920 when the *Galway Express* was taken over by Sinn Féin supporters). The editors of the four main papers vociferously supported the recruitment drive and dedicated lengthy editorials to the War effort.

Thomas Kenny, editor and co-founder of the *Connacht Tribune* in 1909, was originally from Cork but established himself as a central figure in the public life of Galway. The paper was founded by supporters of the IPP and was the most widely circulated and influential in the county. The *Tribune* was an implacable supporter of John Redmond and the War effort and Kenny was possessed of formidable eloquence in his lengthy editorials that spared neither political friend nor foe. Following violent clashes between Sinn Féin members and IPP supporters in October 1914, Kenny wrote, 'Sinn Féin was hitherto treated with generous tolerance in the city, it has grossly abused that tolerance … now the attitude is that tolerance has reached its limit, the puny plotters have only themselves to blame.'[47] Upon the outbreak of war Kenny urged unstinting support for John Redmond's leadership, 'in this moment of crisis Redmond has once more spoken for our own land words of wisdom and justice. The moment may come when even we may be forced into this bloody conflict.'[48]

The *Tuam Herald* was the most widely read paper in the north of the county and was vociferous in its support for the War effort. Richard J. Kelly was editor from the 1880s until his death in 1931 and was grandson of the founder of the paper. From early in the century, Kelly lived in Dublin, leaving the day-to-day management of the paper in the hands of John Burke. Burke was an early member of Sinn Féin and elected for the party to the Tuam Town Commissioners in 1907.[49] Despite Burke's background, the paper consistently expounded Galway's perceived patriotic duty to support the War effort. On the outbreak of the conflict, the paper editorialised, 'the upholding and sacredness of the principal of nationality being one of the main things that is now being fought for in the present war'.[50] The paper published 'Battle Song', upon the outbreak of conflict, typical of the many similar ditties published with regularity during the period:

> Sons of the Gael, where er ye be,
> Let not the alien spoiler rend,
> In twain your ancient land.
> Arm ye! Defend,
> The cairns of them who for her dark hills died.[51]

The *Galway Express* originally represented the views of the small Protestant community in Galway and the paper's editor, H.D. Fisher regularly condemned, what he termed, 'the pro-German section of our community'. Fisher's rhetoric escalated as the War progressed and the paper became increasingly intolerant of any perceived slight to the military. The small signs of Sinn Féin growth during the War infuriated Fisher and he wondered 'why do not our people recognise the fact that they are being driven into rat holes':

> Sinn Feiners cannot be tolerated, they must be absolutely put down if they speak against the protection of Ireland from the enemy. If traitors are in the country, they can only expect the fate of such, and we saw with all sincerity that we trust that when any signs of traitorous conduct are evinced, or any meetings held which are pro-German, all the parties should be held up as people who are enemies and who are playing into the hands of the brutal and anti-Catholic Huns.[52]

Estimates of the number of Irish-born soldiers who fought in the War have varied, but it is clear that 210,000 represents a conservative estimate.[53] Figures are problematic due to the number of Irish-born men who enlisted in Britain, America, Canada, Australia and New Zealand. Canadian researchers have found that 19,000 Irish-born men fought in the Canadian Forces, while Australia had nearly 5,000.[54] We have no comparative figures for the number of Irish-born recruits for the two largest centres of Irish migration, the United States and Britain. In terms of casualties, the Irish Memorial Rolls, compiled in 1923, lists 49,435 Irish War dead; however, the list is compiled from those who fought in Irish regiments only and includes men not born in Ireland while omitting the large number of Irish who fought in non-Irish regiments. To complicate matters further, there is no means of quantifiying the number of Irish-born men, who were conscripted or enlisted abroad, who gave their British address as place of origin.

Rural Irish people were less likely than those in other parts of the United Kingdom to join the army and those in Connacht were less likely than elsewhere in Ireland. The number of recruits raised in Ireland in the period from 2 August 1914 to 8 January 1916 was 86,277. Of this number, just 3,678 were raised in the 88th regimental district that comprised the counties of Connacht.[55] The distribution of recruits to the army and navy between 2 August 1914 and 15 December 1915 highlights this regional disparity with police estimating the figures as: Ulster, 49,760; Leinster, 27,458; Munster, 14,190; and Connacht, a mere 3,589.[56]

In terms of the War dead listed in the Irish Memorial Rolls, 743 men with Galway addresses are included. The Galway dead fought in a range of regiments; however, the largest number by some margin fought in the Connacht Rangers, with some 270 casualties. Galway casualties are listed in sixty-eight different regiments, with casualties concentrated in the Irish regiments, in particular: Irish Guards (75); Leinster Regiment (39); Royal Dublin Fusiliers (37) and Royal Munster Fusiliers (35). Of the 743 Galway casualties, 94 were killed in the initial five months of the War; 179 were killed in 1915; 179 in 1916; 157 in 1917 and 120 in 1918.[57] For the reasons previously discussed, however, it is clear that these figures represent a significant under-estimation of the true number of participants and casualties.

Originally raised in 1793 as the 88th Regiment of Foot, the Connaught Rangers were stationed at Renmore on the outskirts of Galway town. The vast majority of recruits were farmers' sons and the sons of the working poor of the towns who joined for economic reasons. Both of the regiment's regular battalions served in the War with four additional battalions formed in 1914. The Connaught Rangers saw service at some of the most iconic battles including Ypres, The Somme and Gallipoli, as well in more far-flung theatres of war including, Egypt, Palestine and the Mesopotamia campaign.[58]

The 1st battalion 'Connaughts' were stationed in Karachi before the War erupted and were posted to the Western Front. The 2nd battalion was based at Aldershot and took part in the original British Expeditionary Force (BEF) that arrived at Boulogne on 14 August 1914. Due to heavy losses, this battalion was merged with the 1st battalion in December 1914. The combined 1st and 2nd battalion fought at the First Battle of Messines in October 1914 and the Second Battle of Ypres in April 1915. The 1st battalion subsequently fought in the Mesopotamia campaign.

The 3rd and 4th reserve battalions were formed at Renmore barracks and Boyle, County Roscommon respectively. The 3rd battalion was based in Newcastle, England, and the 4th battalion moved to Scotland with both subsequently amalgamated into the larger battalions. The 5th battalion Connaughts fought in the disastrous second offensive at Gallipoli in August 1915. This battalion was mainly composed of new recruits and landed at what became known as Anzac Cove on 5 August. The battalion suffered heavy casualties before being withdrawn in September. The battalion subsequently served on the Salonika Front, fighting the Bulgarians in southern Serbia at the battle of Kosturino on 7 December 1915. The battalion was later stationed in Palestine. The 6th service battalion Connaughts fought on the Western Front from 1916 to the end of the War and participated in a number of campaigns, including The Somme, Third Battle of Ypres (Passchendaele) and Cambrai. The battalion suffered such heavy losses that it had to be disbanded in April 1918.

'An honest and manly stand': the Irish Volunteers, 1913–16

The early years of the War saw a marginal republican presence in Galway coalesce around a small number of active Irish Volunteer companies in the south-east of the county. Some of the most active IRB figures in the county at this time were in the Athenry district with Dick Murphy acting as the head centre (organiser) for the county. Along with Murphy, Jack Broderick, Larry Lardiner and Stephen Jordan from Athenry set up Volunteer companies in neighbouring districts. Eámonn Corbett and Patrick Callanan from Craughwell, Tom Ruane and Mick Newell from Carnmore, Micheál Ó Droighneáin from Spiddal, Liam Langley from Tuam, Joseph Howley from Oranmore and George Nichols from Galway town comprised the leadership of a conspiratorial network of rural IRB militants on which the new organisation was built.

The Galway town branch of the Irish Volunteers was founded at a public meeting in December 1913 with Roger Casement and Eoin MacNeill leading a torch-lit procession of students through the town, headed by the brass band of the St Patrick's Society and the Bohermore Fife and Drum Band.[59] Following the customary speeches and the election of a provisional committee, hundreds of men joined the new organisation. The apparent success of the meeting was an illusion, however, and most new recruits never became active, as Volunteer Thomas Hynes later recalled: 'that was all was heard of most of them'.[60]

The establishment of the Volunteers was not initially viewed with a great degree of alarm by either the police or their political rivals in the UIL. There was little that was actively conspiratorial about their activities and training exercises were carried out in full view of the authorities with some ex-servicemen perceiving their efforts as a means of eventually encouraging young men to join the British army.[61] Companies occupied themselves with route marches at weekends, with drill practice on weeknights and officers elected by the rank and file. Companies had few rifles, leading to frequent problems with boredom and indiscipline as recruits found the excitement they anticipated failing to materialise.

Volunteers who enrolled in the new force were overwhelmingly the sons of the rural poor, small farmers and rural labourers – young men for whom the camaraderie provided a welcome release from the tedium of servitude.

A striking feature of the initial phase of the movement was the small but significant number of clergy who played considerable roles in organising companies. Fr John W. O'Meehan of Kinvara was central to the formation of his local company and supplied the group with caps and suitable reading material. Fr Henry Feeney of Clarinbridge became a close confidante of Liam Mellows with his parochial house used for IRB meetings. Fr Connolly of Garbally College, Ballinasloe, was also consulted by the IRB leadership regarding their plans.[62]

Under Tom Kenny's guidance, the IRB in Galway had been centred around the twin rural pre-occupations of hurling and land agitation. Tony Varley has noted that Kenny 'personified in the eyes of many the Fenian tradition of pursuing nationalist and agrarian concerns together'.[63] Through more than a decade of land agitation, Kenny laid the platform for his younger acolytes to develop the Volunteer organisation. Michael Newell recalled that in the Castlegar circle of the IRB:

> The principal matters discussed at the meetings were, the recruiting of new members and land division. At this time there was a great deal of agitation for the division of land. The IRB took a leading part in the agitation and carried out numerous cattle drives, also the breaking down of walls on the farms of landlords and land-grabbers, whose houses were also fired into.[64]

Volunteer Peter Howley noted that he had little trouble in recruiting eighty men from around the Ardrahan district as 'there was a continuous war being waged against the landlords and the RIC in County Galway, right up to the formation of the Volunteers in the year 1914'.[65] Tom Kenny's role as chairman of the county board of the GAA was central to spreading the new movement. Volunteer Pat 'the Hare' Callanan was eventually to fall out with Kenny, but recalled the heady mixture of land and freedom in the Galway IRB: 'The principal matters discussed at meetings [of the IRB] were, land division, methods to be adopted to compel landlords to sell holdings to tenant farmers, which included cattle driving, breaking walls and the firing into the houses of landlords and their supporters.'[66]

As the Volunteer movement grew, their main concern, as elsewhere, was lack of arms. The IRB ensured that all senior members in the county were IRB men, as Larry Lardiner, Captain of the Athenry company recalled:

> Arms were now what was required and all went to work to collect funds to buy them, each company made a collection [and] on the whole realised a

fair amount of money, particularly as a good number of the aristocratic class who did not agree with Carson and the Northern Volunteers subscribed generously. The difficulty now was for the officers and men who were in the IRB and Sinn Féin and keep counsel over all the companies and also control all the funds and the arms.[67]

The takeover of the Volunteers by the IPP in May 1914 led to a fundamental change in the nature and political complexion of the organisation, as Larry Lardiner recalled: 'this upset everything, immediately and it was with the greatest difficultly that a complete smash up was avoided'.[68] The leadership of the IPP gave their official support to the Volunteer movement in May, precipitating a national wave of enthusiasm as UIL members joined Volunteer branches in their thousands, or in most cases, set up new ones in areas where none previously existed. Within a few weeks of the initial re-organisation, the organisation was 3,033 men strong and organised into thirty branches across Galway.[69] The rapid expansion of the force became a major source of concern to the authorities in Dublin Castle and in a far-sighted note of warning, the Chief Inspector of Police for Ireland wrote:

> The rank and file of the Irish Volunteers are drawn from the very class with whom the police have frequently come into collision during agrarian disturbance. In Ireland, the training and drilling of the male population is a new departure, which is bound, in the not too distant future, to profoundly alter the existing conditions of life. Obedience to the law has never been a prominent characteristic of the people. In times of passion or excitement the law has only been maintained by force and this has been rendered practicable owing to the want of cohesion among crowds hostile to the police. If the people become armed and drilled, effective police control will vanish. Unless the population which is now being drilled and armed is placed under some responsible leadership or control, these trained bands of men will be used for cattle driving or other similar illegalities.[70]

The expansion of the Volunteers saw individuals join the movement who ostensibly made extremely unlikely supporters and who brought new motives and agendas into the organisation. The Galway police noted, 'In the towns, the ranks are recruited from shop assistants and labourers with a small proportion of shopkeepers and tradesmen, and in the country localities, farmers and farmers' sons dominate the ranks … The force is badly organised however and with not much discipline.'[71] Volunteer committees attained a new social and political character with leading merchants and prominent figures among the new county leadership. Parliamentary representatives who had previously ignored the Volunteers appeared on public platforms and leading merchants such as Máirtín Mór McDonogh became officers.

Members of the Galway gentry perceived the force as a possible future component of the British military and their attempts to influence the movement were obvious, if not widely shared, and the support of the gentry was a mixed blessing.[72] Members of the old landed elite, such as Sir Henry Grattan Bellew, became chief inspecting officer for the county, with Captain Charles Philips and Major James Cheevers acting as his assistants.[73] The police reported, 'members and leaders of the local gentry in Athenry and Mountbellew who were formerly looked upon as unionists are foremost members and leaders and have subscribed large sums of money towards the purchase of arms and equipment'.[74]

The evolution of the organisation into a mass movement generated palpable excitement and a newfound confidence among young men who enrolled. The authorities noted with alarm the less deferential attitude that membership inspired among some recruits and the police noted that Galway was, 'in the grip of the Volunteer movement recruited in nearly every branch by moonlighters and other seditious and undesirable characters'.[75] Police were fired at on a number of occasions in the village of Clarinbridge and a frustrated county inspector noted, 'these people seem to be under the impression that all law has been abrogated in this area because they are Volunteers and that they can indulge in the amusement of firing at the police without fear of consequences'.[76]

July 1914 marked the highpoint of the enlarged Volunteer organisation with rapid progress made in terms of numbers, influence and support. A formal command structure consisting of ten battalions was aspirational, however, rather than a reflection of the reality of membership. In theory, these battalions consisted of seventy-eight companies with each company based on the parish or half-parish; however, only twenty-eight of these areas were represented at the Volunteer county review at Athenry in June and it is likely that many existed on paper only.[77] The public reluctance of sections of nationalist opinion to openly support the movement had passed, however, and supporters of the IPP eclipsed the separatist influence within the movement. Thomas Kenny of the *Connacht Tribune* called the county review, 'unquestionably the most historic and impressive event that has taken place in Connacht in the last fifty years with 5,000 men present to watch the 2,000 Volunteers'. The rural character of the organisation was apparent with Kenny noting, 'Galway city was well represented but when the question of population is considered, it lost badly in comparison with the County contingents and in fact the little village of Craughwell had as many members.'[78]

The split in the Volunteer movement following John Redmond's declaration of support for the British War effort at Woodenbridge on 20 September resulted in the immediate collapse of the Volunteers in Galway as the overwhelming majority of companies declared in favour of John Redmond and formed the rival National Volunteers. The same companies also voted in favour of not joining the War effort by immediately leaving the new movement in such large numbers that the National Volunteer force immediately collapsed. The police reported that in Galway:

> The extraordinary falling off of enthusiasm with which the Volunteer movement was conceived is undoubtedly due to the fact that the members will not enlist in the army and they believe that if they go on drilling, they will in some way or another be forced to enlist for services at the front. They make a great parade of their eagerness to defend the shores of Ireland, knowing that there is very little danger of them being called on to do so, but their warlike ardor vanishes rapidly at the idea of fighting against Germany abroad or indeed against anybody else.[79]

According to the Galway RIC, every Volunteer company in the Galway west Riding, comprising 4,892 men, declared for John Redmond, compared to only 685 Volunteers who opted to join the breakaway separatists in the Irish Volunteers. In the east Riding, 56 branches of the movement comprising 4,712 men declared in favour of Redmond, with only 360 men in favour of Eoin MacNeill who remained the nominal leader of the hardline faction.[80] The decline of Volunteer numbers resulted in a scenario in which the original IRB-dominated companies at Athenry, Clarinbridge, Castlegar, Claregalway, Killeeneen, Ballycahalan and Ardrahan remained loyal to the IRB-dominated Irish Volunteers. The police reported how the faction was 'bitterly opposed to Redmond's announcement and ... bitterly disloyal and will do all in their power to prevent recruiting'.[81]

Recourse to violence between rival factions characterised the split in some districts. The split in the Volunteer movement in Galway town became particularly bitter following the disruption by republicans of a public meeting called by Redmond's supporters in October.[82] The power lines to the town hall were cut by members of the IRB and the gathering degenerated into mayhem as hecklers abused their rivals and scuffles had to be broken up by a large body of police. The meeting was plunged into darkness and stink bombs were hurled among the delegates, sending the hall into a panic with people charging out through doors and windows.[83] Determined not to be outdone by their rivals, the meeting was reconvened on a makeshift platform and, after hurling William O'Halloran, the secretary of the local labourers' union, off the platform, MP Stephen Gwynn addressed his followers. Denouncing, 'Eoin MacNeill and the self-elected leaders of the provisional committee of the Volunteers', he declared the allegiance of the Galway Volunteers to Redmond and amid raucous scenes, closed the meeting by 'asking the assemblage to repeat after him, God save the King, and this was done with spirit and gusto and a voice in the crowd echoed, God save Ireland'.[84] It was at this point that the *Connacht Tribune* announced:

> Sinn Féin has hitherto been treated with generous tolerance in the city: it has grossly abused that tolerance and the great majority who consider themselves free to act as sane and practical men, in order that they may reap to the full the benefits which the Irish Parliamentary Party has won, now take the attitude that tolerance has reached its limit. The puny plotters have only themselves to blame.[85]

The Irish Volunteers' contempt for Galway's nationalist elite did not pass unchallenged, however, and the sabotaged meeting precipitated the collapse of the Irish Volunteers in the town. Days later, while the Irish Volunteers assembled for a meeting, IPP supporters gathered to fling insults at their rivals. Determined not to be intimidated, sixty Volunteers emerged in formation and fist fighting duly erupted. Volunteers received beatings as fighting raged around the town. Windows were smashed along the streets and groups of IPP supporters moved out of the town centre and attacked the homes of known republicans. Volunteer John Hosty recalled, 'Missiles began flying – crash – crash – crash goes the glass in the windows over the shop. Members of the Company began to clear out running the gauntlet so to speak – until about half a dozen were left.' The Volunteers had to contend with both the police and their political rivals as Hosty continued, 'We got a short way only when the rush came with the RIC in the rear, urging the mob on.'[86] Describing the event as 'guerrilla warfare on a small scale', the *Connacht Tribune* reported, 'Every house in the city, the occupants of which were known to have been in sympathy with the Sinn Féiners was visited and had its windows put in by stones.'[87] The small republican element in the town struggled on, but never recovered its strength, often being forced to rely upon rural Volunteers from Castlegar for much needed muscle. Volunteer John Hosty recalled 'the remnants of the Galway company as a unit, ceased to function'.[88]

The enmity between the two groups continued to manifest itself over Volunteers' disruption of recruitment meetings and Volunteer Thomas Courtney recalled, 'the whole town of Galway went recruiting mad. It was not a question of will you join up, but what regiment are you joining.'[89] The minority group concentrated their energies on an anti-recruitment drive, while the National Volunteers led a vigorous campaign of propaganda, with the full support of the town council. The Irish Volunteers' rival campaign involved young members putting up posters, disrupting recruitment meetings and organising rival speakers. Their campaign did not endear them to the townsfolk as Volunteer Thomas Hynes recalled, 'we tried to break up recruiting meetings but we generally got beaten up ourselves as at least eighty per cent of the population were hostile to Sinn Féin, for a number of their husbands and sons were in the English army and navy'.[90] Volunteer Thomas Courtney acquired recruiting forms for the British army and went to the houses of those who had signed up to leave for the front and tried to dissuade them. When this proved unsuccessful, Courtney filled out the remaining blank forms in the names of prominent supporters of the recruitment drive, later noting 'It was noticeable how some of them cooled off in their recruiting efforts after that.'[91]

Violence between nationalists and republicans was not confined to Galway town and in early 1915, the police reported that in north Galway, 'Cummer and Turloughmore are in a state of disturbance and terrorised by secret society and moonlighting gangs.'[92] The situation became volatile due to the split in the Volunteer movement and the subsequent bravado of local leaders in provoking a number of riots and shootings. Tensions exploded early in the New Year when a riot broke out in Turloughmore after publican and district councilor Patrick Murray, 'proclaimed himself a pro-German' at a social gathering in the village, subsequent to which the police were attacked and fourteen men sent for trial for rioting and assault.[93] Some of Murray's supporters were later shot at while returning to their homes with two men sustaining wounds and three houses attacked by armed men.[94] Numerous gun attacks took place in connection with the dispute with violence peaking in March when the police reported, 'a strong faction has been organised to crush Murray and William O'Brien'.[95] The provision of extra police contained the situation and the authorities later noted, 'Turloughmore has been kept in order by the large force of police, the elements of disorder are there and the slightest relaxation of police watchfulness will result in crime.'[96] The feud led to an incident recalled locally as 'the battle of Murray's fort', when rival Volunteer companies attacked each other from their strongholds in their respective public houses.[97] The RIC were forced to fire over the heads of the men involved and several police and rioters suffered head injuries as stones, sticks and hurls were used as weapons. Once again, a large number of Murray's supporters were arrested and the number of extra police in the area was increased, with the county inspector noting, 'at Turloughmore and Cummer, the peace is only protected with incessant police vigilance, and no less than two head constables and fifty extra police have been drafted into an area of a very few square miles'.[98]

The GAA in Galway also broke into rival organisations following the split in the Volunteers. The administration of the GAA, and hurling, in particular, was heavily influenced by members of the IRB who were also senior Irish Volunteers. Following the split in the Volunteer ranks, the bitterness resulted in the majority of clubs and officials in south Galway joining the short-lived National Gaelic Athletic Association (NGAA), which was established as a rival to the more politically advanced GAA. In 1915, the County board of the GAA consisted of ten men, six of whom were among the most prominent IRB men in the county. Patrick Murray, previously discussed in connection with the Turloughmore dispute, William Cannon of Tuam, Stephen Jordan and Larry Lardiner of Athenry, and George Nichols of Galway Town, were all committee members, as well as prominent Irish Volunteer organisers, and the Chairman of the Board, Tom Kenny, was the fearsome former head centre of the IRB in the county.[99] There had been heated exchanges at county board meetings for a number of years as south Galway members, in particular, resented Kenny's authority over the association. Martin Ward of the Loughrea club, who was also a UIL town councilor and a close associate of MP William Duffy told a gathering of delegates:

> The old enthusiasm for the game was gone, owing to the way it was run by one or two men in County Galway. This was not to be wondered at, as the principal it was manipulated under was wrong: using their position to inculcate into the minds of young men doctrines, which at this crisis in our history, should not as much as be mentioned among them.[100]

The Galway affiliate of the NGAA comprised ten south Galway clubs and was dominated by representatives of the UIL. Of the seven-member executive, at least four were prominent UIL representatives, with Martin Ward, Thomas Coen and James Mulkerrins, all UIL councilors, and Brendan Cawley, a prominent UIL activist from Craughwell, acting as treasurer.[101] The ten clubs involved in the breakaway group continued to play matches among themselves for a number of years afterwards, with the movement dying out in 1918. On a national level only a small number of breakaway clubs from Sligo and Kildare joined with the Wexford, Dublin and Galway clubs; however, the clubs that broke away in Galway represented a serious challenge to the association and the bitterness of the affair soured an already tense situation, adding extra spite to local rivalries.

Foundation of Cumann na mBan

Women played an important and under-estimated role in the early growth of the republican movement. The first branch of Cumann na mBan was founded in Athenry in January 1914 and was led by Julia Morrissey. Morrissey was typical of the young, unmarried women who became enthusiastic leaders of the new organisation. Cumann na mBan tended to draw members from the same districts and extended families as the Volunteers themselves, and in this respect, most members were related or on close terms with their male counterparts. These familial bonds were fundamental in terms of secrecy and trust. The terms 'girls', rather than 'women' was employed both by the women themselves and the Volunteers when referring to Cumann na mBan, reflecting the youth of the women involved.

In terms of training, cooking, field signalling and first aid were emphasised and the women occasionally joined with the men on route marches and 'were trained in the secreting of despatches which might be entrusted to them'.[102] The organisation of Ceilidhs and dances provided an important social role for the organisation, facilitating the building of closer social bonds within the wider movement of activists within an appropriately sober, Catholic and Gaelic environment. Bridget Ruane, *née* Morrissey, recalled that when she joined the organisation she was told that she would, 'take aid lessons and help at sports and hurling, sell badges and attend sewing classes … and later helped make tricolour badges, small flags, kit bags, etc.'[103] Activism fostered independence among the young recruits; however, their primary role was to support the work of their male counterparts. Ruane recalled, 'Our duty was to attend the Volunteers, cater for them and help them in every way possible; by collecting funds, helping at sports, at hurling matches, and selling tricolour badges':

> People were very poor at that time. We could give a cup of tea and a jam sandwich for one shilling (having profit at the same time). The badges only cost one penny and the dances two shillings to get it. There were plenty of boys and girls who played music with melodeons, yet all the

monies taken were handed over to the brigade to buy arms, ammunition and steel to make pikes.[104]

When the split in the Volunteers occurred in September 1914, Cumann na mBan pledged their loyalty to Eoin MacNeill and the local Fenian faction. The movement remained small and diffuse until the War of Independence and constituted around fifty active members in the Athenry/Clarinbridge districts.[105] These districts were the heart of the secret society/hurling nexus from which the Volunteers also emerged. In August 1914, a rare public meeting was held in Galway Town Hall and addressed by Elizabeth Bloxham; however, with the split in the wider movement in September, the small number of middle-class 'respectable' members quickly left.[106]

Liam Mellows

The Galway Volunteers received a significant boost in March 1915 when Volunteer GHQ sent Liam Mellows, with Alfie Ó Monacháin – who arrived in January 1916 – as his assistant, to help organise the county. Mellows and Ó Monacháin were an unlikely duo to lead a revolution in Galway. Both were outsiders, urban and un-initiated in rural ways. Mellows was born in Hartshead military barracks, Ashton-under-Lyne, Lancashire.[107] Three generations of the Mellows family served in the British military and Liam's father, William, was born in Gondah, India, where his father was serving. William Mellows met his future wife, Sarah Jordan, a dressmaker, while stationed in Cork in 1882 and married in Fermoy in 1885. Sarah Jordan, was the youngest of eighteen children to Patrick Jordan, a land agent from Monalug, Wexford. The couple moved to Ashton-under-Lyne in 1889 after stints in Manchester and Glasgow. The family moved again to Dublin in 1894, thence to Cork where Liam and his older brother Frederick attended Wellington Barracks military school. By 1900, Liam and his family were back in Dublin where he continued his education in Portobello garrison school. Sergeant William Mellows' hopes that his son would become a military officer were to be subverted by the boy's love of Irish history but the itinerant lifestyle and martial culture in which he was nurtured framed his years as a republican activist. In terms of Mellows' father, republican Robert Brennan later reflected that, 'concerning the treasonable activities of his family, Mr Mellows was puzzled but tolerant. The mother, however, declared that since she was a Wexford woman she could be nothing but a rebel.'[108]

Mellows' route to republicanism was through his involvement with the Fianna Éireann boy scouts movement which he joined in Dublin in

1911.[109] The organisation was established to counter the pro-imperial boy scouts movement established by Robert Baden-Powell in 1907. The Fianna provided Mellows with a practical vehicle for his military upbringing and allowed him to instil the same martial values in young recruits. Travelling across Ireland establishing local units and organising events, Mellows attained the experience and personal qualities that made him a competent Volunteer organiser.[110] Fianna comrade Alfred White recalled Mellows as possessed of 'a rock like uprightness, a serious minded unflinching adherence to fundamental loyalties'.[111] Mellows' lifestyle during this period foreshadowed his later role in the Volunteers and White recalled, 'He covered on average 60 to 70 miles a day on his bicycle, starting in Wexford and then working towards the west.'[112] Annie Fanning, who later helped him escape from Ireland in the aftermath of the 1916 Rising, observed a characteristic fatalism in Mellows, recalling that, 'In later years I met Liam Mellows at a banquet in his honour in Tullamore … he then said … that people who helped him always got into trouble or died: these are not his words, but something near.'[113] Mellows replaced Liam Gogan as national secretary of the Volunteers in early 1914, working alongside his brother, Barney, and Eimar O'Duffy, a role he occupied until he became a full time organiser and was dispatched to Mrs Broderick's boarding house in Athenry.[114]

The arrival of Mellows represented a formative boost to republican morale and organisation and his commitment and charisma made an indelible impression. Mellows had a vision for the movement beyond many of his contemporaries, as Volunteer organiser Robert Brennan reflected:

> To some of us who had been many years in the IRB the prospect of a rising seemed remote, but Mellows' optimism was infectious. We would get our chance soon he said, when England and Germany would go to war. On the parade ground Liam was a stern, rigid disciplinarian, he drove the boys hard. Off duty he was light hearted harum-scarum practical joker and he was a punster.[115]

Mellows' deputy, Alfie Ó Monacháin, a poster and lithographic artist by trade, was a native of Balfour Avenue on Belfast's Ormeau Road. Appointed initially as Volunteer organiser in Cavan in 1915, he was arrested and held on remand in Crumlin Road jail in October and sentenced to three-months hard labour under the Defence of the Realm Act.[116] On release in January 1916, he 'got instructions from GHQ to go to Galway to assist Liam Mellows. From this it will be seen that GHQ had reasons for having Galway very specially organised and equipped for the coming Rising. My district being mainly the Gaeltacht.'[117]

Mellows made an immediate impression on the young rural farmers' sons of the Irish Volunteers. Volunteer Pádraig Ó Fathaigh later wrote, 'he was the life and soul of the movement. His magnetic power was amazing and the Galway Volunteers would follow him wherever he led.'[118] Volunteer Francis Hynes recalled, 'I, who had the privilege of being one of his most intimate acquaintances often wondered how a man whose inner thoughts were so deep and so serious could always show such careless, I might say irresponsible front, to his casual acquaintances. I will always remember the first night he addressed our company.'[119] Hynes recalled, 'My impression of him was that he may have been a clever lad – he was about 22 years – but he couldn't be much good at fighting ... before the first night under his command was over they laughed no more, they loved and respected him after that.'[120]

Mellows was to make his mark in the county in 1916 but on the eve of the Rising, he remained a marginal figure in the wider political scene and his control over his own men was to be very severally tested in the coming Rebellion. Fr Henry Feeney of Clarinbridge acted as chaplain to the Galway Volunteers and developed a close bond with Mellows. On the fiftieth anniversary of the Rising he recalled:

Mellows was well below average height, frail looking with fair, almost white hair. He wore rimless glasses of the pince-nez type and did not, at first sight, inspire great respect or confidence. But the thin, frail body was tough and sinewy, immune to cold and hardship. Liam had other qualities which endeared him to the Galway Volunteers. Off duty, he was good humoured and an ingenious practical joker, especially as regards his police escort which he was adept at throwing off the scent.[121]

Political mobilisation in rural Ireland

The British War effort was widely supported in rural Ireland, despite the relatively low recruitment figures in Connacht. Political life in Galway in the early War years was fractious and characterised by frequent feuding that often centred around personalities rather than ideology. In most districts, the Irish Volunteers made little headway and even the small signs of political change generated resentment among more prominent political factions. Urban political mobilisation tended to be conservative and civic organisations were dominated by property owners, professionals and the merchant classes. That the middle classes dominated politics in the towns was not unusual and was reflected in the towns' steadfast support for the leadership of the county's old nationalist leadership but the persistent nature of that support was to prove remarkably enduring. Galway town, in particular, saw the War as an economic opportunity, that imposed a moral duty on its citizens to come to the defence of Britain and prove the enduring spirit of Irish manhood.

The violence, disdain and indignity that frequently characterised local politics highlights the fact that despite the perceived popular acceptance of moderate political leadership at a national level, on a local level, politics had the capacity to generate intense passions. Ideology often played a minor role in determining political allegiances with profoundly local interpretations of rapidly evolving political realities contributing to a complex spectrum of political loyalties. Recruitment meetings provided ready-made battlegrounds for rival groups reflecting the degree of recreational violence tolerated by the community.

The slow but steady rise of the Irish Volunteers during the early War years was fuelled by a heady mix of hurling, land hunger and economic resentment, all of which was exacerbated by the domestic ramifications of the War. The respectable political establishment was vociferously behind the British War effort and the young men who joined the ranks of the military did so in the earnest belief they were fighting for Ireland's glory on the European battlefield. While the majority of young men were motivated by a range of factors other than political considerations, the motivation of the more ideological young recruits did not necessarily differ as radically as might be assumed of those who believed that Ireland was worth fighting for at home. The contempt between nationalist and republican supporters tended to obscure the shared characteristics between both traditions. While enthusiasm for the War effort was most apparent in the towns and the Irish Volunteers remained a resolutely rural phenomenon, it is an oversimplification to regard the constitutional and separatist tendencies as inherently distinct. The irony of the IPP's contempt for the Volunteers' militarism is highlighted by the background of many party stalwarts in the violent land agitation of the late nineteenth century. Local political activists, including MPs William Duffy and James Cosgrave, cemented their personal reputations through their involvement in violent campaigns against landlordism and proudly boasted of having been jailed on behalf of their community. The UIL had a long tradition of supporting violent campaigns against landowners, and in this respect, their contempt for the Volunteers lay in their disdain for the perceived impertinence of an emerging class of farmers' sons and daughters who were determined to defy their parents' political allegiances. Physical force was not a moral or ideological issue and supporters of the IPP did not object to the use of violence against other nationalists when their own dominance of local politics was challenged. Indeed, many prominent commentators revelled in the actions of their most ardent supporters in keeping their less well-heeled rivals firmly in their place.

CHAPTER 3

A Lost Republic: Liam Mellows and the 1916 Rising

Over 300 men were deported from Galway in the aftermath of the 1916 Rising when Liam Mellows led 600 Volunteers and Cumann na mBan in the east Galway countryside. The rebels attacked police at Athenry, Clarinbridge, Oranmore and Carnmore, traversing the countryside until Saturday morning. In the historiography of Easter Week, events outside Dublin have, until recently, received little attention and most studies have focused on events in Dublin. Historian Fergus Campbell has illuminated the remarkable attempts by Liam Mellows to foment armed insurrection in the west.[1] The national aspect of the Rising, however, has been neglected to the detriment of a full appreciation of the ambitions of the revolutionary leadership. A close analysis of events outside the capital illustrates the capacity for a wider rural dimension for Rebellion. The stark variety of responses to the events of the week shines a light on the complex nature of political allegiance in nationalist Ireland.

The events of Easter Week in Galway soured an already poisonous political atmosphere and the diversity of responses to the Rebellion, ranging from widespread support in some rural districts, indifference and hostility in larger towns, to outcry and panic in Galway city was indicative of the complexity of nationalist political allegiances during the revolutionary period. As this episode highlights, what is referred to as the nationalist political tradition concealed a spectrum of divergent allegiances, reflecting a cultural chasm between the rural countryside, where the tradition of agrarian secret societies still flourished, and the urban world of the towns, where the military barracks continued to play a central role reflected in cultural and political allegiances.

The plan for the Rising in Galway was predicated on the successful delivery of several thousand rifles from *The Aud*; however, when the arms landing off the Kerry coast failed, the prospects for a meaningful western dimension to the

Rising ended. The force of over 650 that went out in Galway were armed with thirty .303 service rifles, a few miniature rifles and about three hundred shotguns. Volunteer officer Alf Ó Monacháin later recalled:

> The Galway Volunteers, when they went out, did not hope to do anything big. Badly armed as they were, their only hope was to bottle up the British garrison and divert the British from concentrating on Dublin, and this they succeeded in doing. Outside the big town the Volunteers had absolute control of the County. There were about 600 square miles of Galway Free County, from Galway city to Ballinasloe, and from Tuam to Gort.[2]

The plan for the county had two phases with companies to be armed at central points, returning to their districts to attack police barracks, before proceeding as a larger group into the heavily garrisoned town of Galway. The plan was aspirational but the degree to which it reflected the capacity of the Volunteers for open revolt is unclear. Ó Monacháin explained, 'It had been arranged that 3,000 of the rifles from *The Aud* were to reach Galway, and there was a man in Galway ready for each rifle. Everything had been planned with men on the railway to take the rifles at Kerry and distribute them all along the line right up to Galway.'[3]

Volunteer Michael Fogarty was first told of plans for the Rising when he attended a Volunteer meeting in Limerick on Palm Sunday.[4] Fogarty worked as a railway signalman for the Great Western Railway Company and later stated that the Clare Volunteers were in charge of landing arms from two sloops at Carrigaholt, some of which were to be loaded onto a railway carriage and sent north to be used in Galway. Fogarty's role was to make sure the railway lines were kept open and the train delivering the weapons arrived safely in Athenry. Volunteer John Hosty of Galway town recalled, 'the information we had in Galway on Holy Thursday was that Companies were to move south of Galway, contact Clare and if the expected landing of arms matured, and at that stage there was no reason to doubt – to collect their share and move back again to Galway'.[5] Local companies were then to mobilise to central depots along the railway line to receive their supply of weapons at the Gort, Athenry and Tuam stations. Volunteer Thomas Nohilly recalled, 'the plans for the North Galway Volunteers, as far as I know, were that they would proceed to Athenry on Easter Tuesday night, or the following day. They were to be taken there on a train driven by Volunteer Sam Browne who was a loco engineer attached to the Great Southern and Western Railway Company.'[6] Having carried out the initial phases of the plan, the Volunteers were to link up with Volunteer companies from the midlands, 'along the line of the river Shannon'. Tomás

Ó Maoileoin, commander of the Westmeath Volunteers, recalled 'we were to wreck the rail link to the west and then we were to march to Shannon harbour and effect a link with Liam Mellows' force holding Ballinasloe'.[7]

Larry Lardiner, Captain of the Athenry company and second in command to Mellows, was one of the few Galway officers to record personal doubts about the Galway Volunteers' readiness. Lardiner believed that Mellows was informed at Christmas 1915 that a Rising was imminent, 'however, he never mentioned a word of it to any of the Galway officers, but by suggestion and insinuation he gave them to understand that something was about to happen. The wisdom of his silence is doubtful but possibly he was acting under orders.'[8] Lardiner concluded, 'in going over my plans I discovered that the forces in Galway were entirely inadequate'.[9] Volunteer Patrick Callanan recalled that a few months before the Rising, Pádraig Pearse visited Irish Republican Brotherhood (IRB) organiser Dick Murphy in Athenry:

> In the course of the conversation Pearse told them that a Rising had been decided upon but he did not mention a date for it. Pearse asked Lardiner if he could hold a line on the river Suck near Ballinasloe. Lardiner said he could. Murphy then said they could not hold a position on the Suck for any length of time owing to the poor equipment and armament they had, and that the only chance they had was to attack the local RIC Barracks. Murphy also told me that Pearse seemed very disappointed, and that both Lardiner and he assured Pearse they would be in the fight whenever it took place, and do the best they could.[10]

When news reached the Royal Irish Constabulary (RIC) of the initial Volunteer mobilisation on Easter Tuesday, rural barracks were evacuated with the police flooding into central depots in larger towns including, Tuam, Loughrea and Ballinasloe. In Athenry, the police remained inside the barracks, despite the remarkable events going on around them. The rebel force was given the run of the east Galway countryside and the authorities later concluded:

> That the Sinn Féin insurrection was so quickly put down and that it was confined to so few districts outside the metropolitan area must be ascribed to the fortunate arrest of Sir Roger Casement and the failure of the German ship to land the required arms and ammunition. There is no reason whatever to believe that if these arrangements had not miscarried, the Irish Volunteers in any County would not have held back. In fact, the evidence is all the other way.[11]

Easter Week in Galway

Liam Mellows was arrested in the Athenry home of Julia Morrissey in late March 1916 and taken to Arbour Hill Prison. He was deported under the Defence of the Realm Act to Leek, Staffordshire, where he was he lodged in 10 Rose Bank Street.[12] The IRB arranged his safe return, however, and he was smuggled back through Glasgow and Belfast to Dublin – rather appropriately, dressed as a priest – by Nora Connolly and his brother Barney. He was spirited to Galway on Wednesday of Easter Week and hid out in Killeeneen. News that the Rising was to commence was brought to Athenry on Holy Thursday by Anna Fahy, wife of Volunteer leader Frank Fahy, vice commandant of the Four Courts garrison. The message was written by Pádraig Pearse and addressed to Larry Lardiner, Captain of the Athenry Company; it was written in a code agreed upon in advance: 'collect the premiums at 7 pm on Easter Sunday evening'.[13]

With Lardiner making preparations to notify the Galway companies, Eoin MacNeill's countermanding order calling off the Rising was delivered, causing much confusion. Éamonn Corbett, Captain of the Clarinbridge Company recalled, 'We immediately proceeded to Killeeneen to tell Liam [Mellows] who was mystified with the news.'[14] A second dispatch from Pearse was subsequently delivered to Athenry informing Lardiner that the Rising had merely been postponed until Monday. The confusion provoked Lardiner into making the journey to Volunteer headquarters in Dublin to ascertain the situation; he was unable to get a definitive answer, however, and returned to Galway none the wiser. The final notice to 'come out' arrived late on Monday night and following a 'council of war' held in Killeeneen, Mellows dispatched word that the rebels were to mobilise on Tuesday morning.

The first shots of the Galway Rising were fired at just after seven a.m. on the morning of Easter Tuesday when a group of Volunteers led by Mellows and numbering approximately 100 attacked the police barracks in the village of Clarinbridge. On reaching the village, the Clarinbridge and Killeeneen companies cut telegraph poles, blocked the main road and partially destroyed the main bridge in the town. Mellows selected a vanguard of younger men, some as young as 17, who rushed the door of the barracks, successfully gaining access to the building with four RIC defenders forcing a partial retreat. One Volunteer told the *Connacht Tribune* in 1966:

> Mellows, a great believer in the élan and courage of youth, picked twelve fellows of about seventeen years of age from the many who offered themselves. He was to be proved wrong in his estimate. The élan and

courage was there but not the craft of experience. Some of the older men suggested getting sledges and breaking down the door but Mellows was anxious to press on to Oranmore and vetoed the suggestion.[15]

During the course of the attack, Fr Michael Tully, who was saying mass in the village, pleaded with Mellows to call his men off. The group was unable to breach the barrack's defences and after several hours of sniping, the main body of rebels departed, marching seven miles to the nearby village of Oranmore, leaving a small force to keep the building under intermittent fire. The rebels took with them three RIC who were caught unawares while on patrol.[16]

As the group approached Oranmore, they were joined by the Oranmore and Maree companies and when word reached the village of the rebels' approach, the four police on duty barricaded themselves into the barracks. Once again Mellows selected a group of younger Volunteers who approached the building and tried to rush the door; however, as one veteran remembered, 'the spirit of the men was high and, led by Lieutenant Costello, a party rushed up to Smyth's doorway and tried to smash it in with a crowbar. The folly of this attack was seen when the police fired through the doorway and wounded one of the Oranmore Company. Both garrisons then began systematically firing at anything that moved.'[17]

Frustrated once again, the Volunteers kept the building under intermittent fire until a contingent of the Connaught Rangers arrived from Galway to relieve the beleaguered police. The force consisted of a party of police under County Inspector Clayton and a party of ten Connaught Rangers under Captain Sir Andrew Armstrong. A brief firefight ensued and the police and army charged down the main street, wounding one Volunteer.[18] The rebels had commandeered a number of motorcars, vans and traps and rather than face the better-armed troops, they evacuated in the direction of Athenry. The group was a remarkable sight as it made its way through the east Galway countryside; as one veteran recalled, 'Along the road to Athenry, Mellows led his men, some riding on the motley collection of carts, drays and sidecars. Riding on one of the cars were the Cumann na mBan who had accompanied them from Killeeneen.'[19]

At Athenry, Volunteers and Cumann na mBan from surrounding districts had been arriving throughout Tuesday, including companies from the Derrydonnell, Newcastle, Athenry, Cussaun, Rockfield, Kilconieron, Kiltulla and Killimordaly districts. Over 300 were busy preparing bombs and equipment, yet, no attempt to attack the RIC barracks was made. Volunteer Frank Hynes explained:

Anyone reading this account would be inclined to think that we were acting in a rather cowardly manner – why did we not attack the barrack in Athenry? Why did we keep retreating, etc, etc. The Volunteers who were out in Galway numbered between five and six hundred. We had about fifty full service rifles and about thirty rounds for each rifle, about one dozen pikes and a good many were not armed at all, so that if we wasted our ammunition on attacking the barracks, we had nothing to fight with after that; and as for bombs, we made some hopeless attempts at making bombs. [20]

As word reached Athenry that Mellows and his contingent were approaching from Oranmore, the large group, as Hynes later explained, 'decided to retreat towards Oranmore and meet Mellows and his contingent and leave it to him to decide what was best to do'.[21] As the group approached the Athenry Model Farm, they heard the first boom from the big guns of HMS *The Laburnum* in Galway Bay. The navy shelling of the coast between Oranmore and Castlegar continued all week, increasing the sense of drama. Many Volunteers believed their 'gallant German allies' had arrived in Galway Bay and the booming was the sound of a naval battle between German U-boats and the navy.

With Mellows and his group joining the large Athenry rebel contingent at the Model Farm, the camp was a hive of activity and morale was high: 'Many men who had not been in the Volunteers at all joined up to fight and all were in the best of humour and full of pluck.'[22] The Volunteers were accompanied by the women of Cumann na mBan, and as one recalled, 'Even sleeping was no problem. The women lay in the beds normally used by the students and many of the leaders and men also found orthodox beds. For the others there was plenty of hay and straw to make cosy shakedowns.'[23] Liam Mellows later wrote:

The greatest enthusiasm prevailed amongst the Rebels. About thirty girls, members of Cumann na mBan, accompanied their brothers-in-arms the whole week. Their spirit and determination was wonderful. Nothing could dampen the spirits of all who were 'out'. Songs and recitations could be heard on all sides when resting. Laughter and fun never deserted them. The police, in abandoning several of their barracks and huts, were in such a hurry that they left uniforms, clothing and boxes and kits behind them. Several of the irresponsible mirth makers amongst the Volunteers dressed in 'peelers' uniforms and strutted about imitating the authoritive airs of the sergeants – the little Caesars of their district.[24]

While the main body of the Volunteers massed at the Athenry Model Farm, about six miles east of Galway town, the Claregalway and Castlegar companies, under the command of Thomas Ruane, had mobilised and billeted for the night in the small village of Carnmore, awaiting their orders from Mellows. When news of their position reached Galway town, a group of RIC formed a convoy and drove to confront them, leaving Galway early on Wednesday morning. Volunteer Mick Newell recalled the gun battle that took place:

> The enemy advanced up to the cross roads and Constable Whelan was pushed by District Inspector Heard up to the wall which was about four feet high, the District Inspector standing behind Whelan and holding him by the collar of his tunic. Constable Whelan shouted, 'surrender boys, I know ye all.' Whelan was shot dead and the District Inspector fell also and lay motionless on the ground. They got back into the cars and went in the direction of Oranmore. The enemy then made an attempt to outflank our position but were beaten back. The enemy then retreated and continued to fire until well out of range of our shotguns. They got back into the cars and went in the direction of Oranmore.[25]

Following the confrontation, the contingent made their way to Athenry to link up with their comrades. By now the group numbered almost 650, posing major problems in terms of food, sleeping accommodation and arms. Mellows took the decision to march to a more readily defendable location and the group marched in military formation from Athenry to Moyode Castle, located between Athenry and Loughrea, arriving late on Wednesday. One veteran later told the *Connacht Tribune* in 1966:

> Life was grim in Moyode. There was only open fireplaces and small grates to cook upon and utensils were very scarce indeed. The provisions brought from Oranmore and the Farmyard were soon consumed and the potatoes, a new variety, proved uneatable, even to hungry men.
>
> Only about one in four had an overcoat and during the cold April nights, they suffered severely from cold. Life was grim. Drinking was forbidden and the only amusement in the camp was provided in the drawing room of the mansion where the officers and ladies of Cumann na mBan danced for a few hours under the eye of Father Feeney.[26]

The officers were unhappy with the capacity of the old mansion to withstand an assault, however, and they were beginning to have difficulty keeping the

force motivated. Hunger affected morale, forcing Mellows to address his force
on Thursday night, asking anybody who wasn't happy to leave. Ailbhe Ó
Monacháin recalled, 'Some men, for whom there was no arms, decided to go
home, and one whole company went away. This was at ten o'clock at night.
The company that went away was back again about 3 o'clock next morning.'[27]
With food becoming scarce, Mellows ordered the requisitioning of a bullock
from a local farmer, as he later described in characteristically romantic fashion:

> Commissariat and transport departments had to be organised. The former
> was put in the charge of Lieutenant Jack Broderick of Athenry. He took
> up his duties with a zeal and enthusiasm wonderful to behold. In a short
> while he had a staff of several butchers and other helpers. He organised
> commandeering parties and dispatched them for anything considered
> necessary. Cattle were slaughtered but no more than were absolutely
> needed. The girls of Cumann na mBán were set baking bread and rations
> were issued to the men. Each company appointed orderlies and cooks
> to draw rations and prepare meals. One of the cooks developed a genius
> for making stew and the quarters for the Athenry Corps, to which he
> belonged, was generally invaded about meal times by men from all the
> other corps, attracted there by the savoury smells. Officers, going about
> their duties were hailed on all sides by amateur cooks, with cries of 'Ate a
> Bit of this Captain, tis Grand,' 'Try a little of the Castlegar mate'.[28]

Mellows upbeat description of this episode is contradicted by the testimony
of veterans given to the *Connacht Tribune* for the fiftieth anniversary of the
Rebellion, and as one noted:

> The slaughtering and cutting up [of the bullock] was done by Michael
> O'Connor, a butcher who had been captured with his van and was kept
> prisoner in the belief the campaign would be a lengthy one and his services
> would be required. But the cooks burned the meat badly, and no one was
> anxious for more beef after this experience.[29]

Mellows was reticent to commandeer more livestock despite the efforts of IRB
leader Tom Kenny to persuade him and one veteran later noted:

> Strangely Mellows was reluctant to slaughter bullocks for his men and
> his reluctance was not entirely due to the poor cooking on the previous
> occasion. When [Tom] Kenny [Fenian leader] had ridden in with four

bullocks, Mellows had given them back to the owner who had followed Kenny asking for his bullocks to be restored.[30]

By Thursday, the initial euphoria of the week was fading and the sobering realisation sank in for many ordinary Volunteers that it was only a matter of time before they would have to face infinitely better equipped British troops. Mellows was determined to keep his force out, however, and one officer later recalled, 'As far as I remember he said he could hold out for a month by moving south to the Clare hills.'[31] Volunteer Michael Kelly recalled:

> I remember that Mellows and some officers went out by car on Thursday night in the direction of Ballinasloe on reconnaissance as it was rumoured that British Military were advancing on Moyode. The rumours about the British advance and the uncertainty, along with the withdrawal of the two hundred men, had a disturbing effect on all the Volunteers at Moyode on the Thursday night. We got no sleep that night as we were called out a few times during the night and lined in our Companies for roll call.[32]

The appearance of the influential Fenian leader Tom Kenny compounded Mellows' leadership crisis, as the battle for hearts and minds was under way between the outsider, Mellows, and the old Fenian Kenny, as Frank Hynes explained:

> This man did his best to get us to give up and go home and have sense. He brought one particular rumour that five or six hundred soldiers were marching on us from Ballinasloe. We called an officer meeting and I'm afraid that one or two of our officers were anxious to take him seriously and take his advice and go home. Liam [Mellows] got disgusted and said he would not disband his men. He handed over command to Larry [Lardiner] but Larry would not disband them. Liam, after about an hour took over again.[33]

Mellows would not be moved by the arguments of his officers and Frank Hynes found, 'that dedicated man, who made no secret of the fact that he had come back to offer up his life for Ireland, could not understand that anyone would wish to do less':

> They had been told they were to take part in a route march and now they found themselves in armed rebellion. They had been told too, that they

would be away from home for only three days, now they were already four days gone and it was the intention of the leaders to carry on a prolonged campaign. Those of Athenry who stayed – and there were many of them – dragged their overcoats from those who were going away and were the lucky possessors of such garments. They needed them for the campaign to which they had committed themselves.[34]

Once again, Mellows' own account of the night represents a romanticised version of events:

On the night of the second last day of the Rising in Galway, things looked so black, that it was felt incumbent I should address the men and put the situation clearly before them so that it could not be said they had been led on in ignorance, made dupes of and fooled. Can I ever forget the scene. Several hundred men drawn up in the courtyard of a castle residence that was our headquarters, at two o'clock in the morning, a weird light cast on the assemblage by several torches of bog deal. They were armed with every conceivable type of weapon, rifles, shotguns and pikes. I spoke to them at length, putting the situation clearly before them, and ended by saying that any man that did not feel he could go further with us could go home and he would not be thought any worse of, he had risked everything in coming out and no man could do more. There was a dead silence for a few minutes and then a big powerful countryman, one of the simple, honest, and so many I know here would denigrate, uncouth and ignorant fellows, stepped to the front and said, 'we came out to fight for an Irish Republic, and now, with the help of God we are not afraid to die for it.'[35]

On Friday, Mellows took the decision to march the reduced force further south in the forlorn hope that the Clare Volunteers had risen. The group left Moyode, marching south in formation, eventually garrisoning at Limepark, an old shell of a big house near the small village of Peterswell, close to the Clare border. It was during the march to Limepark, that Mellows decided to disband the women of Cumann na mBan. One Volunteer recalled in 1966:

The Cumann na mBan were not in the column. Knowing the hardships that had to be faced it had been decided to leave them behind. But knowing too that these ladies would refuse to be left behind, a stratagem was employed to make them go home. They were sent to the Hynes home in Cregaturla on the pretext of being needed for some martial project and so were absent when the men marched away. Only Julia Morrissey remained with the rebels.[36]

Fr Henry Feeney of Clarinbridge, who had been with the Volunteers all week, was joined on the march to Limepark by Fr Thomas Fahy of Maynooth College and the pair pleaded with Mellows to disband his men before the military encircled them. Revd Henry 'Harry' Feeney (1898–1945) was a native of Castlegar and served as curate in Clarinbridge. He acted as spiritual guide to the men throughout the week and was held in high regard by the Volunteers; he and Mellows developed a deep personal bond.[37] When Mellows refused the priests' pleas, Fr Fahy persuaded him to allow them to put their case to a meeting of brigade officers. Volunteer Michael Kelly recalled:

> I heard one of the priests telling all the officers assembled about the surrender in Dublin. A discussion then arose mainly between the priest and Mellows. The priest was trying to convince the meeting that, as the Volunteers in Dublin had surrendered, the Galway Volunteers should disperse as the position was hopeless in the circumstances. The priests asked Mellows whether he would be agreeable to put it to the men whether they would disperse or carry on. Mellows said that he had already put it up to the men in Moyode and that every man in Limepark had agreed to carry on. The priest said that as Dublin had been dispersed, the British Forces could concentrate fully on Galway. Mellows still refused to go to the men for a decision as he maintained it had been already taken. The priests asked him then if he would allow them to put it to the men and after some hesitation he agreed.[38]

Fr Thomas Fahy left his own description of the final conclave:

> Mellows said that it would be better to fight it out now as their lives were all forfeit anyhow. He also pointed out that the six local RIC prisoners would be able to identity every one of the Volunteers. After deliberation these six RIC men gave an undertaking they would give no information to their authorities, which undertaking I was glad to be afterwards authentically assured, was honoured. All the officers at the meeting with the exception of Liam Mellows and Alf Monahan voted for disbanding. I asked Mellows to convey the decision to the men. He begged myself to do so, saying that he was reluctant to ask a single one of them to go away. I

then addressed the men, telling them the decision and advising them to break up immediately and save their equipment for another day. Mellows did not address the men. He was very depressed; the news from Dublin had upset him greatly.[39]

Volunteer Frank Hynes recalled the disbandment:

I wouldn't like to witness again the scene that was created by the disbandment. I saw big six-footers weeping. There was terrible confusion but in the midst of all of it, the rifles were thrown here and there on the ground. I went round and made my men take them up and bring them with them. They brought them and hid them on the way home.[40]

The Galway Rising ended in the early hours of Saturday morning despite Mellows' pleas to stay out. The group saw no prospect of making a realistic stand with so few rifles and the news that Dublin was falling into the hands of the Crown Forces. While Mellows, Patrick Callanan and Frank Hynes sought refuge in the Slieve Aughty Mountains, their men trudged wearily to their homes. Over the course of the following week over 400 were interned in Galway jail before being transported to Richmond Barracks in Dublin. Around 330 were deported to prisons across England and Scotland before being interned together in Frongoch.[41]

'Our Citizen Army': the conservative response

While the rebel force was massing in the east Galway countryside, events in Galway town were taking a very different turn. Cut off by rail and road from the rest of the country and with telegraph lines down, news of rebel activity created a sensation, with rumour and hysteria taking hold. The *Connacht Tribune* reported, 'on a muggy day, [with a] dry atmosphere and serene sky':

All in all, one had the sense, the vague sense that one was living through an historic hour. That for a day, the town was recalling the stirring days of Emmet and Lord Edward Fitzgerald and the men of '67, with this taking of police barracks, these conjectural Risings and marchings and the same dependence on primitive methods, the dispatch rider and rumour, which characterised the happenings of those times, as if we were not living in the days of motorcar, telegraph and telephone.[42]

Business premises closed their doors and work came to an immediate stop. Amid fears of a repetition of events in Dublin, the post office was placed under armed guard and a notice of martial law was posted stating all licensed premises in the urban district were to remain closed forthwith and all persons to remain indoors between the hours of five in the morning and eight at night.[43] Members of the Redmondite National Volunteers were explicitly exempt from the emergency regulations and the military curfew added to the sense of unease, as one reporter noted:

> Men were no longer able to concentrate their minds on their business, and all and sundry fairly took to the streets. Comfortable merchants went about, and the streets were filled. Straight away shutters were seen to be going up. And other premises commenced to close of their own accord so that the town presented the appearance of a city preparing for an investment. Preparations were made for meeting and repelling the invasion and anxious people found themselves drifting towards the Square and looking in the direction of Oranmore and keeping a close eye on the opening from Foster Street.[44]

On Tuesday afternoon, a public meeting was called by the urban district council attended by over one hundred people in the Town Hall. A resolution passed at the meeting noted:

> That this public meeting declares the actions of ill-advised persons in the County of Galway, who have at a time when the valour of Irish troops had done so much to shed glory on the arms of Empire, chosen to shock and outrage public opinion by bloodshed and civil strife: that we declare our opinion that the advice of Mr John Redmond indicates the course which true political wisdom has shown to be right; and we call upon the authorities and people of Galway to co-operate to crush by every means possible the efforts of the disaffected fanatics and mischief-makers.[45]

Thomas Kenny of the *Connacht Tribune* began the meeting by decrying that 'they had been plunged into a state of civil war in which armed people threatened and were threatening to invade the town', before comparing the actions of the rebels with the bravery of the Irish soldiers at the Western Front. Of the Dublin Rising, he informed the audience:

> A whole lot of men had, according to rumour, tried to hold up the public offices, the post office and places like that in Dublin. What on earth effect

that could have in ten or twenty years as regards the government of this country? Was it not a million times better to allow things to go on the way they had been and not try and take the law into their own hands.[46]

Another speaker told the gathering, 'Irishmen as a rule are not fools but unfortunately a large number of young men throughout the country were led astray by gentlemen who should know better and he for one did not blame the ignorant countrymen.'[47] Another speaker agreed, adding, 'they have been led into a trap and it is only afterwards when a settlement is reached, that they will realise what a mistake they have made in supporting the irresponsible hot heads of the country'.[48] Several speakers expressed the widespread sentiment that the rebels were a movement not 'for the benefit of Ireland, but for Prussia, it seemed to be one not to free Ireland but to hand over the country to Prussia and that at a moment when the national prosperity of the country was greater than in any other country in Europe'.[49] T.C. McDonogh of the urban district council echoed the theme of the ingratitude of the farming community, 'The Irish farmer just now had everything he wanted. They had the land purchased out and got good prices for their crops, and yet at the bidding of people who ought to know better they rose up in Rebellion and everything that had been done for their country was of no avail.'[50]

A 'Committee for Public Safety' was formed to liaise with the Crown Forces and to organise a civilian response to the 'crisis'. The meeting was addressed by Mártín Mór McDonogh and citizens were urged to offer themselves for enrolment as 'special constables' under the command of the regular RIC, or 'in any way the authorities may consider, they may be useful in the present crisis'. The 'specials', acted as a reserve force for the police and the *Galway Express* thanked forty-seven men whom they claimed, 'did much to relieve the police and give the latter a well-deserved and much needed few hours rest'.[51] Throughout the week, meetings of the Committee for Public Safety were held at the Town Hall amid growing anger at the perceived isolation of the town and the fear of an impending 'bread famine'.

Police who had evacuated the surrounding countryside poured into Galway town and their numbers were boosted with the arrival of over 100 RIC from Belfast. Dr Sandys, divisional surgeon, and Mr O'Dockery, superintendent, in conjunction with St Johns Ambulance Brigade, took over a number of houses and a full staff of trained nurses and assistants were placed in a state of readiness.[52] Groups of National Volunteers under Captain J.P. McNeill donned their uniforms, marching around the town in military formation with rifles and bayonets provided by the military. In an article entitled 'Our Citizen Army' the

Galway Express noted that, 'one of the brightest spots in the present lamentable affair is the manner in which Galway civilians have risen to the occasion. A fine citizen army of special constables, dispatch riders, assistants in first aid, etc, have cheerfully given their service to the local authorities in their hour of need.'[53] Magistrate Joseph Kilbride later wrote to the Chief Secretary, 'I swore in fifty reliable men as special constables. They performed their duties assigned to them well and willingly.' Kilbride was less successful with the Catholic Bishops, however, noting, 'I did all I could to induce the Catholic Bishop of Galway, Dr O'Dea, to assist in putting a stop to the outbreak without success. I induced one of his priests, Fr Davis, to attend the meeting and to speak. The whole body of public opinion was at all times perfectly sound and opposed to the Sinn Feiners.'[54]

Known republicans in Galway town, including most Volunteer officers and senior IRB figures were arrested on Tuesday. Volunteer Thomas Hynes remembered:

> There was great confusion. We did not know what to do and, as far as the city was concerned it was too late to do anything as RIC and military were already alerted. It was our intention to take a few prominent men – Martin McDonagh (Màirtin Mór), Joe Young, etc., and occupy the Post Office. This was George Nichols' plan. He seemed to know more about what they intended to do in Dublin than the rest of us did.[55]

Volunteer Thomas Courtney, who had been trying to organise the Volunteer companies in Moycullen and Spiddal found Volunteers were unwilling to obey his orders:

> The police searched carts or large parcels. They would not let a bag of flour out of the town. The east end of the town leading to Oranmore, Athenry, Dublin was well guarded. The soldiers had a machine gun behind the wall at one spot. The town was full of special police. Everybody was talking of the rebel army which was supposed to be marching on the town. Rumours of a German landing, etc.[56]

By Wednesday, the RIC aided by the special constables had arrested a motley crew of IRB suspects, Sinn Féin supporters and Volunteers. IRB organiser, Micheal Ó Droighneáin; solicitor and IRB centre, George Nichols; future MP Pádraic Ó Máille; and a German linguistics professor, Valentine Steinberger were among the most prominent. Volunteer Frank Hardiman recalled 'as each prisoner's name was called out, a charge of treason was read out by a naval lieutenant. He told us that the penalty if found guilty would be death, and warned us that any prisoner trying to escape would be immediately shot.'[57] The men were tied up and loaded onto open-top vehicles and paraded for the entertainment of hostile local people. Volunteer John Hosty recalled, 'Mud, stones, etc., etc., were not good enough when the locals were leaving by boat.'[58] Micheal Ó Droighneáin recalled, 'In that way they drove us to the Docks, our car leading. The second car was pelted with and off the streets by the mothers of men serving with the British Forces – [Frank] Hardiman and [Seamus] Carter receiving lumps of mud in their faces.'[59] The prisoners were transferred on board HMS *The Gloucester*. On Friday the prisoners were transferred to the sloop, *The Snowdrop* and brought to Cobh harbour.

On Tuesday afternoon, a navy vessel, *The Laburnum*, began bombarding the Galway coastline at Maree and Oranmore and the sound of the shells increased the sense of anxiety in the town. The shelling provoked unease in the communities living around Galway Bay and people began to move to the perceived safety of the town. The *Galway Express* reported, 'Even as we write, streams of peasant refugees are fleeing from their once peaceful homes in the tranquil countryside from Oranmore to Castlegar and vicinity to seek the shelter denied to them by the folly of their own friends and neighbours.' The paper later reported that the village of Oranmore, 'is being gradually deserted until now it is a veritable wilderness'.[60] The *Connacht Tribune* assured their readers, 'citizens can now rest in perfect security, should it ever have been broken, it is of course, obvious that this vessel could easily turn her guns, not only on Oranmore, but on Athenry, with the most effective results'.[61]

Lack of solidarity for the country 'refugees' in the 'besieged' town was evident and the *Galway Express* noted, 'A new type of blockade has been established in Galway. Country people coming from the direction of the recent Volunteer activities have been forbidden to bring any provisions or household supplies home, lest any of these commodities would find their way to the enemy's camp. The procedure appears to be an effective one.'[62] As the week progressed, more naval vessels arrived in the Bay and on Wednesday, a man-of-war carrying a company of Royal Munster Fusiliers was given an official welcome by the urban council.[63]

By Friday life began to return to normal as the rebel threat failed to materialise and the market resumed as usual in Eyre Square. On Saturday, public houses were given permission to open and schools were ordered to resume. At Saturday's meeting of the 'Committee for Public Safety' a telegram of thanks from the military was read and the committee updated on the progress of the round-up of suspects. A relieved Thomas Kenny declared, 'In this matter considered civil opinion will weigh with the authorities, for the civil element in the city has stood loyally by law and order.'[64]

Aftermath

Local newspapers were uniform in their condemnation of the Rising. In an editorial entitled, 'Poisoning the Wells', the *Connacht Tribune* explained, 'The reason we are not all rebels is that we are fortunately sane enough to see that the dreams of Ireland as a sovereign state is hopeless. About five per cent of the nation has not seen it. That is a matter for regret. But surely an occasion for the other 95 per cent of the public to treat them as if they had sold their soul to the devil. Attached to England, we must remain.'[65] The *Tuam Herald* described the week's events as 'a melancholy exhibition of midsummer madness' and the rebels as, 'degenerate sons'.[66] The paper published a verse, *The Stay at Home Soldiers* mocking the Volunteers:

> Content in vile ease at his country's mishap,
> Refuses to budge and fill up a gap,
> Leaves Erin's battalion's to fight on alone,
> All thoughts of his fathers, all spirits hath flown,
> Tho' tales of their doings in Belgium is told.[67]

Support for the authorities during Easter Week was not limited to Galway town and at Craughwell, Turloughmore and Loughrea, the National Volunteers – 'the true Irishmen, not rebels and pro-Germans' – as the *Galway Express* noted, came out to support the RIC.[68] In Loughrea, the *Tuam Herald* reported that:

> But for the National Volunteers, the town would have been handed over to the crowd for mischief and worse. Their conduct is eminently credible, for it was a trying and courageous act on their part. Great credit is due to Mr William Duffy MP and his local and patriotic helpers for having got his men to show themselves true National Volunteers and not the advance guard of looting and murderous Germans.[69]

National Volunteers manned the police barracks in the village of Craughwell and the *Tuam Herald* commended, 'the Craughwell men's loyalty to Ireland', especially since, 'they knew well little mercy would be shown some of them, if those lunatics got into the village'. The paper specifically praised those men who 'tore themselves away from a fond and loving wife, whose kisses were still on their lips'. 'Cowardice,' the paper concluded, 'would not allow those German hirelings enter where they knew a warm reception awaited them.' The paper was surprised at this turn of events, noting that Craughwell was, 'previously considered a hell on earth by men who knew it not'.[70] At Turloughmore, an area 'not noted for its loyal sentiment' the *Galway Express* reported, 'notwithstanding its reputation, the village and district of Turloughmore were quiet during the Rising. The local National Volunteers armed themselves and placed their services at the disposal of the police.'[71]

There were several casualties of the Galway Rising that, to varying extents, remained obscure family tragedies. Martin Reaney, a Volunteer from the Weir, in the Kilcolgan district, took part in the Rebellion but appears to have suffered a mental breakdown during the course of Easter Week necessitating the care of Cumann na mBan.[72] Returned to his parents, he took his own life a week later.[73] He was 23 years of age and a boat builder and small farmer's son. At the inquest into his death it was reported that events of Easter Week 'had clouded his mind' and that, 'returning from the Rising, he was strange in his manner'.[74] He left his home early on the morning of 16 May, tied himself to an anchor and threw himself into the ocean.

Valentine Steinberger, professor of romance languages in University College Galway was arrested during the Rebellion and briefly deported to England. He was one of a handful of staff and students including Dr Thomas Walsh and student Cornelius O'Leary to be arrested.[75] A cultural nationalist, Steinberger was not a member of the Volunteers but actively supported the movement at public meetings. Following the outbreak of the Rebellion, then aged over seventy years, he was seized by police in his home and deported to England. Already weakened by poor health, he developed pneumonia during his two week confinement. The University lobbied for his return and he was released in the last week of May but died in November. A Galway student who had been imprisoned alongside him claimed, 'he treated with calm contempt the gibes and jeers, the insults and indignities he had to undergo and was never in the least afraid of the worst that could be done to him'. His coffin was carried through the town by students who printed an angry obituary in the college magazine:

Treated like the vilest criminal as a prelude to much further treatment of a similar sort. We need not ask why this was done – we know and we will not forget. His health at the time was poor and the treatment he received then and during the weeks that followed weakened him considerably and left him easy prey to pneumonia which carried him off a few months after his release.[76]

Constable Patrick Whelan, who was shot dead by the Volunteers at Carnmore, was a native of Whitewall, Kilkenny, and was formerly a member of the Irish Guards.[77] District Inspector George B. Heard stated at the inquest into his death that Whelan was one of thirteen police, along with a party of soldiers, sailors and civilians, who accompanied him to Carnmore on 3.15 a.m. on Wednesday morning.[78] He was buried with military honours in Bohermore Cemetery in Galway town on 27 April accompanied by detachments of the Connaught Rangers and Royal Marines.

Leslie Edmonds, who was alleged to have directed the shelling of the Oranmore coastline, was shot dead by the Anti-Treaty IRA on 23 July 1922. The *Irish Times* noted the killing and speculated that Edmonds was unlucky to have driven into an IRA ambush set up for the National Army and mistakenly killed in the belief that he was an army officer.[79] He was killed at the wheel of his vehicle along with Jack Jordan, aged 19, a driver for the National Army.[80] A native of Birmingham, he was chief inspector of the Congested Districts Board (CDB) for Counties Clare and Galway.[81] Material alleging that Edmonds was an informer was deposited in the archives of University College Galway by TD Gerald Bartley in 1967.[82]

Following their confinement in Galway jail the Galway prisoners were brought to Richmond barracks in Dublin. A number were court-martialled and sentenced to between one and ten years' penal servitude. Following the court-martials, over 320 were deported to eight prisons across England and Scotland. Two groups were sent to Wandsworth Prison in south west London on 9 May and 2 June. Two batches were interned in Wakefield Prison, West Yorkshire on 13 May and 2 June. The prison was used as a home office work camp during the War and housed soldiers held on criminal charges. Another group was sent to Stafford Prison in Staffordshire on 13 May. The republican prisoners were among the last to be housed in the prison and the decrepit facility was closed for several decades following their departure. Three batches of prisoners were sent to Knutsford Prison in Cheshire on 2, 15 and 21 June. A group was sent to a temporary detention barracks in Woking, Surrey on 20 May. Another group was sent to Lewes Jail in East Sussex on 20 May, along with several prominent leaders of the Rising including, Éamon de Valera and Harry Boland. Two groups were dispatched to Scotland on 20 May with one group sent to Perth Barracks and another to Barlinnie Prison, north east of Glasgow City.[83]

Michael Kelly recalled a mixture of defiance and anxiety among the prisoners as they crossed the Irish Sea:

We were a gay party singing and dancing. Some more serious-minded of the prisoners were of the opinion that the British were taking us out to sea to sink us, and others said we were put on the cattle boat so that the Germans, if they sank the boat, would take it for what it was and would not make any attempt to rescue us.[84]

The hostility of onlookers was remarked upon by many. Volunteer Michael Newell from Castlegar recalled:

We were surrounded by a very hostile crowd of both men and women, who jeered us, called us nasty names: they also spat at us. One of the soldiers dropped his rifle to the trail position and struck three of the hostile crowd, knocking them out. He then shouted 'Up Carraroe, Up Connemara'. He was John Keane, a native of Carraroe. I heard afterwards that he was tried for this assault and sentenced to two years' imprisonment, but instead was sent with a draft to the Dardanelles. He was not heard of again.[85]

The prison routine came as a shock to many. Tom B. Cleary from Athenry described the daily routine in Stafford Prison in a letter to his wife Mary:

We are very well. Just as well as one could expect under the circumstances. There is very little time for thinking during the day. All bustle ... congregation almost as thick as you would see in an ordinary church on Sunday. Everyone with his own story. All the newspapers that are in print in England or Ireland. Letters and parcels continuously going and coming. Writing, reading, singing, marching, praying, bathing, sweeping, mopping, card playing, smoking, yarning. Bed at ten. Up at 5.30. Every hour has its excitements and its strict duties.[86]

The majority of the Galway prisoners were released throughout late 1916 and early 1917. In many other parts of the country, returning prisoners were received with a rapturous welcome in an Ireland utterly transformed. In Galway, many of the men and their families suffered genuine hardship and there were few celebrations. Thomas Ruane, who led the Volunteers in their fatal clash with the police at Carnmore, was granted early release from Lewes Prison on the grounds of ill health and his police file noted, 'there was no one to meet him off the train in Oranmore, just a couple of family members but no supporters'.[87] Gilbert Morrissey, of the Athenry Company put the subsequent inactivity of his area during the War of Independence down to demoralisation following the Rising:

> Many of the Volunteers in Co. Galway suffered a great deal of hardship subsequent to the Rising of 1916. At that time, a great many of them were in poor circumstances. Many of them were bread-winners for their families and, when they were imprisoned after the Rising, the families suffered. The neighbours at that time were not as sympathetic as they became as the fight progressed, and there were no funds out of which any provision could be made towards the amelioration of their conditions. Many of the interned Volunteers belonged to the farming class. At that time, they were not as well-off as they became two or three years later. They could not afford to pay hired men and their crops were left unattended until the general release in December, 1916. They and their families underwent a great deal of hardship which might have affected their later service in the Irish Volunteers and Irish Republican Army, only for the fact that the general public became imbued with their spirit, and the general morale of army and people alike was raised to a high level.[88]

Mellows in exile

Following the events of Easter Week, Liam Mellows made his way to New York via a circuitous route that involved hiding out in the south Galway and Clare countryside before making his way to Liverpool dressed as a priest and earning his fare as a seaman. His time in the United States represented a torturous exile that had a profound impact on his political and personal development. While in exile in New York he became involved in Irish-American political activism and spoke at many Clan na Gael, and subsequently, Irish Progressive League meetings. He was to remain in New York for four unhappy years, returning home following the death of his father in October 1920.[89] Irish Citizen Army veteran Frank Robbins recalled, 'He was recognised by all the 1916 Exiles, as we were termed, as our leader.'[90] Mellows made an immediate impact on John Devoy, the leader of the New York Fenians. Pat 'the Hare' Callanan introduced Mellows to Devoy and recalled, 'He was very pleased with Mellows and said he was the most capable man who had so far arrived in America.'[91] Devoy employed Mellows in the *Gaelic American* newspaper and he was in demand as a speaker, as one admirer noted, 'Though not a high-flown orator, he was such a powerful and convincing speaker that he could hold an audience of Americans, many of whom had no connection with Ireland, spellbound during an hour's speech.'[92] The *Gaelic American* was the main American conduit for information about the activities of Clan na Gael and the Irish Volunteers. Devoy gathered a cadre of émigré revolutionaries around the newspaper, including Mellows, Frank Robbins and Patrick McCartan.

In October, Mellows was arrested and imprisoned in the Tombs Prison, New York for entering the United States without correct documentation. He endured confinement for twenty-two hours a day until his release in November when supporters pledged a bond of $7,000.[93] Fellow Irish exile John Brennan believed that Clan na Gael deliberately left Mellows to languish in jail: 'Mellows and McCartan were left in prison in the Tombs and the story was put out by the Clan na Gael that they did not want to be released on bail.'[94] Brennan noted that Nora Connolly, daughter of James Connolly and a close friend of Mellows, visited senior members of the Clan and 'asked them to put up the bail, and they had given her the same answer which we had got that he did not wish the bail to be raised'.[95]

Mellows' relationship with the American Fenian movement was fraught and the stress of his absence from Ireland damaged his health. He resented the insipid infighting and personality clashes that characterised the Irish-American movement and found the absence from the rapid advance of the republican movement at home traumatic. Mellows wrote to Fenian leader Joe McGarrity in 1920:

> I feel too disgusted with the situation in the Friends of Irish Freedom to mention it but Mrs O'Brennan will give you a picture of how things really are. At a meeting organised by me here the other night $5,000 was raised in a few minutes but there are hundreds of people here who will not touch the bond issue if it is handled by the men who have grabbed the funds of the Friends of Irish Freedom.[96]

John Brennan formed a close alliance with Mellows when he eventually fell out with Clan na Gael over the issue of conscription. Brennan claimed that:

> it was as a direct result of Mellows' determined stand on the conscription question that he was called up by the heads of Clan na Gael. He was offered the alternative of ceasing his connection with these [Clan na Gael] meetings or losing his post on the *Gaelic American*. Without hesitation he

made the choice. He would continue his propaganda for the Irish cause on the streets of New York.[97]

Mellows was subsequently expelled from the American Fenian movement and for a period, ceased his involvement in republican politics entirely. Brennan recalled, 'After this, he went out in search of a job and, after failing to find a suitable one, had to accept the heavy work of an unskilled labourer, for which he was not fit. One day he collapsed at his job. His weakness was due to starvation.'[98] According to his close friend Frank Robbins, 'Mellows was subject to spells of despondency and was inclined to be neglectful of himself.'[99] Mellows possibly suffered a bout of anorexia brought on by depression or nervous tension, but Robbins was anxious to discount the rumours that Mellows had starved himself:

> This starvation story was the product of imaginative-minded women, had no basis or foundation and was a terrible libel on our good Irish folk living in New York, not one of whom, no matter how strongly they might have disagreed with him, would [not] have done everything possible to help him during his illness … Finally, a Mrs. McCarthy who was a member of the New York Cumann na mBan and a nurse, did learn about his illness and from that onwards helped to bring him back to good health.[100]

Despite his personal torment, Mellows described the Rebellion in Galway in heroic terms in the *Gaelic American* in January 1917, while privately he felt profound anguish. Robbins recalled Mellows' anguish over the morality of the actions of the secret military council that planned the Rebellion, blaming Mellows' change of mind on the influence of Volunteer leader Patrick McCartan:

> I noticed that he [Mellows] was in very low spirits and I jokingly said to him, 'A penny for your thoughts Liam, or are they even worth that much', to which Mellows replied in a very despondent manner, 'If I had known as much in Easter Week as I know to-day I would never have fired a shot'.

> With that he told me that the Revolutionary Military Council had taken unto themselves powers to which they had no right; they had usurped the authority of the Supreme Council of the IRA which was the only authority with power to declare the Insurrection, and they had set themselves up as a military junta and ignored everyone else.[101]

Mellows finally arrived back in Ireland in October 1920 after working his passage as a stoker aboard the *Philadelphia*. Return to Ireland was not the exhilarating release he had hope for and the death of his father in August added to the urgency of his return. His experience of the United States advanced his emerging socialist analysis, developed his ability as a leader while his absence from the formative early events in the Independence struggle at home strengthened his determination to give all in the fight for the Republic.

The complexity of wartime allegiances in rural Ireland

The Galway Rebellion was doomed once the *Aud* failed to land her cargo of rifles and ammunition off the Kerry coast. Liam Mellows faced an impossible task and the Rising in the Galway can only be understood in this context. Mellows' achievement in keeping so many of his followers out for so long was a reflection of his abilities as a leader. Looking back after forty years, his deputy still believed the county could have been taken and 'if the original plans had been carried out, it is probable that all the barracks in the County could have been taken without a fight'.[102] The Galway Volunteers' actions during Easter Week, however, suggest that the force would have faced considerable obstacles even if the planned arms had arrived. A successful campaign would have demanded effective communications over a very wide area, including districts that had no Volunteer companies. The group was unsuccessful in the attacks they carried out and the lack of detailed planning, the unpreparedness of ordinary Volunteers and the ambiguity, and even outright hostility, of the rural community, stymied Mellows' plans. In this respect, the traditional orthodoxy that the confusion caused by Eoin MacNeill's countermand order prevented a nationwide rising from erupting, should be treated with caution.

The events of Easter Week in Galway shine a light into the complex political allegiances of rural Ireland and the sheer variety of responses to the Rebellion attests to disparate political traditions. Historian Martin Dolan interviewed many veterans of Easter Week for the fiftieth anniversary of the Rebellion on behalf of the *Connacht Tribune*. He concluded:

> The Galway Rebellion differed from that in Dublin in one important respect. It was not a 'rising' of intellectuals, of teachers, of poets, of scholars. In it there was only one teacher, there was only one priest, there was a rate collector, and a shopkeeper's son. The rest of the rebels were farmers and sons of labourers and tradesmen of all descriptions. It was a Rising of

common men who had learned their patriotism from their parents, from patriotic teachers, from those who were steeped in the traditions of secret societies that had always existed ...[103]

If the men and women who came out with Liam Mellows in 1916 were indeed the 'common' people of the countryside, then equally, the young men and women who rallied to the call of the Committee of Public Safety, who cheered the navy and RIC, and who gathered to throw mud at republican prisoners, were for the most part, 'common' working people also. Republicans did not have a monopoly on the political imagination of the poor and the hostility of so many 'common people' during Easter Week exposed republican ideologues' idealisation of themselves as the embodiment of the downtrodden. The political chasm between the rural and urban political milieus in Galway was profound and nationalism in 1916 encompassed diverse strands that reflected the rural tradition of violent defiance of the authorities, alongside an urban tradition that constituted a distinctly western variety of empire nationalism.

The rhetoric of both nationalists and republicans during Easter Week was characterised by bombast, exaggeration and bluff. The degree to which the Committee for Public Safety genuinely believed that an 'invasion' of Galway town was imminent is open to question and their verbose pronouncements should be treated with scepticism. Local commentary on the Rebellion was flavoured with a heavy dollop of social snobbery and the nature of insult employed on both sides is revealing. While the elites of the Parliamentary Party were firmly represented by Galway's mercantile elite – the so-called 'shoneens' of republican propaganda – the latters' depiction of their republicans rivals as 'dupes', 'degenerates', 'lunatics', 'Huns', 'peasants', 'fools', 'penniless wanderers' and 'desperadoes', reflects the inherent class bias of those for whom the Rebellion represented a challenge, not simply to the military authorities, but to the old political leadership and the social order of local society itself.

CHAPTER 4

The Rise of Sinn Féin and the Volunteers, 1916–20

The ignorant country boys have learned a lot since 1916 …

Sinn Féin representative Stephen Jordan, Galway County Council, June 1920[1]

There were a number of political and economic developments that facilitated the rise of Sinn Féin and the Volunteers in Galway before the outbreak of the War of Independence. Republicans in Galway decisively defeated the IPP in the 1918 General Election and their success was driven by a series of political and economic factors, of which, the War was the formative catalyst. The veteran leaders of Galway's political establishment faced a younger, more energetic cadre of opponents – many of whom had been incarcerated for their political beliefs. As Fergus Campbell has shown, the wave of land agitation that gripped the county in the early months of 1918 benefited republicans enormously as the party became associated with a mass campaign of land agitation by the rural poor.[2] Republicans supplanted the traditional role of the UIL as leaders of the rural poor against their traditional oppressor – the petty landlord and the bullock. The threat of conscription, however, more than any other factor led to the rejection of the IPP and facilitated the rise of Sinn Féin.

From 1917 until early 1919, the focus of the republican leadership concentrated on building up the Sinn Féin organisation while drawing as little attention to the growing Volunteer movement as possible. From a situation prior to the Rising where many Volunteer companies defied and antagonised the police, the 300 prisoners who returned from Frongoch and other British jails initially adopted a less visible approach with drilling and parades ceasing and public disorder avoided. 1917 was a year of quiet re-organisation as the last of the prisoners returned to civilian life with a significant minority playing key roles in building a popular republican movement.

Sinn Féin's electoral triumphs in a series of national by-elections in 1917 had formative repercussions that proved to be definitive developments in terms of the evolution and political approach of the Volunteer movement.[3] The electorate's endorsement of two relatively obscure republicans in North Roscommon and South Longford convinced the Volunteer leadership that Sinn Féin could be successfully mobilised as a formidable electoral machine. Participation in successful electoral campaigns ameliorated the disappointment felt by many rural republicans following the events of Easter Week 1916. As leading republican Richard Mulcahy explained, following Éamon de Valera's successful election in East Clare in July 1917, 'All feelings of frustration for the Clare, Limerick and Kerry Volunteers arising out of the disappointment of Easter Week had been completely thrown aside. Into the defensive organisation set up to secure success in the east Clare election, a definite element of defiance had entered.'[4] Many Galway Volunteers from the south and east of the county travelled to Clare to participate in de Valera's successful campaign gaining a valuable morale boost and practical knowledge.

By late 1917, Volunteer leaders acknowledged that co-operation between broadly defined sections of nationalist opinion was both possible and necessary to facilitate the emergence of a broadly based political force that could be allied to the Volunteers. A national re-organisation of Sinn Féin was initiated in October and a new constitution formally ratified. A governing executive and parish-based cumann structure was organised with the electoral ward becoming the unit of organisation in urban centres.[5] The issue of Sinn Féin's dual monarchy policy presented a stumbling block to unanimity between militant republicans and moderate supporters and a compromise formula whereby the party committed itself to securing 'Irish Freedom' and allowing the electorate to choose their form of government was agreed. The election of de Valera as president was highly significant as the influence of Arthur Griffith, whose perseverance had sustained the party, was superseded by more militant voices.

Aftermath of rebellion

The failure of the IPP in the General Election of 1918 in Galway was unsurprising to local commentators, with Sinn Féin gaining 31,271 votes compared to the IPP's 9,225.[6] In advance of the 1918 General Election, the national executive of Sinn Féin formed the nascent nucleus of a future government cabinet with leading members taking responsibility for various economic departments, compiling reports and announcing social and political policies at weekly meetings. By late 1917, Sinn Féin pronouncements were dominated by the impending economic crisis that rising prices for basic commodities were generating. The War provided a major boost to strong and middling farmers, and in Galway, the police reported, 'farmers were never in their lives in more prosperous circumstances owing to high prices for their stock and farm produce'.[7] As new Sinn Féin cumainn sprang up across the county in late 1917, the authorities became convinced the party would become 'dangerous if allied to some popular land campaign'.[8] The War had serious repercussions for those on the economic margins and the suspension of emigration dashed any hope of escape from poverty for many young people. Land purchase was effectively stopped as the work of the Congested Districts Board (CDB) was put on hold and the Board withdrew its impending offers for 159 estates comprising 267,500 acres and subsequently rented land to large landowners or simply left farms idle.[9]

While the rural poor traditionally produced the bulk of their own foodstuffs, most urban families could not fulfil all their food requirements and were forced to purchase food stuffs from shopkeepers and markets. As strong farmers and shopkeepers increasingly profited from rising food prices, rising prices for bacon and potatoes stimulated popular fears over food shortages and profiteering stimulated the popularity of Sinn Féin's anti-government rhetoric. By early 1918, speculation in basic foodstuffs was increasingly commonplace and indignation and fear over food prices stimulated widespread land seizures in counties across Leinster, Munster and Connacht. Seizures were carried out by young farmers, farmers' sons and labourers, many of who had recently joined Sinn Féin.

Land seizures began spontaneously in January 1918, becoming widespread in Counties Clare, Galway and Roscommon, in particular.[10] Seizures involved large groups forcibly entering grassland farms belonging to larger landowners and the CDB put their own livestock out to graze, and from March onwards, ploughing the land and sowing potatoes. Cattle and sheep drives often accompanied seizures, as owners' stock was driven off in large and elaborate drives that exhausted police resources with the Royal Irish Constabulary (RIC) obliged to retrieve the unfortunate animals. Newly formed Sinn Féin cumainn were to the fore in the seizures and land occupations were often 'claimed for the Republic'. Land seizures formed occasions of communal solidarity and were often accompanied by brass bands and cheering crowds; violent clashes between the police and agitators amplified Sinn Féin's anti-RIC rhetoric.

From 1917 onwards Sinn Féin and the Volunteers steadily eroded the civil role of the RIC and the courts system and constructed an alternative counter state with the establishment of a system of Dáil courts and republican police. The boycott of the police and courts was an incremental process and created a parallel system of administration. The boycott of the RIC was crucial as people increasingly turned to the republican movement for the redress of personal grievances. The administration of justice and the 'punishment of crime' by the Volunteers rather than the police led to the collapse of the courts system by early 1920. This process was compounded in the first six months of 1920 as Sinn Féin took control of local public administration by winning the overwhelming majority of seats on local councils and Boards of Guardians.

The engine of the republican movement in Galway remained the young rural proletariat, guided by a significant group of younger clergy, several of the county's leading Gaelic Athletic Association (GAA) officers and a seasoned group of older Irish Republican Brotherhood (IRB) members. The growth of the movement was confined to the rural poor with the RIC reporting in 1917: 'no responsible men or persons with a stake in the country attending their meetings'.[11] From having only one cumann at Craughwell at the beginning of the year, Sinn Féin had fifty-one cumainn with a total membership of 3,044 by December 1918.[12] The GAA, led by IRB member Stephen Jordan from Athenry, played a crucial role in energising the party with hurling matches and other GAA competitions allowing republicans to defy War-time military regulations concerning public gatherings. The police believed the growth of the Volunteers intimidated those who had not previously countenanced joining the movement:

> What is bad about the situation at present is that the older and more respectable people are getting afraid not to be Sinn Féiners. It must be remembered that these people have to live amongst the Sinn Féiners, who are going through men and young priests and for the most part are bullies. The Sinn Féin policy here is to get a good grip of the County and when their numbers are very strong, they will see what they can do, and they can do a good deal by shooting at night. That is the Galway habit, firing at persons and firing into dwelling houses.[13]

The events of Easter Week remained fresh in many Volunteers' minds, and in December 1917, farmer Luke Flynn was shot by raiders in his home near Oranmore. During Easter Week he refused to hand a shotgun to the rebels and allegedly threatened to shoot the first man who tried to take it from him.[14] The bitterness between the Volunteers and MP William Duffy's supporters in Loughrea continued to fuel violence, and at a variety performance organised by the local 'Sinn Féin clergy' in May 1917, Duffy's supporters interrupted proceedings by 'chanting for the red, white and blue of England and denouncing Sinn Féin'.[15] Performers were followed to their lodgings by a hostile crowd, 'shouting loyal expressions' and the manager of the company was arrested for drawing a revolver on the mob.

The GAA in Galway suffered a serious blow following the Rising with the deportation of many of the organisation's leading members and the police initially noted that the movement 'had not regained its old activity and importance since the Rebellion'.[16] In a matter of months, however, the organisation was growing in parallel with Sinn Féin due to the tireless work of returned prisoners. The authorities identified the connection between Sinn Féin and the GAA, and hurling in particular, believing, 'the GAA is only a cover to advance the interests of the Sinn Féiners',[17] and 'it is most disloyal and it gets at the young as no other organisation does'.[18]

The degree to which the GAA could be used as a vehicle for all manner of disputes was illustrated by a hurling match held in Corofin in April 1917. Defying War-time restrictions, a prominent IRB member assembled hurling teams from Anabally and Annaghdown. The match was organised to taunt the authorities and demonstrate the ability of the Volunteers to assemble a large group of men without the knowledge of police; however, police claimed that the game was organised to intimidate local tenants who got farms from the CDB on the Blake property at Corofin. As a local farmer, the IRB leader applied for a division of land on the property but failed to be included in the division, 'on account of his history and antecedents'.[19]

The terrible violence of the War was brought home to the people of west Galway in tragic fashion on 15 June 1917 when nine fishermen were blown up by a mine they retrieved from the sea near Inverin on the southern shores of Connemara. Such was the violence of the explosion that only two bodies could be identified and the body parts of seven victims were buried in an unmarked grave in Bohermore cemetery in Galway town. The group was exploring the coastline for salvage near Lochán Beag beach when they spotted the mine close to shore. Thinking the mine was a barrel, it was rolled ashore from a boat. The explosion was heard over ten miles away and the unfortunate victims were literally blown to pieces. A passing doctor attended the scene but there was nothing that could be done for the deceased. It remains unclear whether the mine was British or German but local suspicion that the mine was British – and not German as claimed by the military – was compounded by the haste in which the coroner's inquest was held and the lack of publicity or propaganda attached to the tragedy by the authorities. The fact that the victims were poor

Irish speakers from the western seaboard compounded the official and popular disinterest in the tragedy.

The explosion was the single biggest loss of life in the west of Ireland during the period and the relative obscurity of the events surrounding the deaths reflected the widespread disinterest in the affairs of the remote Irish-speaking communities of Connemara. While a financial fund was supported by *The Galway Express* and *Connacht Tribune*, there was little obvious outrage among respectable society and the tragedy never became part of the wider consciousness of the community outside the close environs of the close-knit community in South Connemara.[20] The men who died were:

An Lochán Beag: Éamonn MacDiarmada (53); Tomás Hoibicín (30); Seosamh Ó Flaithearta (32); Tadhg Ó Céidigh (30); Colm Ó Féinneadha (18)

An Teach Mór: Peadar Ó Cuálain (17)

Na hAille: Mánus Ó Fathartha (20); Éamonn Ó Laoi (17); Pádraig Ó Laoi (17)[21]

Further maritime tragedies followed and on 19 December 1917, four fishermen from Galway town lost their lives aboard the Neptune after hauling up a mine in Galway Bay. Martin McDonagh, aged 60; William Walsh, aged 40; and his son Patrick, aged 16; and Bartley Gill, aged 50, lost their lives. The following year, on 31 May 1918, another fishing vessel, the Pretty Polly, was torpedoed in Galway Bay with the loss of skipper Joseph Canavan and four other members of the Canavan family: Joseph (aged 20); Mark (aged 26); his cousin Mark (aged 37); Mathew (aged 37); and Tom (aged 37), along with crew members, Joseph and Patrick MacDonagh.

Insult and the rise of Sinn Féin

Political debate during the War tended towards personal insult and the rise of Sinn Féin generated bitter resentment among many supporters of the IPP. Motifs of insult employed in anti-Sinn Féin rhetoric can be classified into four categories. Republicans were derided for their roots in the rural poor and the supposed poverty of their supporters formed the basis of frequent insults; they were accused of being too young and too immature to have legitimate political opinions and the fact that most of their members were not active during the Land Wars of the late nineteenth century was a recurring source of criticism;

Sinn Féin was dismissed as being part of a wider conspiracy by 'pro-British reactionaries' and members were frequently labelled the puppets of 'the crowbar brigade', 'Freemasons', 'Tories' and the Orange Order; finally, republicans were derided as physical cowards who lacked the courage of their convictions as evinced by their opposition to the War effort and the chaotic events of Easter Week.

At a United Irish League (UIL) meeting in Ballinasloe in late 1917, a local nationalist representative described Sinn Féin members as 'fellows who the Land League had given a touch to in the past'.[22] At a meeting of the Ballinasloe Board of Guardians during the same month, a member remarked, 'I never saw them [Sinn Féin] carrying a Land League banner or anything else to advance the movement, except their straw hats, it is the landlord crowd that is behind them, they were in their swaddling clothes when we were fighting the land fight.'[23] At the same meeting, a nationalist member exhorted a colleague who had declared his support for Sinn Féin, 'to get rid of these undesirable men in the Sinn Féin ranks who were making with them and voting with them, for these are the fellows that will sell you and sell Ireland and bring down bitter ruin. Put them in prison and hang half them … Sinn Féin are only a crowd of gossoons who play football and hurley and now think they can run the country.'[24] Chairman of Galway Urban Council Philip McDonnell echoed these sentiments, and at a public meeting in April 1918, declared, 'unlike the diehards, [they] did not live in a balloon or go on chasing rainbows'.[25]

The *East Galway Democrat* was published in Ballinasloe and adopted a particularly aggressive tone towards Sinn Féin, noting that, despite the best efforts of 'that Englishman Mellows', 'the old leaders and the old methods will prove that the currency of idiots will not pass as genuine coin'.[26] The paper described Sinn Féin as 'the descendants of Castle Catholics, rent office hangers on, toadies, flunkeys, grabbers, policemen and disappointed office seekers'.[27] The editor warned against the release of the Galway prisoners following the 1916 Rising, noting, 'the mad mullahs represented a danger to the country'[28] and later published an editorial on the rise of Sinn Féin under the headline, 'Suckling Youths':

Big noises may be heard nowadays by suckling youths who have not so much brains as the head of a pin. Entering into politics and trying to put political opinions down the necks of the people is becoming sickening. A well-to-do farmer mentioned to us some time ago that he had changed his business from Ballinasloe to another town on account of the babbling nonsense of one of the class we have just referred to … In our town, the wings of shoneenism were always extended and under these wings clustered the brood of the backboneless, fearing a fight at any time, they turned and scut. Is it to the care of such that our future is to be trusted?[29]

While younger priests played a crucial role in the emergence of Sinn Féin, republicans did not have a monopoly on clerical support. At a meeting in support of north Galway IPP candidate, Thomas Sloyan, a local priest unfurled a green flag and asked the audience, 'Are you going to desert the green?', claiming 'the national cause they represented was the only cause that had brought comfort, consolation, benefits, and anything that was good to the country'.[30] Monsignor Patrick McAlpine of Clifden was a prominent supporter of MP William O'Malley and advised his constituents that it would be strange, 'if we followed the thoughtless crowd whose rainbow chasing policy no matter how well intentioned, courts defeat and spells disaster, whose aims are impossible of attainment, as wild as they are chimerical'. McAlpine concluded, 'it is simply sickening and disgusting to find that our people don't open their eyes and see for themselves that many of the apostles of the new evangel were bred and reared in the rent office; they are the pliant tools and willing agents and the landlord and the sheriff when the poor were being evicted'.[31]

With the UIL floundering and the IPP in disarray, conservative nationalist opinion in Galway town found expression in the formation of the National Club. The Galway National Club was formed at a meeting attended by around fifty 'influential nationalists' organised by Thomas Kenny of the *Connacht Tribune* and chaired by Philip McDonnell of the Galway urban district council in November 1917.[32] The Chairman told the meeting that, despite the rise of Sinn Féin, 'there is still a very substantial and weighty proportion of the community still prepared to give loyal adhesion to the old movement'. The purpose of the club, the chairman continued, was to help Ireland achieve 'the fullest and most complete freedom within the empire'. The organisers intended to provide a club where 'rational nationalists may meet and discuss the events of the day, where ... everything that is sanely patriotic, and everything that makes for our moral and material welfare along the path of security may be promoted.' The club hoped to keep the National Volunteers intact through its auspices and announced that an 'early opportunity be availed of to have the arms seized by the authorities restored'.[33]

The inaugural meeting of the new club was attended by many of Galway's leading 'public men'. Extensive premises were secured in a prominent location, which, they claimed, would be guaranteed to 'attract the best class of people' with rooms for billiards tables, latrines and space to seat four hundred. Club subscriptions were set at £1.1s – sufficiently high to be beyond the means of most working people. Members were required to sign a club pledge stating that they 'were in full and active sympathy with Ireland's claim to her full and complete control of her internal affairs'.[34] By the end of their first month, eighty-three members had applied for membership and the *Connacht Tribune* lauded their efforts under headlines such as 'money talks' and 'under the old flag', leaving readers in no doubt of the club's social character.[35]

The organisation of the club was given added incentive by the decision of the electoral boundary commission to bring an end to Galway town's status as an electoral borough with its own MP (Newry and Kilkenny also lost their borough status) and incorporate the town into the Connemara electoral constituency. The ending of Galway's borough status deprived nationalists of an almost guaranteed seat in Parliament. Thomas Kenny of the *Connacht Tribune* claimed the decision was an 'atrocious betrayal' and 'the ascendency had begun to reap some of the fruits of a victory … in the face of divided Irish opinion'.[36] Writing under an obvious pseudonym, a member of the National Club wrote a typically searing letter to the *Connacht Tribune* in early 1918 claiming, 'only for Mr John Redmond and the Irish Party, the fathers of some of our young clergy who are now attacking him, would not have been in a position to give them the education they attained'.[37] The club gave a platform for prominent nationalists to meet and make speeches that could be printed in the *Connacht Tribune* without incurring the fear of public insult – a perennial problem at public meetings. In April 1918, P.S. McDonnell told a meeting of 'men that were in the fight when some of these latter day politicians were unheard of', that, despite reports that 'Galway had gone politically mad, it was perfectly obvious that they had maintained their sanity and were maintaining it still, they did not live in a balloon and had no desire to go rainbow chasing.'[38] Noting the 'swollen heads of young Sinn Féiners' at a meeting in July, members were told to be conscious that because of 'the traitorism of educated men like Eoin MacNeill and others who tried to flitch away the temperaments of young uneducated countrymen … the heart of the country will soon ring deep with sorrow and her indignation would turn on these fellows for their treachery.'[39]

The new land war

While the organisational structure of Sinn Féin and the Volunteers was put in place during 1917, the early months of 1918 saw a wave of popular land protests that was to provide the impetus for the movement's unprecedented growth. In February 1918, the west Galway chief inspector of police wrote to

Dublin Castle warning that 'were it not for the presence of troops in Galway and Gort and the operation of aeroplanes at Oranmore, it would be difficult for the police to keep an upper hand'.[40] The source of the unrest was Sinn Féin members' involvement in land seizures, cattle drives and raids for arms, which generated unprecedented clashes between the RIC and large crowds of determined agitators, often armed with shotguns and accompanied by cheering women and children.

The seizures were fuelled by the rising cost of food, and prices for basic commodities reached an all-time high at the beginning of the 1918 with the *Connacht Tribune* reporting that while, 'there was no fear of famine everybody knows that the people in the towns are in a bad way'.[41] At a meeting of urban tenants in the town of Tuam, it was reported that, 'scarcity of food was serious in nature … the workers cannot even get potatoes on market day' and the meeting proposed the provision of an allotment system whereby urban tenants could grow their own potatoes.[42] Amid the scarcity, shopkeepers were regularly prosecuted for breaking statutory regulations governing the prices of meat, potatoes and other basic necessities.

The agitation was not limited to land seizures or cattle drives and incidents of violence were extensively reported. During January alone, landowner J.G. Alcorn of Kilroe House in north Galway was wounded in a gun attack;[43] shots were fired at a land steward at Castle Taylor in east Galway;[44] a house on the Menlo estate of Valentine Blake was burned;[45] and at Dunsandle, farmer Thomas Murphy was wounded in a gun attack.[46] Raids for arms by the Volunteers escalated, with police reports of raids by masked men in the districts of Gort, Kinvara and Claregalway.[47] The link between the emerging land war and the Volunteers was apparent, with the RIC warning, 'Sinn Féin is now being worked as an agrarian movement for the forcible repossessing of land. Land is being openly commandeered for grazing and for personal occupation. This new phase of Sinn Féin will bring many young men into the movement which previously held no attraction for them.'[48]

As the agitation spread, the growth of Sinn Féin became a source of concern to the authorities. In April, the RIC in West Galway noted:

The number of Sinn Féiners is growing in this County and younger members are beginning to show a spirit of defiance, egged on to it and stirred up by the younger members of the Roman Catholic clergy. This policy at present is to supplant Redmond's party and they will succeed in Galway as they have succeeded in Roscommon and Longford … they recognise the futility of open rebellion but they think that much may be accomplished in other ways by a strong and determined party once the military law has been withdrawn.[49]

Sinn Féin cumainn continued to spring up around agitations and former UIL supporters were prominent at cattle drives and land seizures. Sinn Féin and the Volunteers acted as stewards and organised deputations, and according to police, they were 'muttering discontent and preaching sedition and disloyalty, secretly encouraging outrage and appealing to the basest elements of an irreconcilable people'.[50] While the republican leadership had their reservations about the land seizures, they were powerless to stop the spread of protests and benefitted from the popularity the party was rapidly gaining. The Volunteers came into the open for the first time since Easter 1916, and in many districts, the police were helpless as people began to treat them with open defiance, as the county inspector for West Galway reported:

> The police in moving about are treated with contempt and are jeered at. No one is allowed to speak to them and information as to the recurrence of outrages has to be dragged out of the injured persons. The opinion is prevalent that the police cannot do anything and would not be allowed to do anything. At night the lives of the police are in danger all the time while on patrol and I am in daily fear of hearing that some man has been shot by means of some foul and cowardly treachery. All this is due to the Sinn Féin rebels who went out in 1916.[51]

The leadership of the IPP took an alarmist approach to the unrest. In a letter to the *Freeman's Journal* published in February entitled 'Ireland and the Bolshevik Conception of Freedom', leader of the IPP John Dillon, declared:

> However attractive to romantic and political young men [seizures] would inevitably lead the people to disaster and chaos such as that which reigns in Russia at present ... In the present state of Russia we have a full illustration of the form of liberty which these leaders desire to be introduced into Ireland, and which is characterised by wholesale murder, unpunished robbery, universal civil war and the dispersal by machineguns and bayonets of the lawfully elected representatives of the people.[52]

As increasing numbers of small farmers and tenants became involved in cattle drives and the occupation of land, new Sinn Féin cumainn began exercising a degree of social control. The unrest generated an acute sense of insecurity for landowners as police became powerless to prevent farms from being taken over. Former UIL representatives who had been scathing in their criticism of Sinn Féin, stated that land occupations were justified as, 'they must rely on themselves alone. They must take, till and do everything they wanted with the lands and not be relying on the British government. They will never get fair play until they were governed by Irishmen.'[53] Court cases associated with the agitations formed occasions of communal support for arrested men and prisoners often refused to recognise the court and defiantly mocked the proceedings.

Concerned at the scale and ferocity of land seizures and anxious to disentangle the movement from the escalating wave of seizures, the national standing committee of Sinn Féin issued instructions on 23 February that no cumann had the authority to organise or conduct a cattle drive without placing their case before the Comhairle Ceantar of Sinn Féin and all clubs should immediately refrain from raids for arms in private houses.[54] Richard Mulcahy later explained the leadership's thinking, 'It [the executive] was concerned with the public's appreciation of the function of the Volunteer organisation and their establishment of its prestige and of its authority in the eyes of both friend and enemy. It sought to foster popular cohesion and sustain the defiant spirit of the people generally.'[55]

The new Sinn Féin dictate was followed days later with a similar memorandum forbidding Volunteers from involvement in land seizures; however, in Galway seizures continued unabated. Following the republican ban on their members participating in agitation, a new organisation, 'The United Irish Tillage League' was established at a public meeting in the village of Creggs on the Galway/Roscommon border and a written manifesto sent to large grassland farmers in the district. The programme demanded that owners hand over a portion of their land to the people for tillage and claimed that some form of compensation would be paid.[56] As the early summer of 1918 progressed, however, the police claimed an increased military presence in the county 'had a sobering effect', and life returned to normal, although the RIC found it difficult to get the necessities of life 'where local priests were to the fore as they attempted to make the RIC's lives unbearable'.[57]

Sinn Féin and the Volunteers instigated the establishment of republican courts in early 1918 to mediate agrarian disputes between tenants and small farmers, and larger landowners.[58] The courts were to come into their own in the second wave of land agitation during the spring of 1920 but the fundamental mechanisms were established in response to the first phase of the new land war. The courts involved a respected member of the community mediating between landowners and local tenants clamouring for access to land. The courts were to become the most remarkable achievement of the revolutionary movement in the county and the widespread acceptance of their rulings in 1920 attested to their seminal role in gaining Sinn Féin the allegiance of property owners. By initially supporting and benefitting politically from land seizures in early 1918, the establishment of the courts provided a further political boost for the party as they could portray themselves as a safeguard against the violence of the rural poor. Far from being Bolsheviks – as their most ardent opponents claimed – the courts allowed Sinn Féin to be seen as the only legitimate safeguard against a potential plebeian revolution. The courts increasingly dealt with regular criminality, and in March 1918, one of Sinn Féin's own members was tried for an assault following a Sinn Féin rally in Athenry. The accused was sentenced to two weeks' hard labour in the Killeeneen parish hall supervised by the local Volunteer company.[59]

The conscription crisis

The conscription crisis of April and May 1918 ushered in a new political landscape and exposed the duplicity of the government and the impotency of constitutional nationalism. The crisis provided a renewed impetus for nationalist solidarity at a time when rural society was at a turbulent crossroads. The anti-conscription campaign and the role of younger clergy, in particular, in organising public opposition to the impending Conscription Bill brought Sinn Féin a crucial measure of public respectability that it hitherto lacked.[60] It is unclear if the land hunger that erupted in the early months of 1918 would have been sufficient to carry Sinn Féin to electoral dominance; however, the conscription threat that emerged in April, just as the wave of land agitation abated, provided a continuity of popular political momentum. Throughout the latter part of 1917, the UIL in Galway was reported to be 'losing ground every day',[61] and in September, the police pronounced the organisation 'practically dead in influence'.[62] With a vacuum in political representation, the conscription crisis became the most significant political stimulus in the rise of Sinn Féin. The crisis brought the party into the political mainstream, and by April 1918, fear of conscription provided Sinn Féin a platform and relevance it hitherto lacked, as British policy threatened to impinge on ordinary people's lives in previously unimagined ways. By shouting loudest against the threat, republicanism became relevant to the broad mass of the people with an immediacy that proved far more successful than ideological arguments.

As a vast series of anti-conscription meetings was organised across the country, a national general strike on 23 April was observed by businesses and workers. An anti-conscription pledge formulated by the newly founded Mansion House Committee consisting of all ranks of nationalist opinion became intrinsically associated with Sinn Féin. The party enthusiastically canvassed on public platforms, after mass and at fairs, marts and markets. The crisis brought Sinn Féin into firm agreement with the Catholic hierarchy for the first and only time.[63] Representatives of the Mansion House Committee attended meetings of the Catholic hierarchy at Maynooth, with the Bishops issuing a stern manifesto, 'We consider that conscription forced in this way upon Ireland is an oppressive and inhuman law which Irish people have a right to resist by every means that are consonant with the law of God.'[64]

As the crisis gathered momentum, the ranks of the Volunteers became swollen with new recruits, most of whom who had previously stood aloof. Volunteer Sean O'Neill recalled that the more prosperous section of society in north Galway emerged as unlikely supporters:

> The well-to-do and former supporters of Redmond and pro-British types were all now looking to the Volunteers and Sinn Féin for a lead. Bank clerks, excise men and such would come to me and discuss conditions in the trenches of Flanders and Gallipoli and when they'd stroke their well shaved chins and comment on the difficulties of having a decent shave or bath in a slushy trench in Flanders I could not resist laughing into the faces of these gloomy looking men. A very large number of 'would not be soldiers' flocked into the local Volunteer Company.[65]

The crisis mobilised and politicised young people as no previous political issue and the *Tuam Herald* noted in April, 'the country is aroused as never it was before in living memory'.[66] Five hundred young men marched through the town in early April under the banner, 'We will not have conscription.' The *Herald* noted, 'it was a remarkable gathering considering the spontaneity of the event and that it was mainly confined to the town'.[67] The meeting was followed by a public meeting of the Volunteers, an indicator of the political conversion the conscription threat aroused in towns that displayed little obvious republican support. The *Herald* was careful to insulate the IPP from criticism and checked its earlier commentary, claiming, 'If the Sinn Féiners kept quiet, and did not go about drilling and marching, armed men from one County into another showing what they could or would do and challenging the government, we should never had heard of conscription. It is the general opinion by this sort of silly display we brought it on ourselves.'[68] Rival nationalists also attempted to blame Sinn Féin for the crisis and MP William O'Malley claimed, 'it is unquestionably the drilling of four hundred thousand young men as de Valera claimed that must have its effect upon the government. The Irish Party will oppose it tooth and nail.'[69]

Throughout the crisis, younger clergy emerged as ardent opponents of the government and the most passionate and effective critics of the proposed bill. The anger generated by the crisis saw the government and police denounced in previously unthinkable forums. In north Galway, Fr Malachy Brennan of Caltra warned his flock not to have anything to do with the RIC, whom he memorably referred to as 'pimps and spies and a disgrace to the country that produced them'.[70] At Loughrea Cathedral, Archbishop Thomas Gilmartin announced, 'Ireland is a nation and she has a right to determine on what conditions she is going to give the blood of her sons. Now it is proposed to treat her as if her sons were slaves.'[71] At a meeting in Ballinasloe, Archbishop Gilmartin told a public meeting, 'Ireland is a distinct nation from England geographically, economically, socially distinct. If England has no right to conscript us against our will, we have a right to resist such an outrage by the most effective means at our disposal. Not only have we a right to resist but a duty.'[72] Father Owen Hannon told an audience at Tuam, 'stick to one another like men when conscription is killed and you will have a free country'.[73]

Conservative nationalists who bitterly opposed Sinn Féin made clear their determination to oppose the Conscription Bill; however, their previous support for the government saw them indelibly identified with the act, and in many cases, blamed for the crisis. Galway's incumbent MPs, William O'Malley, Stephen Gwynn and William Duffy were forced to denounce the government on anti-conscription platforms throughout April and May after having urged unstinting support for the War-time government over the previous four years. Gwynn's stance had evolved considerably, as in July 1915 he told a gathering in Loughrea, 'While you and I would prefer to serve in an army voluntarily recruited, I would sooner have conscription than national defeat, humiliation, ruin and disaster. If men could not be got by voluntary appeal, they would have to be got by compulsion and I would not oppose it, if it came of necessity.'[74] In late May 1918, he attempted to publicly backtrack, writing to the *Tuam Herald*, claiming that at no time did he support conscription being introduced.[75] Anti-conscription meetings were impressive affairs and over 1,000 men marched twelve miles from Corrandulla to Galway to attend a public meeting in late April. The Bishop of Galway, Dr Thomas O'Dea, wrote an open letter to the meeting noting that 'conscription forced upon Ireland was oppressive, inhumane and impossible and the people had a right to resist it by every means'. Bishop Thomas Gilmartin wrote, 'they were all at one in what promised to be the most determined and united campaign that was ever organised in any country against the threatened infringement of a nation's fundamental rights'.[76]

A further timely propaganda boost for republicans was provided by the so-called 'German plot' that began on 12 April 1918, when police arrested a mysterious stranger attempting to land a small craft off the coast of County Clare. James Dowling of the Connaught Rangers had been taken prisoner on the Western Front and subsequently joined Roger Casement's Irish Brigade at Limburg. Dowling was removed to London on charges of 'voluntarily serving the enemy' and subsequently sentenced to death; his arrest was heralded by the British government as proof of a 'German plot' to invade the west coast of Ireland with the aid of the republican movement.[77]

The belief that a German landing in Galway was a possibility and that the Volunteers were preparing for such an event was firmly held by the RIC in the county, who continually warned Dublin Castle of such a threat. District Inspector Ruttledge wrote to Dublin Castle in February 1917: 'the rebels must have some information that the Germans are about to attempt a landing because that alone would move them now after the lessons they learned in April 1916'.[78] Ruttledge noted, 'The released Sinn Féiners are keeping out of sight, having a great dread of court martial. But they are still anti-British and would rise again if the Germans landed on this coast, not otherwise, as they recognise the futility of coming into conflict with the British Army without the solid backing of German soldiers.'[79]

On 17 May, a number of leading Sinn Féin members were arrested in connection with the so-called plot and the government announced that Sinn Féin was implicated in a pro-German conspiracy. A coterie of Galway's leading republicans were arrested, including the editor of the *Galway Express* George Nichols; General Election candidate Dr Bryan Cusack; Colm O'Gaora (Rosmuc); Thomas Ruane (Carnmore); Stephen Jordan (Athenry); Michael Trayers (Gort); and Brian Fallon (Loughrea). Several of the men were deported to England under the Defence of the Realm Act.[80] The affair added additional impetus to the republican surge in popularity and the arrests and deportations provided Sinn Féin with a significant boost while further discrediting the authorities at an already fraught juncture in popular opinion.

Sinn Féin possessed an array of talented orators including several lawyers who made easy political capital from the affair and strongly alluded – unjustly so – to rival nationalist opponents' complicity in the arrests. The *Galway Express* warned, 'there is a danger, however, that the Irish Party may return to Westminster using as an excuse that they go there to see justice done to the Sinn Féiners … certainly the Sinn Féiners at home and in jail don't want anyone to make an appeal on their behalf. Much as they will suffer and as great as the personal loss for each, they would rather rot then for their principles then be restored to freedom by the negations of them.'[81] Labelling the arrests as 'kidnapping', Louis O'Dea told a public meeting, 'it was a strange state of affairs that at the dead of night, these men should be taken out of their beds and brought away on a charge, which on the words of the charge itself, could not be proven'.[82] Noting that the men were 'treated as criminals' even though there was no charge against them, O'Dea fired a warning shot at local IPP stalwarts: 'slaves who tyrannised were more tyrannical than tyrants themselves. There was only one course possible.'

1918 General Election

The writing was firmly on the wall for the IPP in Galway long before the General Election in December 1918. The *Galway Express*, rebranded a republican newspaper under the editorship of George Nichols of Sinn Féin, announced that rather than being a battle between Sinn Féin and the IPP, the election 'was a fight between Sinn Féin and the British government. Aiding and abetting the government will be the Irish Domestic Party.'[83] Sinn Féin candidates were publicly conspicuous from early 1918, speaking on public platforms across the county. Dr Brian Cusack (1882–1973), who was elected for North Galway in December, was originally from Granard, County Longford and was a medical doctor and a founding member of the Volunteers in University College Galway where he completed his medical studies. With a practice at Turloughmore, he represented educated, socially mobile and respectable republicanism and was not a militarily significant figure. Likewise, Frank Fahy (1879–1953), subsequently returned in Galway South, was a native of Kilconickny, Loughrea, and graduated from UCG.[84] A Gaelic League activist, he became a national school teacher and achieved popular nationalist acclaim in the aftermath of the 1916 Rebellion after serving as senior officer under the command of Edward Daly in the Four Courts garrison. Pádraic Ó Máille (1876–1946), who was to defeat William O'Malley MP in West Galway, completed the trio of respectable, socially mobile candidates and was the older brother of the first professor of Irish at UCG, Tomás Ó Máille. The Ó Máille family home at Muintir Eoin in north-west Connemara was to be an important base for the West Connemara Flying Column. Ó Máille, unlike Fahy and Cusack, was a significant military figure in west Connemara and was active throughout the period, becoming a member of the most active flying column in the county.[85] Liam Mellows was to be elected unopposed in the East Galway constituency despite remaining in exile in New York.

Sinn Féin's newly found respectability was demonstrated as early as the first week of January when sixteen priests sat on a republican platform in Eyre Square, Galway, to hear de Valera speak.[86] Throughout the year, newly formed Sinn Féin clubs made public repudiations of the county's old political stalwarts. The Kiltullagh Sinn Féin club typified the mixture of anger and lingering deference when, in January, it called upon local MP William Duffy to resign:

> Mr Duffy has long since ceased to represent the views of the men of Kiltullagh. That while thanking Mr Duffy for former services we are forced to the conviction that he and the party to which he belongs have, by their action in recent years, brought discredit on the manhood of Ireland, and we are determined to do our part to wipe out the disgrace.'[87]

Under the editorship of IRB centre and Sinn Féin leader George Nichols, the *Galway Express* pushed the political line that Sinn Féin was the only legitimate political voice of nationalist Ireland. In January, he noted that, in respect of the South Armagh by-election, only an 'unholy alliance of officialdom, unionism and Redmondism' was preventing Patrick McCartan from defeating the '"effete" Parliamentary Party'.[88] Nichols' editorship of the *Express* turned the paper's longstanding conservative character on its head, and through a mixture of humour and invective, he proved himself an equal of the *Connacht Tribune's* Thomas Kenny in presenting a compelling case for his political cause.

Women played an important role in the 1918 electoral march of Sinn Féin and were prominent at republican meetings and in the distribution of election literature. Galway town established a new committee of Cumann na mBan early in January consisting of young working-class and lower-middle class women. A weekly social in the Sinn Féin Hall on Prospect Hill provided the organisation with an opportunity to attract new members in a less stoic environment.[89] Social gatherings were an important aspect of Cumann na mBan's work, and at a concert held in Athenry in July, both Cumann na mBan and the Volunteers displayed an impressive array of talent with exhibitions of 'jig dancing', reels, hornpipes, arias, 'racy and topical songs', piano and violin recitals and 'histrionic sketches' enthusiastically received.[90] Cumann na mBan organised a 'sports and regatta' at Menlo during the same month, described in typically ostentatious fashion in the *Galway Express*, as 'a garden party, a picnic, a tournament, an alfresco reunion, a riverside fête, an amphibious excursion, a band promenade, a courting map, and so on'.[91] The paper noted it was 'the first regatta held on the Corrib under republican auspices and we have no doubt it will not be the last'.[92]

There were social boundaries beyond which Cumann na mBan could not expect to be tolerated. A 'well known Catholic lady' was refused entry to the Galway Golf Club in August 1918 on the grounds that she was associated with Sinn Féin. A writer to the *Galway Express* noted that republicans had only themselves to blame for associating with the 'felon setting fraternity'. Criticising two members of Sinn Féin who remained in the club despite the rebuke to their comrade, the writer scolded, 'the shoneens know well that the golfing Sinn Féiners will hold on to membership no matter what kicks they themselves or their principles get'.[93]

George Nichols employed vindictive humour to target the old guard of the IPP in advance of the election, with MPs William O'Malley and William Duffy mocked as 'the weary Willies' and MP Richard Hazelton as 'Dandy Dick'. Following a successful election rally in Headford in March, the *Galway Express* noted, 'the people of the constituency of Dandy Dick from Carolina now recognises that Sinn Féin is at once the repository and the exponent of the Irish national cause'. Nichols informed the audience, 'it was pure nonsense to say that Sinn Féin stood for red revolution, for it had on its side some of the most illustrious Church men in Ireland'.[94]

A violent undercurrent existed throughout the extended election campaign. At a political meeting in Clifden in early March, the RIC baton-charged opposing factions ostensibly meeting to discuss a land dispute over the Clifden Castle demesne.[95] Monsignor Patrick McAlpine, a strong supporter of MP William O'Malley, chaired the meeting and began by claiming that Sinn Féin represented 'latter day hillsiders'. MP William Duffy or 'Willy wagtails' as the *Express* described him, noted that local land agitators who joined Sinn Féin represented, 'the wild, headlong, mad rush of young inexperienced men ... the cherished hopes of Ireland in our generation may be saturated in bloodshed and socialism and ruin'. With fighting erupting between nationalists and republicans gathered outside, a force of fifty RIC baton-charged the opposing groups. George Nichols subsequently gloated, 'although Clifden was supposed to be the only stronghold the Parliamentary Party bosses held in Connemara, the meeting eventuated in the greatest moral, intellectual, and physical triumph which Sinn Féin has yet scored in Iar Connacht'.[96]

Pageantry and spectacle formed an important part of republican meetings. At a Sinn Féin meeting in the village of Woodford, 'on all sides were to be seen banners of green, white and gold. The Sinn Féin clubs from Abbey and Derrybrien formed up on the Fair Green headed by the Ballinakill Fife and Drum Band.'[97] At a meeting in Headford, election candidate Frank Fahy addressed the crowd from, 'a spacious platform gaily decorated with bunting in the republican colours and a massive flag which spanned the space at the rear of the structure which bore the legend "on our rights we will insist"'. A body of horsemen carrying Sinn Féin flags arrived at the platform as the meeting commenced, 'and from the adjoining houses the green, white and orange insignia was given to the breeze'.[98]

Control of the *Galway Express* allowed Sinn Féin to circulate details of their political meetings that had been ignored in the main nationalist papers. At a public meeting in the republican stronghold of Athenry, election candidate Frank Fahy was flanked by seven clergy when he justified the land seizures sweeping the county: 'there was a cry for more food and when the people took the land to provide that food there was a cry of anarchy in the anti-Irish press across the water. There was no cry of anarchy when three millions of their people were driven from their farms in fifty years.'[99] Fahy's depiction of the land seizures as justifiable historical retribution for post-Famine clearances drew wild applause. Conscious of the strong clerical presence on the platform, Fahy tempered his tone, telling his audience, 'he did not want outrages and did not advocate the indiscriminate seizure of farms' and 'we are not out for any class or creed but for all Ireland'. Sinn Féin candidate for West Galway Pádraic Ó Máille told the audience, 'there were only two parties in Ireland, those who were in favour of the English connection and England, and those who wanted a completely free and independent Irish Republic and it is time to separate the sheep from the goats'.[100]

Stephen Gwynn, MP for Galway borough, was a particular target for the *Galway Express* and its contempt was unrestrained. Gwynn's ambiguity over conscription and his outsider status made him an easy target and it was obvious from early on that he was doomed should he look to stand again in the county. Gwynn's courageous decision to defy his age and join the War effort in May 1918 – he was one of only five MPs to do so – drew the contempt of *Galway Express* who gloated, 'Stephen Gwynn's number is up. His goose is cooked as the Yankees say "he is all in." His political future is behind him. His £400 per year is in jeopardy. And so he has joined the army again.'[101] That Gwynn's goose was indeed cooked became painfully apparent in May when his previously loyal supporters in the Galway urban council denied him a hearing on the topic of voluntary recruiting at their monthly council meeting.[102] To be so publicly reproached in his own constituency by the old guard of the

IPP was a watershed moment, illustrating the depth of feeling created by the conscription crisis.

Gwynn raised republican ire to a frenzy by making ambiguous comments in the House of Commons in October 1918 on conscription. Noting the 'great betrayal' the *Express* wrote, 'when we commented on Stephen Gwynn's political manoeuvres in Galway during the last few days and suggested the chicanery which lay at the bottom of them, we were unaware, like the rest of Galway, of the cold blooded, callous and dastardly perfidy of which he had been guilty'.[103] Urging followers of the IPP to switch allegiances, the *Express* made an inevitable sectarian appeal: 'they owe it not only to their self-preservation, in the face of the most menacing crisis they ever encountered, but to the honour of Ireland, to the support which has been pledged to them by their townsmen and to the loyalties of their religion'.[104]

Struggling to win younger voters engaged in land agitations, MP William Duffy sought to associate himself with the land struggles of the 1880s and continually reminded voters of the advances that party had made on behalf of the tenants. At a meeting in Loughrea in October he told his supporters:

> During the past forty years we have battled for every class in the community: for the farmers in breaking down landlordism and setting the peasants free; for the small holders in securing a substantial increase in their holdings without a penny of cost and starting anew independent men; for congests in changing them out of their wretched bogs and swamps onto rich lands with pleasant surroundings and neat comfortable houses to shelter and make them happy.[105]

From having only 3,394 members at the beginning of 1918, Sinn Féin had 7,486 members across eighty-three cumainn by election time and benefitted from a youthful vigour which their opponents simply had no appetite for or capacity to match.[106] As the election campaign gathered momentum, republican Sean O'Neill recalled, 'Our branches and members were as well trained and as eager as an All-Ireland team entering the playing pitch at Croke Park.'[107] In November, the police noted that over 1,000 people attended a Sinn Féin meeting to hear Frank Fahy plead the case for a republic in Loughrea. The decision to hold the meeting in the 'anti-republican' town was a direct challenge to MP William Duffy who could only attract 150 people to an election rally a few weeks later.[108] Volunteer Martin O'Regan of Loughrea recalled:

Sinn Féin had many enemies in the town at that time, almost all the better off section of the community were ranged against it as well as the recently demobilised British soldiers and their friends. The people showed their hand long before polling day. They were allowed full scope for the anti-Sinn Féin activities by the RIC. The doors of Sinn Féin supporters were often smeared at night with anti-national slogans such as 'To Hell with Sinn Féin'.[109]

In the run up to the ballot it was clear from the tone of nationalist commentary that the poll would be unfavourable to the old establishment. Pointing out the 'utter futility and criminal folly of rebellion', MP William Duffy told his followers a few days before the ballot, 'the unfortunate steps that had dogged Ireland in the past were about to be brought upon her again by the false misguided leadership of her own misguided sons'.[110] On the eve of the election, the *Connacht Tribune* left Galway voters in no doubt of what the election represented:

It is a straight fight between rival policies. Sinn Féin is struggling hard with one object in view. However carefully that object can be screened or camouflaged, it stands out today in all its nakedness. It is to overthrow the Irish Party, to bring wreck and ruin to the one political combination whose leadership has anything to show the people of Ireland as if they were the evil emissaries of that fate that seems to hand over our country, blasting our hopes when they seem to brighten. The Sinn Féin leaders have considered no device or trick too mean, no lie too hideous, no abuse of public men too vile to achieve their object.[111]

Sinn Féin's margin was impressive with republicans winning all three contested constituencies and taking a fourth unopposed. Of a total of 40,496 votes cast in the contested constituencies, Sinn Féin won 31,271, compared to the IPP's 9,225.[112] Pádraic Ó Máille triumphed in Connemara with 77.15 per cent of the vote; Frank Fahy won in south Galway with 85.90 per cent; and Dr Bryan Cusack won the north Galway constituency with 68.99 per cent. Liam Mellows was returned without a ballot in east Galway.

Election day was marked by street fighting in Loughrea as republicans and nationalists clashed during two days of violence. Republican 'peace patrols' armed with sticks initially clashed with nationalists; there was hand-to-hand fighting before both groups began fighting the police. Only when military reinforcements arrived from Galway was order restored. Fr J.W. O'Meehan was attacked, with his car windows smashed, and three priests who were present subsequently wrote to the *Connacht Tribune* to decry the behaviour of MP William Duffy's followers.[113] Ex-servicemen and their wives were prominent in the disturbances and fighting was only broken up with the military fixing their bayonets and training a machine gun on the respective factions.[114]

The War and political revolution

In the aftermath of the 1918 General Election, the *Tuam Herald* concluded that the IPP's disastrous performance was the result of 'an absence of legislative performance, the presence of questionable transactions, the stoppage of land redistribution and the failure of the Home Rule settlement':

> The country was certainly getting ahead of the old men and old minds that of late controlled its policy and regulated its destiny. Their methods of managing matters was not calculated to inspire public confidence and their manipulations of elections by the machinery of so-called conventions, of which we had wretched instances in this County were bound, sooner or later, to be resented by the people whose trust was sorely abused. The closed borough arrangement under which no independent young man dared to attempt to get into their ranks or was likely to be accepted by their party bred a sort of worn incapables who were fast losing public confidence.[115]

The tenor of the *Tuam Herald*'s analysis reflected the degree to which the problems that befell the 'auld stock' of Irish politics in 1918 had long-standing causes. The war brutally exposed their weaknesses and pushed nationalists forward in terms of their aspirations for their country, and in the aftermath of the 1916 Rebellion, the IPP was no longer capable of articulating that reality. Fergus Campbell has argued that the rise of Sinn Féin reflected the emerging radicalism of the rural poor that had its roots in the wave of agrarian revolt that swept districts in the west in the years 1918 and, subsequently, 1920.[116] In this respect, Tony Varley has noted, 'Sinn Fein, in the co-ordinated tillage land campaigns it ran in 1918, proclaimed itself ready and able to do what the UIL and the CDB had failed to do – end the food crisis and destroy the large-scale grazing system.'[117] Sinn Féin's rise to power was driven by several formative factors, however, and the conscription crisis of April and May 1918 was compounded in Galway by the blundering of the authorities in arresting a series of republican leaders just as the former crisis receded. Furthermore, political events precipitated by the War may not, on their own, have been sufficient to overturn the political status quo had Sinn Féin's successful candidates in 1918 not been fundamentally stronger than their opponents. The republican movement was able to field younger, more energetic representatives who were untainted by scandal and reflected the aspirations of an emerging, impatient generation whose fundamental values of social mobility and respectability were to triumph over the coming years.

In the eyes of a resentful and brooding rural community, the IPP ceased to represent the views of ordinary nationalists from 1916 onwards. The moribund state of local organisation was a natural result of the stasis their dominance of national politics had inculcated. The increasing chasm between the political stance of the IPP and the reality of constituents' opinions represented a betrayal of ordinary UIL activists who had provided tireless local leadership, and when a cadre of energetic and talented young clerics began to side politically with their own generation against the 'auld stock' of politics, change was inevitable.

As the IPP became increasingly concerned with the conduct of a war for which ordinary people had diminishing sympathy or understanding, their abandonment of the local in favour of the international left them vulnerable to legitimate challengers. That Sinn Féin, through less than two years of organisation, was able to transform politics was indicative of the moribund state of their constitutional rivals. If the new political force was decidedly proletarian, it was no less representative of society than the UIL had been and the latter had consistently provided genuine representation for the rural poor over two decades of successive land reform. The difference by 1918, however, was that Sinn Féin's rivals could be dismissed as the garrison and its hangers on, with the IPP indelibly associated with the War, the conscription threat and political ineptitude.

CHAPTER 5

War of Independence I: Fighting for Ireland, 1920–1

In terms of the regional distribution of republican activity during the War of Independence, a key theme of the literature has been the regional variations between so-called active and non-active areas, not only between different parts of the country, but within counties themselves.[1] Republican violence in Galway involved sporadic attacks against the police, and to a much lesser extent, the military, by a relatively small force of active Volunteers concentrated in distinct areas. There were few militant companies in the towns and all attacks on police took place in rural districts, apart from one occasion when the Volunteers ventured into the town of Clifden to attack the police in March 1921. As the conflict escalated, the pool of active Volunteers became smaller as the intensity of state reprisals grew more ferocious and the nature of republican violence became more lethal.

The Volunteers killed eighteen people between January 1920 and the Truce in July 1921, fourteen of whom were shot in the east of the county. Nine of the victims were members of the Royal Irish Constabulary (RIC) who were killed while on duty, one was an auxiliary policeman, three were members of the Crown Forces and five were civilians. Of the civilian fatalities, three were believed to be informers, one was the wife of a district inspector of the RIC fatally caught up in an ambush, and one was a farmer, Martin Cullinane, who was shot dead during a raid for arms on 4 March 1920.

In Galway, as elsewhere, women played a crucial but under-appreciated role, acting as messengers, accumulating intelligence and passing information to the Volunteers on the activities of the Crown Forces. Margaret Broderick-Nicholson, one of a small group of republican women in Galway town recalled, 'the job I hated most was enticing British soldiers down the docks in order to have them relieved of their arms by Volunteers, one of whom, an officer, happened to be my brother'.[2] Most women who supported the Volunteers in terms of providing shelter, food and first aid, and who assisted in intelligence work were not members of any organisation but acted out of loyalty to their family and community. In this respect, details of the membership lists of Cumann na mBan are misleading and underestimate the number of women involved. Their stories are among the least recorded and most forgotten and the contribution of poor rural women, in particular, has not been recognised.

Direct control over the Galway Volunteers by GHQ in Dublin was weak and the relatively low-level of training and support inhibited their capacity to prosecute their campaign. Popular support was largely dependent on whether the Volunteers were in the ascendancy or decline in their battle with the RIC and an ebb and flow of support between the rival institutions of the state and the revolutionary movement is apparent. Even in areas where there were no attacks on the police, the boycott of the RIC represented an effective tool of communal solidarity. The County Inspector of the RIC for West Galway described the conditions under which his officers were working before the arrival of the auxiliaries and the Black and Tans:

> The life of the police is scarcely bearable. They are shamed and boycotted and for the most part cannot get the necessities of life unless they commandeer them. They are held up and shot at every opportunity. The order is to destroy them and during July two young men were shot dead in circumstances of cruelty and treachery. The people generally are out for a republic and they propose to get it.[3]

Leadership and structures

Until November 1920, the Galway Volunteers were structured as one brigade organised by an eight-man executive led by Dublin native Seamus Murphy, who was also editor of the Sinn Féin-controlled, *Galway Express* newspaper. At the beginning of the campaign, the brigade staff comprised men who had been involved in the movement from its infancy. One of the main obstacles during the early months of their campaign was cautious leadership, and under Murphy's regime, older leaders were reluctant to authorise attacks. Throughout 1920, the leadership repeatedly restrained more hasty officers from acting independently. With hierarchical control exercised by the brigade staff until November 1920, local initiative was discouraged and repeated requests for attacks were vetoed by the leadership as local officers, who sought to 'get things going' were rebuffed by their superiors. During this early period, restraint and a reluctance to take human life characterised republican attacks as the main objective of operations remained the capture of supplies and the destruction of barracks, and it was not until July 1920 that RIC were killed by republicans.

As officer commanding the county until September 1920, Seamus Murphy was neither a popular nor an effective officer and his decision to flee to his native Dublin in September 1920 became the source of bitterness with many officers blaming him for the inadequacy of their early campaign. A native of Rathmines, south Dublin, Murphy was an active member of the Gaelic League and a member of the Teeling circle of the Irish Republican Brotherhood (IRB). He served as second lieutenant under Éamonn Ceannt during the 1916 Rebellion in Dublin. He was sent to Galway to take charge of the Volunteers in early 1920 but failed to endear himself to the long established local factions. Despite being in charge of the Galway brigade until September 1920, he later left a nine-page witness statement with the Bureau of Military History making no mention of his time in Galway.[4]

The Galway brigade was restructured as part of a national re-organisation in August 1920 with several new brigades formed and a new command structure put in place. The restructuring was an acknowledgement of the failure of the old leadership. P.J. McDonnell recalled that after a long meeting with Richard Mulcahy:

> He informed me that it had been decided at GHQ that for administrative purposes the County as a unit was too unwieldy, that communications to outlying battalions – like mine, through brigade headquarters were held up unduly, and it was decided to divide the County into several Brigades all to be in direct touch with GHQ; that it would mean better communications between the various units and headquarters, that complaints would get a sympathetic hearing, and that headquarters would be able to give the officers practical advice on their problems.[5]

The new structures placed fresh emphasis on local enterprise and were designed to limit the role of the old leadership which had stifled the early prosecution of the campaign. These structures evolved rapidly with the arrival of the Black and Tans in July 1920, transforming the nature of the republican struggle by making it much more difficult to launch successful attacks on Crown Forces. Brigade and battalion structures composed of companies based on the parish, organised by officers with military titles, created the impression of a wide and sophisticated military network. In reality, however, the level of activity, commitment and enthusiasm varied greatly between districts and the command structures do not necessarily reflect military capacity. Likewise, the character of individual officers varied greatly with divergent understanding of what was expected of them and their men. Some officers clearly interpreted their role as the prosecution of an aggressive military campaign against the police, while many more, without the arms, training or support, were satisfied with playing a more limited role involving the maintenance of public order, enforcing the boycott of the police and playing occasional supporting roles to active service units.

The north of the county, excluding Connemara, became the north Galway brigade led by Michael Fogarty and Michael Moran and consisted of two battalions, Tuam and Glenamaddy, comprising ten parish companies each. James Maloney became commanding officer of the Glenamaddy battalion with Tom Dunleavy commanding officer of the Tuam Battalion.[6] These battalions were among the most active and combined republican policing and administration of republican courts with a series of attacks on the Crown Forces. Many of the most active members of the Tuam brigade came from the Milltown and Dunmore districts and Volunteer Seán O'Neill recalled, 'Tuam town itself was not a model of tenacity and grit. That grit was to be found mostly in the sons of small farmers, simple honest souls who meant to do their duty and who were always ready to respond and were even superior to those who, by subterfuge, reaped a reward as a result of such confusion.'[7]

Connemara was divided into two battalions in August 1920, with the east Connemara battalion led by Micheál Ó Droighneáin of Spiddal, and the West Connemara battalion, initially, led by Colm O'Gaora with P.J. McDonnell leading the battalion in late 1920.[8] Meetings were frequently held at the home of West Galway MP Pádraic Ó Máille at Muintir Eoin near Leenane. The nucleus of this group went on to form the west Connemara flying column in 1921 and initially consisted of the Leenane company under Pádraic Ó Máille; the Rosmuc company under Colm Ó Gaora; the Roundstone company under Jim King; and the Clifden company under Gerard Bartley. This group carried out three lethal attacks on the police and used their knowledge of the mountainous terrain to evade capture until the truce in July 1921.

The Galway Number One brigade covered the countryside to the east of Galway town from the parish of Castlegar, north along the banks of the Corrib as far as the Headford district. The most active companies in this area were the Headford, Castlegar, Carnmore, Claregalway and Oranmore companies that were led by Louis Darcy, Brian Molloy, Joseph Howley and Martin Newell, among others. The Galway town company was led by Seán Broderick who acted as adjutant of the brigade. Both Howley and Darcy were shot dead by Crown Forces and a group of committed fighters from these areas combined to carry out a series of attacks at Loughgeorge RIC barracks on 25 May 1920, at Oranmore on 21 August 1920 and at Kilroe on 19 January 1921.

There was a small group of active Volunteers in Galway town including Seán Turke, Seán Broderick, Thomas Courtney and Joseph Togher, who carried out intelligence work and low-level arson attacks on military stores. One auxiliary was shot dead in the town on 9 September 1920 but they possessed insufficient strength to prosecute a concerted campaign. Galway was heavily garrisoned and the military and police enjoyed the social life of the town, carousing in the city's many pubs without fear of attack. Volunteer Peter Greene recalled, 'Galway city was one of the most heavily garrisoned places in Ireland, and I regret to say that enemy had a lot of sympathy from people in the city, who certainly were not of our way of thinking.'[9]

In the south of the county, the Gort battalion under Thomas McInerney consisted of ten companies stretching from the parish of Ardrahan, along the coast to the Slieve Aughty mountains and the Clare border. The battalion was led by a number of committed officers, including Peter Howley of Ardrahan, John and Thomas Fahy of Peterswell, Joseph Stanford of Gort, and Daniel Ryan, Thomas Keely, Michael Reilly and Patrick Glynn of Kilbeacanty. This group went on to form the south Galway flying column in early 1921. They carried out two lethal attacks, the first at Castledaly in 30 October 1920 in which one RIC man was killed and a second attack on the police and military at Ballyturin, near Kilchreest on 15 May 1921, when five police and military, including one woman were killed.

There was a south-east brigade covering the Ballinasloe and Portumna districts commanded by Michael O'Keefe of Portumna. O'Keefe fled the district in the autumn of 1920, and as Martin O'Regan recalled, 'as no new appointment was made for a long time, the whole organisation fell into a state of apathy'.[10] The east Galway brigade consisted of the Athenry battalion, initially commanded by Larry Lardiner, and the Loughrea battalion, commanded by Laurence Burke of Kilnadeema. These areas were considerably quieter than the rest of the county and only one major attack was launched when the Bookeen RIC barracks in Kilconieron was destroyed in July 1920.

When the Volunteers were restructured for the final time as part of a national reorganisation in March 1921, Galway's inclusion into divisions dominated by neighbouring counties was indicative of their fortunes. The whole of the county, south of the railway line from Galway to Ballinasloe, was incorporated into the First Western Division, led by Clare's Michael Brennan. The division comprised County Clare with the addition of south Galway but most of the division's officers were from Clare. North-east Galway was subsumed into the Second Western Division dominated by South and East Mayo and led by Commandant Tom Maguire. Connemara became subsumed in the Fourth Western Division under the command of Michael Kilroy comprising West Mayo.[11] The Mountbellew Battalion was included in the South Roscommon Brigade. The re-organisation was ultimately meaningless, however, as it came so late in the campaign and made little practical difference to an inherently isolated and independent collection of dispersed units of committed fighters.

Initial phase of the republican campaign

The republican campaign in Galway can be analysed in three phases that broadly conform to the evolution of the movement in other active parts of the country. In each consecutive phase of the campaign, the pool of Volunteers involved in attacks became smaller, as the less committed, the older, and those with full-time occupations and more responsibilities, increasingly dropped out. In their stead, remained younger men who were generally free from the constraints of careers, property and regular working hours.

The first four attacks in the initial phase of the republican campaign comprised attacks on isolated rural RIC barracks at Castlehacket, Castlegrove, Loughgeorge and Bookeen between January and July 1920. All of the attacks took place at night and were carried out by large groups of badly armed Volunteers. The primary aim was to seize the weapons and stores held by the police and to physically destroy the garrisons. These initial attacks took place in the east of the county and no members of the RIC were killed. All four barracks were badly damaged with the Bookeen and Loughgeorge barracks destroyed by fire.

The Castlehacket and Castlegrove attacks – the first of this period – were carried out in the northeast of the county and were organised by the Tuam brigade under the leadership of Michael Moran who was a student at University College Galway, and Thomas Dunleavy, a small farmer from the Barnaderg district. The Castlehacket barracks, located between Headford and Tuam was attacked by a group of about seventy Volunteers armed mainly with shotguns, early on the morning of Saturday 10 January.[12] The attack was originally fixed for the twelfth night but as Volunteer John Conway recalled, 'as somebody suggested that it was little Christmas night and not a nice thing to have an attack on that Holy night, it was fixed for the following night'.[13] A large group of Volunteers surrounded the barracks, keeping it under intermittent fire, as a small body of police under Sergeant Higgins returned fire and successfully defended the building. The attack lasted several hours and grenades were unsuccessfully employed to blow the door of the building open.

The second operation carried out by the Tuam brigade was a carbon copy of the first attack with a large group of Volunteers attacking the isolated police barracks at Castlegrove, near Milltown, on the night of 26 March. The barracks was situated a few miles from the site of the first attack and like the previous operation, was carried out by a large group of badly armed Volunteers from the surrounding districts of Sylane, Tuam, Barnaderg, Caherlistrane and Cortoon, led once more by Michael Moran. Volunteer John Conway recalled, 'when the explosion or explosions occurred, all at the front opened fire, directing our fire at the windows in front of us and at the doors'.[14] The large group kept the building under intermittent fire for several hours but once again, the small detachment of police did not surrender and the raiders eventually fled.[15]

The Loughgeorge RIC barracks, situated about eight miles from Galway on the main Tuam to Galway road, was attacked by the Galway Number One brigade in the early hours of 25 May. This attack was led by Martin Niland, Nicholas Kyne and Michael Walsh of the Galway brigade and the small attacking party included a number of students from University College Galway. The group possessed only two rifles and a quantity of gelignite. Volunteer Martin Fahy recalled, 'we knew there was no hope of taking the barrack with only two riflemen. The two rifles were the only ones the [University] College [Galway] Company possessed. It was, therefore, more in the nature of an experiment than anything else that we tried the explosives.'[16] The gelignite exploded as planned but failed to shatter the building while the attackers kept the barracks under intense fire until eventually retreating. The outer buildings attached to the barracks were completely burned down.[17] The failure of the attack was a blow to the morale of the Volunteers and Thomas Hynes sought to blame the brigade commander Seamus Murphy, claiming, 'They [the RIC] were prepared to surrender if anybody came through but Murphy would not allow anyone to enter the barracks.'[18] The fallout from the failure of the assault caused a rupture between the brigade and battalion officers, with Nicholas Kyne, battalion O/C, 'chucking his appointment' in protest at the lack of militant leadership.[19]

The Volunteers in east Galway carried out their first attack on the police at Bookeen barracks in the parish of Kilconieron, in the early hours of 4 July, in an operation that bore similarities to the three previous attacks. The attack was organised by Patrick 'Hare' Callanan and carried out by the Craughwell, Leitrim, Killimor, Kilconieron, Kilnadeema, Bullaun and Closetoken companies.[20] As in previous attacks, the assault commenced with an attempt to blow a hole in the outer wall of building that failed due to faulty explosives.

The Volunteers then attempted to set off the gelignite by shooting at it, setting the building alight.[21] The policemen within withstood a prolonged siege lasting several hours, returning fire with hand grenades and rifles before making their escape unhindered. Callanan explained, 'I decided that our objective had been achieved and withdrew, leaving the barracks in ruins.'[22] The building was destroyed and the RIC were fortunate not to have burned to death before making their escape.

The failure of these early attacks precipitated a fundamental change in republican tactics and the Bookeen attack was the last time such large groups of Volunteers were involved in operations of this type. From May onwards, only Volunteers who were specifically selected and fully equipped participated in operations against the police, who were targeted on patrol and, consequently, more vulnerable than in their heavily fortified barracks. These early attacks were carried out with a degree of amateur enthusiasm in a climate of relative innocence regarding the realities of guerrilla warfare that the arrival of the Black and Tans was to shatter.

Adapting to new realities

The Volunteers campaign evolved with arrival of the Black and Tans in July 1920, as the movement's organisational framework began to collapse due to the arrest and/or assassination of leading officers. This led to a period of disorganisation which lasted from September until the New Year and a dramatic drop in activity. As there were not enough active Volunteers to maintain an organisational structure based on parish companies, the internal organisation lapsed while GHQ in Dublin appears to have lost interest. With a limited supply of weapons, some set about 'getting things going', but by October 1920, this was limited to less than two hundred committed officers with many companies concentrating on tiresome local duties involving policing and administration. Seamus Murphy, the commanding officer for the county, fled to Dublin in September 1920 leaving the organisation without any functioning central command structure. In theory, a brigade, battalion and company structure continued to exist but no brigade O/C was appointed to replace Murphy and areas were left to act on their own initiative with no over-arching strategy or leadership. This situation damaged morale and the organisation became dependent on the initiative of individual districts which launched inherently local campaigns.

During this period the Volunteers carried out three lethal attacks on the Crown Forces which bore striking similarity. All three attacks took place in daylight with ambushes of vulnerable RIC patrols carried out by select units of Volunteers. With the withdrawal of the RIC to much larger barracks in the towns, the Volunteers switched from attacking isolated barracks to attempting to ambush vulnerable patrols of RIC men travelling between barracks. These attacks were carried out with a greater degree of professionalism than previous attempts as the attackers set out to intentionally kill policemen for the first time. In this phase of their campaign, the number of men involved in attacks became smaller and consequently better armed, with Volunteers specifically selected.

The first successful ambush during this phase of the campaign was led by Michael Moran and Michael Fogarty of the Tuam brigade on 19 July at a wooded area on the Tuam to Galway Road, known as Gallagh Hill.[23] Sergeant Beatty, along with constables Brennan, Burke and Carey left Tuam barracks for Dunmore in a police van at nine p.m.; they were ambushed three miles outside the town and constables Burke and Carey shot dead. The small group of Volunteers from Cortoon, Barnaderg and Tuam said an act of contrition over the bodies of the two dead men before collecting their rifles and releasing the surviving RIC.[24] The attack was the first lethal operation carried out in the county and provoked a furious response from the Crown Forces who looted and burned premises in Tuam. Dragoon Guards stationed in Claremorris, along with police from Galway town and Vicar Street barracks in Tuam, rampaged through the town, looting public houses, setting fire to premises and shooting wildly, with the town hall, previously used as a Sinn Féin courthouse, among the buildings destroyed.[25] The Gallagh attack was organised by Michael Moran, who was central to the earlier attacks at Castlehacket and Castlegrove RIC barracks, and following the ambush, he was forced to go on the run after the Crown Forces burned his family home. Moran, aged 27, was the most effective republican leader in the county and was arrested in November. An armed escort was taking him from Eglinton police barracks to Earls Island barracks in Galway town on November 24 when he was shot dead, with the military claiming he was, 'shot while trying to escape'.[26]

The Gallagh ambush was followed by two lethal attacks in east Galway. The Volunteers based in the districts of Castlegar and Oranmore and led by Joseph Howley and Brian Molloy successfully ambushed the police at Merlin Park on 21 August, killing Constable Martin Foley and seriously injuring two RIC.[27] In a similar ambush to the previous attack carried out by the Tuam brigade, five police on bicycles were ambushed by a small group of Volunteers, one mile outside the village of Oranmore.[28] Following the shooting, troops and police from Galway ran amuck in the village with a public house and adjoining premises burned, forcing many residents to flee to the surrounding countryside.[29] Republican leader, Joseph Howley, fled Oranmore after the Crown Forces burned his house in the aftermath of the attack. The police eventually killed Howley and a comrade, Joseph Athy, in separate incidents. On the evening of 17 September, Athy was shot dead near Oranmore, with survivors reportedly seeing gunmen in army fatigues fleeing the scene.[30] Howley was also tracked down and killed on 9 December when he was shot dead at Broadstone Railway Station in Dublin as he alighted from the Galway train.[31]

The final ambush during this phase of the Volunteers' campaign took place in south Galway with a small group of Volunteers led by Thomas McInerney attacking an RIC bicycle patrol at the Castledaly crossroads, located between the villages of Kilchreest and Peterswell on 30 November, with one RIC, Constable Timothy Horan killed.[32] There were around twenty-five in the attacking party, armed mostly with shotguns, and the Volunteers retrieved bicycles and rifles from the surviving RIC before releasing them unharmed. The ambush site was originally to have been across from Castledaly Church but was moved to a less advantageous spot, as Volunteer Daniel Ryan explained, 'it was thought that we should not take advantage of consecrated ground'.[33] As in earlier ambushes, the Volunteers acknowledged the police surrender.

Following the Castledaly attack, Crown Forces burned a number of homes in the district. As is considered in the next Chapter, Harry and Patrick Loughnane, who took part in the ambush, were subsequently arrested, tortured and killed by Crown Forces. Two days after the ambush, the Crown Forces killed Eileen Quinn, who was shot dead by soldiers from a passing lorry, near Kiltartan, a short distance from the ambush site.[34] She had been sitting on the front wall of her garden with an infant in her arms and was heavily pregnant.[35] At the court of military inquiry it was found that she was shot dead, 'by one of a number of shots fired as a precautionary measure and in view of these facts a verdict of death by misadventure must be brought'.[36]

This series of attacks, though relatively few, represented an increasing level of professionalism on the part of the Volunteers as carefully selected groups of well-equipped men from neighbouring districts participated. Many Volunteers dropped out of the movement during this period, rather than take part in ambushes about which they may still have had personal reservations; participation in such activities would also have put their own lives at risk. The majority of companies were content with local duties while playing an occasional supporting role in advance of an ambush by blocking roads and disrupting communications. There was occasionally opposition from officers to attacks taking place in their districts and Volunteer Patrick Connaughton remembered, 'the Leitrim company seemed to be intent on drawing us away from their own area to the Ballinakill company area. The Ballinakill company objected to any attack in their area and a row developed between the members of the two companies.'[37]

By the end of 1920, Volunteer officers were increasingly unable to stay in their own homes and were forced to go on the run to avoid arrest. The police noted in November, 'A good deal of sympathy among people with a stake in the country is due to fear and there are indications of a return to sanity and revulsion against Sinn Féin on the part of the more respectable people, now that the government are beginning to get a grip on the situation. As far as Galway is concerned Sinn Féin has largely lost its power.'[38] In this changed reality, the police reported to their superiors that they were beginning to receive valuable information on the activities of the Galway Volunteers, claiming 'the feeling toward the police is much better with the people inclined toward friendship and there is no attempt anywhere to boycott them. I have received bone-fide information of two or three ambushes prepared for the police.'[39]

By late 1920, republican leaders who were on the run began to re-organise their areas under their own initiative with little reference to over-arching command structures; they regrouped into more fluid units composed of more ruthless and committed men from wider geographical areas. Freed from a cautious and cumbersome command structure these groups became resurgent in the spring of 1921 with the emergence of the county's first flying columns composed of committed young men who had been forced to leave their homes and band together in the open countryside. The columns acted independently of external authority and had little contact with each other or the republican leadership. During this phase of the campaign, the physical hardship of being on the run, the level of personal commitment and the obvious dangers to one's family from reprisal attacks meant that only the most committed young men joined active service units. In March 1921, the West Galway police reported:

The IRA are now confined to the outlying, backward areas where Sinn Féin still lives. There is a bitter undercurrent of hatred against the government and Crown Forces. If the present pressure was relaxed, Sinn Féin would once again renew its old sway in a more rigorous and determined manner. It had such a reign of terror that it will take a long period to remove its evil and ruinous affects.[40]

West Connemara flying column

During December 1920 and January 1921, the West Connemara flying column was formed at meetings in the Ó Máille farmhouse in Muintir Eoin attended by West Connemara's leading republicans. There were twenty-six men in the column at various times, hailing from the districts of Leenane, Rosmuc, Roundstone and Clifden.[41] Commander of the column P.J. McDonnell explained the group's motivation after being unexpectedly summoned before an audience with his Archbishop at Clifden: 'the police and military of England were roaming the country to try and exterminate anyone who stood for freedom of their country; that they pulled men out of their homes and shot them on the street, sometimes before the eyes of their families and that any man who had a chance of fighting was a fool if he waited to be pulled out and shot without making an effort to fight back.'[42] More Volunteers wanted to join the unit than could be accommodated and Volunteer Jack Feehan recalled, 'twice the number turned up to what we expected, and each man had his own small contribution, such as a shotgun, gelignite, cartridges. They obtained gelignite while working for the County council. It was sad to turn some of these men away, for we only had accommodation for twenty.'[43]

As the column could only fully equip twenty men, the unit was limited in size and was fully mobilised on 10 March at Aille na Breagh (Aille na Veagh), at the back of Diamond Mountain, seven miles east of Clifden. The site was chosen as it was in easy striking distance of Clifden and offered a vantage point over both roads leading out of the village.[44] The Connemara landscape posed unique problems as McDonnell recalled, 'the roads in Connemara are like the country "bare and bleak" with no sheltering walls where shotguns would get within range of the enemy'.[45] The Clifden battalion was responsible for arranging food supplies to be dropped near the unit's base and the Leenane company was responsible for keeping the hide-away in battle readiness.

The column was composed of men with no experience of guerrilla warfare, and as McDonnell recalled, 'until they had their first fight, that with the exception of the quartermaster and myself, not a man of the column had fired a shot out of a service rifle'.[46] Food occasionally ran out and the column experienced several prolonged periods living off tea and the meagre kindnesses that poor families in isolated communities could offer. The conditions took their toll and Jack Feehan recalled that 'four days under such terrible conditions was telling on the younger men'.[47]

The column killed two RIC in their first attack carried out in the town of Clifden on the night of 16 March 1921 with Constable G.C. Reynolds dying instantly and Constable Thomas Sweeney dying after his right leg was amputated.[48] The attack was carried out in revenge for the execution of Thomas Whelan in Mountjoy Gaol the previous day. Whelan, who was originally from Clifden, was hanged for his part in the killing of a state agent in Dublin in November 1920, and according to Jack Feehan, 'We felt it our duty to avenge his death.'[49] On arriving into the village, the unit spotted six RIC and selected six of the column to attack the group, with the remainder holding the barracks under fire. Feehan recalled, 'It was decided to pick six of the best shots. We thought it fair enough – man to man, six enemy to six IRA.'[50] When fire was opened by the group, only two RIC were visible and both were killed. The column retreated, and in the hours after the attack, at least sixteen houses were burned by Crown Forces and hundreds of young men arrested. A civilian ex-serviceman, J.J. MacDonnell, was shot dead after calling to the police station to appeal for help in dousing the flames engulfing his father's hotel.[51]

Following the attack, it was decided to move the column to the Maam Valley to escape the attentions of the police and attempt an attack on Maam police station, the only other permanent police barracks in Connemara. Travelling across the Twelve Pins Mountains, the column camped at Glencraff, a valley four miles west of Leenane, before making for the Ó Máille homestead at Muintir Eoin, half way between Leenane and Maam and four miles from the police barracks. Travelling across the mountains with little food was difficult for the toughest of fighters, and according to Jack Feehan, 'To be alone and to have lost one's way in these mountains on such a night would be to court death from exposure.'[52]

After a few days' rest, McDonnell decided that a successful attack at Maam barracks was not a realistic possibility given the reinforced nature of the building and the little ammunition at the unit's disposal. It was decided instead to try and ambush a patrol of RIC and the unit departed on 4 April, crossing the Maamturk and Oorid mountains to Gortmore in the Rosmuc district of southwest Connemara. The column billeted at an ambush spot on the Maam Cross–Screebe Road and took some hard-earned rest while local Volunteers stood watch. On 6 April, the column attacked a party of five RIC travelling by bicycle at a location adjacent to Screebe Church where they knew the police passed each week to pay a local RIC pensioner.[53] Feehan claimed the ambush was the unit's personal act of revenge for the killing of Galway priest, Fr Michael Griffin, by Crown Forces in November 1920.[54] The ambush was a partial success with one policeman, William Pearson, a native of New Zealand, dying from wounds.[55] An RIC man who lay prone in a ditch was spared as he begged for mercy while his comrades escaped on foot, some of whom took shelter at nearby Screebe Lodge. Volunteer George Staunton was disappointed with the outcome of the ambush claiming, 'one over anxious member of the column fired a shot on the impulse of the moment which upset the whole target'.[56] P.J. McDonnell was incensed, insisting that a member of the group fired too early and ruined their chances of inflicting a major blow. After failing to locate the escaped policemen, the column collected the RIC's weapons, along with several bottles of poitín. McDonnell destroyed most of the bottles, keeping two for 'medicinal purposes'.[57]

Following the attack, the Crown Forces burned a number of cottages in the vicinity, including those of Volunteer Colm Ó Gaora, Patrick Pearse's holiday cottage, the co-operative store in Camus and the home of the local school teacher.[58] Volunteer Thomas Geoghegan, who joined the men after the ambush, appears to have suffered a breakdown after learning of the destruction of his family home, and according to McDonnell, 'he went completely out of his mind. It took about four men to control him and get him upstairs, put him lying on a bed and tie him down to it. We sent to Leenane to get the doctor … he came along and gave him an injection of morphia which quieted him down.'[59]

Life became harder for the column as George Staunton explained, 'it would be foolish to remain in the one place for any length of time and to look for any kind of comfort was out of question. Any rest we had was during the daytime, for at night time we did all the travelling.'[60] Needing to send money to GHQ to attain more weapons and ammunition, the unit decided to levy a tax on farmers in the district; as Feehan explained, 'we levied a certain sum on each farmer, knowing that he could afford the amount levied'.[61] Some rich pickings were exploited and Kylemore House, the home of Colonel Mark Clifden, was raided and weapons and clothes taken.[62]

The Ó Máille family homestead at Muintir Eoin in northwest Connemara was the scene of the column's final engagement on 23 April.[63] Muintir Eoin was the well-known homestead of one of the leading republican families in Connemara and would inevitably be raided. The men were aware, however, and decided to lay in wait for the inevitable fight; as McDonnell later explained, 'everyman of the column was anxious to have a really good fight and justify our existence as a fighting unit'.[64]

The attack finally came when police arrived for a routine raid. The Volunteers assumed their pre-planned ambush positions and awaited their orders to open fire; however, a premature shot alerted the police to the attacking party and the advantage was lost. McDonnell recalled, 'once again the element of surprise was destroyed despite all my instructions. No man owned up to having accidently or deliberately discharged his rifle.'[65] In driving rain both parties took cover and engaged in sporadic shooting, neither side able to win a decisive advantage.[66] Jane Ó Máille and her two young children remained in an outhouse as over forty armed men fought a gun battle around her. After almost twelve hours of exchanging fire, and with several men wounded and constable, John Boylan killed, a line of police lorries became visible on the horizon. As reinforcements dismounted and with the column almost completely out of ammunition, the Volunteers fled and police burned the Ó Máille property.

Following the battle, the column made its way north to the townland of Tawnaleen, west of Shanafaraghaun, near Lough Nafooey, 'a quiet lonely place' according to Feehan.[67] Camped out among the elements in a canvas tent, on the remote northern side of Killary harbour, the remaining eighteen men received the sacraments from the same priest who had ministered to the RIC during the previous gun-battle. With the days getting longer, the north Connemara district was increasingly patrolled by large convoys, while a spotter plane patrolled the skies. The column's life became more difficult and they were increasingly forced to concentrate their energies on evading capture and destroying bridges, a laborious task, carried out with pick and shovel.

Remarkably, P.J. McDonnell took a day off to get married, with his comrade, Jack Feehan, acting as best man. The ceremony took place at Kilmeena Church in southwest Mayo on 17 May, with both men armed with grenades and pistols. Neither groom nor best man, however, got to enjoy the celebrations and both returned to join the column later that evening.[68]

During the final weeks of the campaign, the column had sixteen rifles and around 200 rounds of ammunition, and was firmly on the defensive. Having to guard against being captured, the unit was broken into smaller units on 9 May 1921 with one group under Jack Feehan moving into south Mayo, while the remaining members were forced to levy farmers in north Connemara to purchase supplies. Feehan recalled, 'we had to make demands sternly, as this area was a poor one and money was hard fought'.[69] After receiving ammunition from GHQ at the beginning of June, it was decided to try and join up the West Mayo column and launch an attack near Leenane. A navy destroyer lay at berth in Killary harbour, a military aeroplane flew continually overhead and large convoys traversed the narrow roads of north Connemara. The column's final days were spent in the northwestern hills of Connemara and the unit were at a spot called Glennagimla with a group of Mayo officers when news of the truce arrived. Jack Feehan recalled, 'there we received a splendid welcome from our friends and were united with them amid tears of joy, thanking God that we were safe and happy'.[70] The hardship of fighting in such inhospitable territory had taken a toll on the health of a number of the men. Two Volunteers were invalided with severe burns from boiling water, William Connelly had shot himself in the leg, Colm Ó Gaora had suffered facial paralysis, Thomas Geoghegan had experienced a breakdown and number had suffered a variety of injuries.

North Galway flying column

The north Galway flying column was formed by a group of officers from the Tuam battalion and was involved in two significant ambushes that resulted in the deaths of RIC.[71] The column was composed of around twenty Volunteers from the Milltown, Barnaderg, Glenamaddy, Belclare and Sylane districts. The unit was led by men who had gained considerable experience, including Patrick Dunleavy and James Maloney, who led the column, alongside Thomas Nohilly, Thomas Ryan and Thomas Feerick. The unit was occasionally strengthened by local Volunteers but kept together as far as possible, separating only occasionally due to lack of accommodation. From early 1921, the column was constantly on the move, taking up positions and waiting for vulnerable detachments of police. Patrick Treacy recalled the hardships the men endured, 'we were at least seven days without undressing and had only snatches of sleep during that time. To add to our hardships most of us suffered at that time from a severe attack of what was then known as Sinn Féin or republican itch, which was aggravated by very warm weather.'[72]

The column ambushed a lorry of auxiliaries near the village of Moylough on 6 June, resulting in multiple casualties.[73] According to Volunteer Thomas Nohilly, the area was chosen as, 'this was a very quiet area and the RIC moved about it freely'.[74] In the build-up to the attack, Pat Treacy shot and wounded a local RIC man near his home on the outskirts of the village. According to Volunteer Thomas Mannion, 'the idea was that when the RIC in Mountbellew heard that this man was disarmed or killed they would come to his assistance'.[75] The ploy was successful and a detachment of auxiliaries was dispatched to the village. Treacy recalled, 'Almost immediately after we opened fire the lorry came to a halt and the occupants jumped out and took cover on the opposite side of the road from where they immediately opened fire on us. They had good cover behind the bank of the road and their own lorry.'[76] A fire fight lasting an hour ensued between the twelve men in the column and approximately twenty RIC. Damp ammunition, however, led to many of the Volunteers' rounds misfiring, almost costing the column dearly. Thomas Mannion recalled, 'The fire from the RIC was very accurate. It was heavy and well sustained. They used rifle grenades, although at that time we did not know what they were. They made a peculiar noise and seemed to be bursting above our heads and behind us.'[77] According to Pat Treacy, 'the RIC fought well but made no attempt to pursue us and we withdrew. Their fire was accurate as near my position I could see the butts of trees on the fence being skinned by their fire.'[78] The ambush was a daring operation in terms of the commitment shown by the column in engaging a numerically superior and better armed force.

The column's most lethal operation was carried out in the small village of Milltown, near the Mayo border on 27 June 1921, when two RIC, Sergeant James Murren and Constable Edgar Daly were ambushed and shot dead.[79] A section of the column, including Thomas Nohilly, Thomas and Timothy Dunleavy, Thomas Ryan, Thomas Feerick, Patrick McHugh and Peter Brennan, had made their way to Carrareagh village, near Milltown, when they got word that a patrol of RIC had left Milltown and were returning through the district. The patrol consisted of six RIC and two were killed instantly. Thomas Nohilly remembered, 'I fired at the flashes made by them when they fired. After about a quarter of an hour, we withdrew as fire was being brought to bear on our positions by machine guns from the RIC barracks in the village, about three hundred yards away.'[80]

The column remained at large until the truce in July without carrying out further successful operations. Forced to sleep in the outhouses and barns of sympathetic farmers, Thomas Mannion recalled, 'the local people supported us in every way possible. They always gave us food and shelter and always responded extremely well in the matter of collections.'[81] According to Patrick Treacy, 'No words of mine could do justice to their kindness and generosity. Food and shelter were ours at all times of the day and night. We were no doubt a burden on them but they regarded it as a great privilege to help us.'[82]

South Galway flying column

In March 1921, frustrated at the lack of leadership in the county, a number of south Galway Volunteers from the Peterswell, Kilbeacanty and Kilchreest districts, led by John Burke and Daniel Ryan, contacted Michael Brennan, commander of the Clare Volunteers, for assistance in help setting up a flying column in south Galway.[83] Stanford, along with a group of ten Volunteers, including Daniel Ryan and Thomas Keely, took the ammunition and arms in their possession and met Brennan on the Derrybrien Mountains on Holy Thursday 1921. The column was initially led by Brennan and consisted of Volunteers from Clare and Galway and was composed of about forty men.[84]

After several unsuccessful attempts to lure the Crown Forces into ambushes, Brennan took his men back to Clare, leaving the column of Galway Volunteers to organise themselves.[85] A fortnight later, Brennan was ordered by GHQ to take full control of the south Galway Volunteers, establishing the south-east and south-west brigades consisting of five companies each.[86] A new leadership was put in place with several younger Volunteers becoming officers for the first time. Thomas McInerney of Ardrahan became commandant, while Patrick Flynn, Derrybrien; Thomas Fahy, Peterswell; John Coen, Kilbeacanty and John Flaherty, Beagh, led their respective companies. Thomas McInerney remained in charge of the south-west (Ardrahan) battalion while John Fahy acted as O/C of the south-east (Gort) battalion, composed of five companies each.[87]

The Ballyturin ambush was planned by members of this new group who were eager to prove their ruthlessness after being frustrated by the slow progress of the campaign. Bagot House was the home of John C. Bagot, a landlord and Justice of the Peace whom Volunteer Patrick Glynn later described as 'an out and out loyalist'.[88] The first major attack by the new unit was carried out at the gate lodge situated at the entrance leading to Ballyturin House, in the parish of Kilbeacanty. The ambush was organised by Joseph Stanford, John Coen and Daniel Ryan, upon learning that District Inspector C.E.M. Blake would be attending a party at Bagot's house. The new leadership believed that Blake came to the area to kill leading republicans and he became infamous for raiding the Catholic Church in Kilbeacanty. During the incident, men under Blake's command chased Volunteer Thomas Keely out of mass, firing shots on consecrated ground and damaging tombstones.[89] It was an incident that Stanford was determined D.I. Blake would pay dearly for. Displaying a ruthlessness, not previously characteristic of the Galway Volunteers, the new leadership plotted to kill Blake before he could strike at them. Upon learning of Blake's presence in the district, Stanford, Coen and Ryan fled to the safety of the Slieve Aughty Mountains where their camp at Gortacornane Wood was in a state of readiness. The small group was composed of Joseph Stanford, Michael Kelly (Gort); John Coen, Patrick Glynn, Thomas Keely (Kilbeacanty); Patrick Houlihan (Clare brigade) and Thomas Craven (North Galway) with John Keely and Martin Cohen (Kilbeacanty) acting as scouts.[90]

The group took over the gate lodge at Ballyturin House with the inhabitants, the Connolly family, remaining with the men in their home. A number of passers-by had been detained in the lodge when, at around 7 p.m., with the Connolly's lying on their beds and the unit a full six hours in position, a motor car arrived at the gate lodge containing D.I. Blake and his party. With the Volunteers holding positions at the windows of the gate lodge and in the surrounding shrubberies and along the angle made by the avenue and the main road, Captain F.W.M. Cornwallis of the 7th Lancers stepped out to open to gate. Daniel Ryan and Patrick Glynn shouted 'hands up, surrender' but Cornwallis dodged for cover before opening fire on the Volunteers with his automatic pistol, grazing Stanford in the leg. Volunteer Thomas Keely recalled, 'There was a long interval between the order, hands up, and the time I fired. I thought we gave them too much time and too much of a chance before we opened fire.'[91] Patrick Glynn, who lay in the undergrowth, along with Stanford and Craven recalled 'we concentrated our fire on the car, doing our best to save the women in it. The men in the lodge killed the man who came to open the gate.'[92]

D.I. Blake, Captain Cornwallis, Lieutenant William McCreery and the District Inspector's wife, Eliza Blake, who were all travelling in the vehicle, were killed instantly. Ryan recalled, 'Blake fell out of the car dead. McCreery also fell out dead and Mrs Blake. Lady Gregory was saved being hit. It looked as if Mrs Blake tried to fire her own gun or Blake's gun. It was known that she carried an automatic and at times threatened people in the town of Gort with it.'[93] A teenage girl, the niece of Lady Gregory, was also in the car but was unharmed. Ryan recalled, 'We found Lady Gregory in a sitting position behind the car. She looked cool and answered "yes" in a cool calm voice when asked if she was alright. She said she wanted to go to Bagot's and we proceeded there with her.'[94] Before fleeing to their hide out in Gortacornane, the attackers dismantled the car and collected revolvers from the dead before delivering a note to the big house stating that if reprisals followed, they would kill Bagot and burn his house. The Connolly family, who lived in the gate lodge and worked for the Bagots, subsequently refused to name the men involved in the attacks despite being offered inducements.[95] Volunteer Patrick Glynn recalled that Ms Gregory knew the identity of the men involved but never disclosed them to the authorities.[96]

In reprisal for the attack, John Kearney, an RIC man based in Gort, who had been passing information to the south Galway Volunteers, was shot dead by his RIC colleagues after arriving at the ambush scene.[97] Kearney had previously alerted the Volunteers about military round-ups and facilitated the escape of most of the south Galway column.[98] It was initially claimed by the authorities that Kearney was shot by the Volunteers; however, local sources confirmed that police boasted about his death and the claim that republicans were responsible was later dropped by the authorities.[99]

Following the attack, the flying column fled to safe houses across south Galway and local people fled their homes in fear of reprisals. Police burned houses along the road from the ambush site leading into the town of Gort and the homes of Volunteer John, who had taken part in the attack, and Michael Fahy and Patrick Callanan, were among those destroyed. The police subsequently carried out extensive sweeps but the column remained at large, scattered across the countryside. Volunteer Patrick Glynn remembered, 'from the time of the Ballyturin ambush until the truce, we were evading the enemy. They were far too strong for us.'[100] Despite the levels of violence, Glynn noted, 'the local people never wavered in their support of the IRA. Day in day out, they supported us in every conceivable manner.'[101]

Fighting for Ireland and the parish

In terms of their military struggle with the Crown Forces, there was some disagreement as to how strong a position the Volunteers were in when the truce was announced in July 1921. P.J. McDonnell recalled, 'I cannot say that we went wild at the news. To say we were stunned would be nearer the mark, until it began to sink in that the British had been forced by men just like us fighting all over the country to agree to a truce.'[102] Despite being reorganised in April, the Galway Volunteers were struggling to function on a meaningful level and Volunteer Daniel Ryan of the south Galway flying column reflected, 'we were on the defensive and it was no easy job. It was our hardest time. There was no enemy party coming our way small enough to be attacked with the arms available to us'.[103]

Throughout 1921, it was far from clear who was winning the battle between the Crown Forces and the Volunteers in Galway. The truce was viewed as a welcome return to normality by most, and for republicans, as a chance for a well-earned rest. It was widely believed that peace would not last long, negotiations would break down and violence would erupt once more. The retrospective notion that the military stalemate of the summer of 1921 represented a victory for the Volunteers would have been viewed with scepticism. As late as the spring of 1922, as National Army officer Laurence Flynn took command of the Loughrea RIC barracks, the departing British officer chided him, 'hurry up and get finished with this farce, we will be back again soon'.[104]

While the capacity of the republican movement was limited, the young men and women who fought against the Crown Forces in Galway were not adventure seekers who remained in the organisation for personal gain or social kudos. The dangers faced by Volunteers who were willing to take part in attacks from July 1920 were very considerable and republican activity offered no prospect of social or economic reward. In order to remain active for a significant length of time, Volunteers needed to be free of parental control to facilitate long periods of time away from their families. From July 1920 onwards, only the most determined young people, generally without the burden of property, dependents or the constraints of standard work commitments could commit to becoming full-time fighters.

The failure of the Volunteers to garner significant support in Galway's towns was notable and no noteworthy attacks were attempted in the larger towns of Galway, Loughrea, Ballinasloe or Tuam. The resolutely rural character of the republican struggle highlights the limited degree of support the movement could reply upon. In this respect, gauging the level of popular support for republican violence is problematic. In their statements to the Bureau of Military History, Volunteers routinely praised the unstinting community support that facilitated their campaign. However, in many large districts, where no attacks were undertaken, local Volunteers claimed a sustained campaign was problematic due to lack of arms and insufficient training. If the failure of so many units to acquire arms and ammunition is taken as a manifestation of a lack of intent, we can conclude than many republican units were reticent about the killing of policemen and were content to play an auxiliary role to the small number of active service units that emerged in early 1921. In this respect, the desire to fight for the republican cause should not always be interpreted as a desire to be involved in the killing of policemen.

Killing should not be employed as a yardstick of the success or failure of the republican campaign. Young people's willingness to play a role in the independence struggle did not necessarily constitute an acceptance that the killing of Crown Forces represented the foremost component in the emerging revolution. To most republicans, the campaign represented far more than simply inflicting casualties and, as is discussed later, the administration of republican courts, the maintenance of law and order, low-level campaigns of theft and arson from the Crown Forces and the implementation of a boycott on the military and police occupied the energies of the vast majority of ordinary republicans. Brian Hughes has noted that republican control could not be achieved without 'minor acts of everyday terror' and 'it is the local and the perpetual which counts; the daily interaction between neighbours, friends and enemies'. In this respect, as Hughes notes, the 'enemy lived nearby, had a face, and had a name. It may have worn a uniform, but often it did not.'[105]

The inability of many active Volunteer companies to launch successful attacks on the Crown Forces masks a number of pertinent realities. Many less successful ambushes and attacks of limited consequence took place across the county as newspaper reports and the testimony of police and republicans confirm. For every ambush in which Crown Forces were killed, many more less dramatic acts of resistance were carried out. Following the collapse of police authority in 1918, the Volunteers became entangled in much of the seemingly less heroic realities that the administration of law and order entailed and involved responsibilities that many never envisaged having to carry out.

Committed activists did not emerge from any specific socio-economic communities but the presence of strong local leadership, often comprising only a few tightly knit families, was the most important factor in mobilising active republican areas. The presence of inspirational local leadership overrode specific social, economic or cultural conditions as mobilising factors. Inspirational officers played a formative role in mobilising their companies and active units tended to become dependent upon a small number of charismatic leaders. The Tuam Brigade under Michael Moran, and subsequently, Michael 'Con' Fogarty and Thomas Dunleavy; the Gort Battalion under Thomas McInerney and Peter Howley; the West Connemara brigade under P.J. McDonnell; and the Galway brigade led by Joseph Howley and Brian Molloy were foremost in the republican campaign under the guidance of enigmatic leaders.

Support for the Volunteers in rural Ireland was always ambiguous and backing the fight for a republic and admiration for local Volunteers did not necessarily translate into a popular belief in the righteousness of the use of violence. Support for the republican campaign was frequently conditional and varied depending on the particular context, locality and time. At the height of the conflict in March 1921, Archbishop Thomas Gilmartin of Tuam expressed his solidarity with the people of Galway, 'in their feelings of horror and indignation at the actions of the Crown Forces'. However, the Archbishop went on to warn his flock against channelling their anger into support for the Volunteers' campaign as, 'what is called the IRA may contain the flower of Irish youth, but they have no authority from the Irish people or from any moral principle to wage war against unequal forces with the consequence of terror, arson and death to innocent people'.[106] The Archbishop's analysis underlined the fundamental problem facing the Volunteers – the absence of popular moral sanction from the community for their campaign against a superior military force, for which the civilian population was punished in violent reprisals. The Volunteers portrayed their campaign as representative of their community in their fight against an alien oppressor, but in reality, the public did not celebrate the killing of policemen and the violent consequences for the community frequently outweighed the limited support for armed struggle. The degree to which ordinary civilian life was disrupted by the Volunteers' campaign should not be overestimated. In many districts, the military and police continued to socialise in local pubs and hotels, and in Galway town, in particular, the officer class remained part of the social scene. The annual social highlight of the year for most Galweigans, the Galway Races, was not significantly disrupted with a strong turnout reported for the big race days in 1920 and 1921. Even in the north Galway countryside where the Volunteers were strong, coursing events, race days and hunts continued as normal and the March Fair in Tuam, held at the height of the violence in 1921, was reported to be 'one of the largest held in many years'.[107]

CHAPTER 6

War of Independence II: Dying for Ireland, 1920–1

The War of Independence in Galway was characterised by a campaign of attrition by the Volunteers against the police, and by the Crown Forces against the civilian population in general, including, but not limited to Volunteers. The Crown Forces rarely engaged the Volunteers directly but inflicted reprisals upon the communities which they believed – frequently incorrectly – gave support to republican fighters, while arresting and killing senior Volunteer officers.[1] While the behaviour of the Crown Forces generated a popular loathing of the police, the unprecedented violence was formative in limiting the scale of the republican campaign as the community became fearful of republican attacks taking place in their districts.

As the British government insisted that the Volunteers were not legitimate belligerents in a time of war, the police, supported by the military, were held responsible for defeating 'outrage' in Ireland. From early 1920 until the truce in July 1921, almost 14,000 men were recruited to bolster the 10,000 strong Royal Irish Constabulary (RIC). While the majority of the recruits came from the British cities of London, Glasgow and Liverpool, as many as 20 per cent may have been Irish.[2] The Black and Tans, so-called due to their mixed khaki uniforms, were recruited in early 1920 and sworn in as police constables to reinforce local RIC. The vast majority of recruits were War veterans with extensive military experience who were used to treating civilian populations with disdain. The upsurge in the republican campaign led to a second wave of police recruitment in July 1920 that saw the creation of an Auxiliary Division which operated independently of the police. While the Auxiliaries were a distinct force, and viewed themselves as superior to the Black and Tans, the public generally lumped both groups together, making little distinction between the two. In terms of reprisals, it is frequently problematic to ascertain to what degree regular RIC, Auxiliaries and Black and Tans were responsible, and most often, it was a combination of the various branches of the Crown

Forces augmented on occasion by the military. Police records show that recruits to both divisions tended to be in their mid to late twenties and unmarried; they generally received cursory training at the police depot in the Phoenix Park, Dublin, before being dispatched to the countryside.

Charles Townshend has claimed that the use of extreme violence by the British authorities arose less from clear-cut decisions at the highest levels than from instinctive reactions on the ground but that 'in consenting to the militarisation of the police, they [Crown Forces] participated in the creation of a force whose behaviour became as immoral as that of the terrorists'.[3] This traditional view attributes Crown Force reprisals to drink-fuelled and War-traumatised police reinforcements who, outraged by assaults on their comrades, wreaked vengeance on civilians. John Borgonovo and Gabriel Doherty have questioned the assumption that police on the ground were to blame for violent reprisals, noting 'a disturbing policy of assassination sanctioned by the highest level of the British government in Ireland'.[4] According to this assessment, the growing incidence of reprisals forced the government to officially sanction the policy in December 1920, only to abandon it in June 1921 in the face of mounting public criticism. Borgonovo and Doherty have noted the lack of academic attention the reprisal killing of republicans and civilians has received and their conclusions suggest the involvement in murderous reprisals of regular, Irish-born members of the RIC. The Crown Forces in Galway had few qualms about using the most repugnant violence against the civilian community and republicans alike in order to subdue the republican campaign. They failed to thwart the Volunteers completely due to the determination of a cadre of young leaders who were committed to maintaining their campaign come what may. This chapter will examine this campaign in detail and the evolution of state violence, in particular.

Analysing events that remain cloaked in conjecture demands an exhaustive trawl through competing and frequently conflicting sources. Researchers must maintain a scepticism of the historical accounts provided in both local and national newspapers, combatants' accounts, police records and ancillary material. A reliable narrative is, however, possible, when a range of sources are assessed and weighed against each other. The inherent danger of treating police records, in particular, as reliable has been highlighted by Pádraig Yeates when discussing D.M. Leeson's study, *The Black and Tans: British Police and Auxiliaries in the Irish War of Independence*, published in 2012.[5] Police records pertaining to Galway are wholly unreliable and represent obvious fictions designed to protect a force involved in the killing of civilians.[6] As we shall see, the records of Military Courts of Inquiry and County Inspectors' Monthly Confidential Reports are particularly problematic as evidenced by the number of Galway civilians whose deaths were blithely explained away by senior officers as 'killed while trying to escape'. Treating such reports as other than functional components in a campaign of state killing is naïve at best and fundamentally distorts the historical record.

The Galway Brigade of the Crown Forces formed part of the British Army 5th Division during the War of Independence. The Division was commanded by Major General Sir H.S. Jeudwine from his headquarters in the Curragh, where he co-ordinated an operational area covering counties Roscommon, Donegal, Sligo, Longford, Leitrim, Galway, Mayo, Offaly, Kildare, Westmeath and Carlow.[7] A detachment of D Company of the Auxiliaries was dispatched to Galway in September commanded by Lieutenant Colonel F.H.W. Guard, DSO, formerly of the Royal Scots Regiment, based at Lenaboy Castle, Galway. The Galway Brigade under Major M.O. Wilson had its headquarters in Renmore Barracks, the home of the Connacht Rangers in Galway town, and Wilson had troops stationed in six towns across east Galway. The 1st Royal Dragoons were based in Athenry and Ballinasloe; the 17th Lancers were based at Galway, Gort and Tuam; the 2nd Battalion Border Regiment was based at the military aerodrome in Oranmore; and the 2nd Argyle and Southern Highlanders were based in Galway town, along with a small detachment of the Connaught Rangers, the No 5 Section of the Armoured Car Company and detachments of the 6th Dragoon Guards (Carabineers).[8]

At the height of the violence in December 1920, there were 453 Crown Forces stationed in Galway town; 352 stationed in Ballinasloe; and 135 in Oranmore; with smaller detachments of 57 in both Gort and Athenry and 46 in Tuam.[9] Detachments from other parts of the 5th Division were brought into specific areas during roundups of civilians. Direct contact between the military and the Volunteers was relatively rare, with the vast majority of these attacks involving ambushes on small patrols of police.

Everyday violence and detention

The experience of rural communities at the hands of the Crown Forces in Galway matches that of some of the most active areas in Ireland, in terms of the extreme nature of the violence perpetrated on civilians and members of the Volunteers.[10] Twenty-six people were killed by the Crown Forces in Galway between October 1920 and May 1921, eleven of whom were active republicans. Twenty-five were killed in the east of the county, including a priest, a pregnant woman, a serving RIC constable and a retired army officer. Attacks against the civilian population and Volunteers can be analysed in three categories. There was a series of killings carried out by Crown Forces travelling in large numbers, taking no care to conceal their actions or identity, with nine people killed by rampaging police in this fashion. A second series of attacks was carried out by small units of men who targeted specific individuals under the cover of darkness and acting on intelligence about their victim's whereabouts; nine men were killed in this fashion. Finally, republicans were killed in the custody of police and military and described by the authorities as being 'shot while trying to escape'; seven Volunteers were killed in this fashion.[11]

Violent reprisals involving shootings, beatings, looting and the burning of property were carried out by Crown Forces in the east of the county at Tuam, Oranmore, Headford, Ardrahan and Gort; and in west Galway in Barna, Clifden, Screebe and Moycullen.[12] These reprisals were carried out following republican ambushes and involved the burning of homes and businesses and the shooting and beating of civilians. The fear generated by these incidents generated a popular dread at the prospect of the arrival of Crown Forces and hundreds fled the town of Gort overnight in anticipation of the arrival of police and military seeking revenge for the Ballyturin ambush on 15 May 1921.

The burning of homes, the destruction of property, floggings and assaults were frequent occurrences from September 1920. Following reprisals in Galway town in September 1920, Bishop Thomas O'Dea and the Bishop of Clonfert, Thomas O'Doherty released a statement condemning the actions of the Crown Forces that noted:

> We, who live amongst the people, see with our eyes, that not only is protection not given, but for months past, a systematic campaign of terrorism, violence and destruction of life and property has been tolerated, connived at, helped and encouraged, so that amongst the bulk of the people, no life, liberty or property is safe any longer.[13]

Public displays of casual violence violated taboos concerning attacks on the clergy, women and Church property. Evidence of sexual violence is problematic; however, given the scale of casual brutality, sexual assaults of vulnerable women were inevitable. Lady Augusta Gregory wrote of her concern in her diary in September 1920 that the parents of girls in the Gort area had decided to keep things 'hush, hush' when their daughters were 'interfered with' by soldiers.[14] The degree of violence, drunkenness and contempt for the norms of war-time conduct made women particularly vulnerable given that they were confined to their homes by their familial responsibilities while their men folk could flee in anticipation of raids.

Following Sunday mass in Moycullen in September 1920, troops separated the congregation, marching them to a nearby field where they were told that the authorities were going to restore Richard Abbott, an agent on the property of Colonel Campbell, to his home and 'if a hair on his head was touched, six republicans would be killed'.[15] In the Tuam area, council workmen stopped working on the roads following an incident in which men were taken from a public house at Turloughmore and whipped in October 1920.[16] Uniformed men visited the villages of Corofin and Cummer on consecutive nights during the same month, dragging twenty men from their beds, stripping them naked and flogging them on the roadside.[17] On the day of Terence MacSwiney's funeral in Cork, Crown Forces ran amok in Loughrea, wounding three people.[18] Following the incident, Bishop O'Doherty wrote to the chief secretary for Ireland, Hamar Greenwood, informing him that, 'a state of alarm existed in the countryside between Ballinasloe and Athlone on the day of the funeral, with shots fired, men beaten and homes destroyed'.[19] On the same day, a number of young women in Ballinasloe had their heads shaved in the first of a number of similar attacks.[20] In early December, a series of burglaries took place in Athenry and Loughrea with whiskey and cash stolen by groups of soldiers at four public houses.[21]

In March 1921, an editorial in the *Tuam Herald* pleaded for a respite from reprisals as 'the country is bleeding to death, bleeding at every pore'.[22] During the same month the Archbishop Gilmartin of Tuam, wrote, 'if the full tale of flogging, burning, terrorism and looting could be told the whole picture would make even savages ashamed'.[23] The violence represented a degree of brutality that occasionally bordered on psychotic. In June 1921, Patrick O'Loughlin, a railway clerk, was dragged from his bed at his home in Loughrea and brutally assaulted by armed men. His captors falsely claimed they were republicans and they had sentenced him to death. He was pistol whipped, burned with hot coals, glass was smashed into his face and disinfectant poured over his body.[24]

Soldiers involved in violence were rarely brought before military tribunals; however, two police were court-martialled in connection with incidents in Galway town. Constables James Murphy and Richard Oxford were court-martialled in May 1921 for the attempted killing of James Egan and J.P. Greene who were taken from a hotel in Salthill. After a lengthy inquiry with numerous sworn witnesses testifying to seeing the men kidnap Green and Egan and march them into the ocean before seriously wounding them, the case was dismissed as 'a purely internal disciplinary matter'.[25]

The authorities possessed superior intelligence about their republican opponents and their ability to arrest senior Volunteer officers and disrupt their organisation was significant. Most of the republican leadership in Galway had been arrested by the end of 1920, fundamentally altering the dynamics of the republican campaign which consequently became reliant on the individual endeavour of isolated units. Pádraig Ó Fathaigh, the senior organiser in south Galway, was arrested in March 1920, with Colm Ó Gaora, organiser in south Connemara, arrested in April.[26] The numbers of Volunteers arrested increased from September 1920 onwards. George Nichols, who was central to the organisation in Galway town, was arrested in late September and Pádraic Ó Máille, organiser in west Connemara, was arrested in October. In a county-wide operation carried out in the last week of November, the police stamped their authority by arresting sixty-one suspected Volunteers in the Tuam, Portumna, Loughrea and Galway districts. Among those arrested were leading officers, Patrick Coy of Loughrea, John Hosty, Joseph Togher and Frank Hardiman of Galway and Michael Moran and James Nohilly of the Tuam brigade.[27] These arrests fundamentally disrupted the organisation and forced senior officers to go on the run. Most of those arrested were held in Galway jail, a makeshift camp in the Galway Town Hall or in Tuam, before being transferred to Dublin or Belfast, with senior officers, such as Larry Lardiner of Athenry, transferred to Belfast, Ballykinlar and elsewhere.

By December 1920, arrests tended to be carried out through large round-ups and many young men with no republican connection were detained. In the first week of January 1921, two prisoners died from 'fever' at Galway Town Hall. Michael Mullins, aged 27, was a farmer's son who was picked up while working on his land. He had no involvement in politics and had played for the Galway Senior Gaelic football team.[28] Patrick Walsh, a Mayo native from Hollymount, died under similar circumstances during the same week. It is far from clear what the actual cause of death was in both cases with coroners reports hastily published with little detail or explanation.

Relatively harmless Sinn Féin representatives were arrested from late 1920 onwards, as town councillors and other innocuous public servants were interned. Large numbers of Sinn Féin members of public boards were arrested at the beginning of December, including many older republicans.[29] Men such as James Flynn, vice-chairman of Loughrea Board of Guardians, were arrested in March 1921. His incarceration served no military purpose but to discourage membership of Sinn Féin.[30] Dr Brian Cusack, who had been elected MP for North Galway in 1918 and was not an active Volunteer, was arrested in Dublin in March 1921, becoming the twenty-third member of the Dáil to be incarcerated.[31]

Despite its reputation as an anti-republican town, Galway witnessed a sustained period of violent reprisals between September and November 1920.[32]

The period became known locally as 'the terror' and was regarded as particularly shocking due to the generally moderate tone of nationalist sentiment prevailing in the city. The military had long played a central role in the town's identity and the Connaught Rangers were a source of much local pride. The role of the Galway munitions factory had helped convince the town's leading citizens that Galway played a notable role in the War effort and the town was accustomed to parades, brass bands and related military regalia adorning their streets. 'The terror' was to shatter these illusions and brought home the reality of the authority's contempt for, and ignorance of, local conditions.

Only one member of Crown Forces was killed in Galway town and his death and the subsequent actions of police led to a five-week curfew that saw the town's inhabitants subjected to a nightly campaign of violence.[33] The atmosphere of menace was heightened by the absence of street lighting, which the council had agreed to shut off, and a rigidly enforced stipulation that lights could not be turned on in homes or businesses. Edward Krum was a military taxi driver and was on duty at the Railway Station. A number of Volunteers entered the station to await a container of explosives due to arrive from Dublin. People had been gathering to collect the evening papers, and when the train arrived, a crowd rushed the platform provoking Krum into drawing his revolver. He was surrounded by Volunteers and shot dead Seán Mulvoy before he was himself killed with his own gun by republicans.[34]

Following the shooting, the Crown Forces went on the rampage across the town, assaulting civilians and looting and smashing homes and shops, including the Thomas Ashe Sinn Féin Hall. The office of the *Galway Express* was ransacked and the paper ceased publication. Crown Forces arrived at the lodgings of Seamus Quirke, a 23-year-old Volunteer from Cork, dragged him to the docks, shot him and threw his body into the water.[35] A group arrived at the home of Volunteer Seán Broderick who was shot a number of times, managing to survive by feigning death. The intruders shaved his sister's head before locking family members in an upstairs room and setting fire to the house.[36]

The military subsequently imposed a curfew lasting from nine at night until four in the morning and what the *Connacht Tribune* described as, 'fifteen nights of unexampled terror' followed.[37] In a letter read out to his parishioners, Bishop O'Dea subsequently denounced the police for:

> The persistent shooting and flinging of grenades in the city and for miles around, almost every night since curfew began, the systematic campaign of house burning, destruction of property, eviction of families from their homes, dragging of people from their beds at revolver point and forcing

them to act as spies, violence against weak women and girls, and I don't know what other forms of terrorism.[38]

Tension in the town was heightened by the arrival of 300 troops from the Argyll and Sutherland Highlanders.[39] Following the initial outbreak a 'citizens' enquiry' was organised and notices urging people to come forward with testimony were posted.[40] As the meeting was about to get under way, soldiers surrounded the building and District Inspector Richard Cruise ordered the crowd to disperse. A standoff ensued with the organisers refusing to abandon the meeting until clergy persuaded Sinn Féin representative Louis O'Dea to relent. O'Dea's legal business was subsequently ransacked and set on fire. A black cross was placed at his home, similar to ones placed at the homes of Volunteer Michael Walsh and Fr Michael Griffin – both of whom were subsequently shot dead.[41]

Low-level violence continued for a number of weeks as shops and businesses were targeted by incendiary fires, with arson and burglary becoming a nightly occurrence. Amid the violence, the funerals of Volunteers Seán Mulvoy and Seamus Quirke were presided over by Bishop O'Dea and were among the largest ever seen in the town. Businesses and public houses closed and work was suspended in sympathy. The *Connacht Tribune* noted, 'even the employees of the County Club drew all the blinds and went forth to attend the requiem mass'.[42] As the coffins wound their way towards Eyre Square, police on horseback dispersed mourners, sending panic-stricken crowds running through side streets. The scenes were incomprehensible to the families of the town's many military veterans as the authorities turned on some of their most loyal supporters.

October saw an upsurge in violence following the abduction by the East Connemara Volunteers of national school teacher Patrick W. Joyce, on 15 October.[43] Joyce had made little secret of his antipathy towards republicans and had campaigned to have Micheal Ó Droighneáin, a republican officer from Spiddal, removed from his post as a primary school teacher. His fate was sealed when letters he wrote to the police outlining Ó Droighneáin's movements, as well as allegations against other Volunteers, were intercepted by Volunteer Joseph Togher in the Galway post office.[44] Ó Droighneáin formally asked Volunteer GHQ for advice over what steps to take as 'he did not want to have the responsibility of taking appropriate action in such a case'.[45] Volunteer John Geoghegan, who was later shot dead by the Crown Forces, was formally ordered by Volunteer leader Richard Mulcahy to execute Joyce.[46] In the interim, three more of Joyce's letters were intercepted by Togher, addressed to the officer in charge of Renmore barracks, the officer in charge of the 17th Lancers at Earls Island and a third to the Chief Secretary's office. Upon receipt of the second batch of letters, Ó Droighneáin had a priest brought to a disused cabin between Barna and Moycullen. Joyce was taken from his home by masked men with a canvas bag placed over his head. He was 'tried' by a three-man Volunteer court, convicted, taken into the bog and shot dead.[47]

In the aftermath of the killing, the local community displayed little sympathy and the police noted, 'we have, not alone received no assistance, but in some instances the attitude of those questioned has been insolent and defiant'.[48] The Crown Forces frantically searched districts west of the city, with civilians beaten and property damaged. Notices were pinned up in Eyre Square stating that if Joyce was not returned 'somebody would be made to pay the penalty' – that somebody was to be Fr Michael Griffin.[49] On the night of 14 November 1920, an unknown person called to the parochial house shared by Fr Griffin and Fr J.W. O'Meehan. Fr O'Meehan was not sleeping at the house owing to threatening letters he had been receiving.[50] After a conversation with the caller in Irish, Fr Griffin departed on what he thought was a sick call to one of his parishioners and was not seen alive again.

It was initially believed that Fr Griffin was being held prisoner by the Auxiliaries in Lenaboy barracks in revenge for the earlier disappearance of Joyce. Fr Patrick Davis of Rahoon visited the authorities and pleaded there be no reprisals for the kidnapping.[51] Following the disappearance, local people organised by the clergy searched the countryside to the west of the city. Six days after he disappeared, Fr Griffin's body was found by a search party buried under rough ground near Barna village. He had a gunshot wound to the head. Micheál Ó Droighneáin recalled, 'the priests, came out, and with the aid of lanterns, the clay was removed with spades and shovels, and the body taken up, later that night, the body was placed on a donkey cart, and brought in'.[52] A row of thatched houses was burned by the police after the body was recovered and the clergy refused to give possession of the remains to Crown Forces.

It was popularly believed that the caller who lured Fr Griffin to his death was a local man, William Joyce, no relation to the aforementioned P.W. Joyce. The killers used a local civilian to collaborate as Ó Droighneáin recalled, 'I know definitely that he [Fr Griffin] had decided to refuse to leave his home at the behest of British forces and more especially of any stranger. Therefore my opinion is that the individual who called him was known to him.'[53] Likewise, Volunteer Joseph Togher recalled, 'it was an inside job concocted and carried out by the local company of Auxies stationed at Lenaboy':

> We were convinced that the caller (a tout for the auxiliaries) was none
> other than William Joyce ... I intercepted a letter from Joyce to an Auxie,

which, after being broken down, revealed that Joyce had the RIC cipher that was in use that particular month. Michael Staines, our liaison officer, confronted Divisioner Cruise of the RIC with this information, as Cruise had continually denied Joyce's association with the RIC. Had we had this information earlier, Joyce would have been executed.[54]

William Joyce was well known in the town for associating with the Crown Forces and had been seen accompanying them on their raids, helping them navigate the small local roads and identifying local people. Shortly after Fr Griffin's disappearance, Joyce joined the 4th Worcester Regiment and departed with them to England. He subsequently achieved infamy as the Nazi propagandist, Lord Haw Haw, and was hanged at Wandsworth Prison in January 1946.[55]

Random killing

Civilians were frequently the target of reprisals following republican attacks. Two days after a republican ambush at Castleday in the south of the county at the beginning of November 1920, the Crown Forces shot dead Eileen Quinn from a passing lorry, a short distance from the ambush site.[56] She had been sitting on the front wall of her garden with an infant in her arms and was heavily pregnant.[57] At the court of military inquiry it was found that she was shot 'by one of a number of shots fired as a precautionary measure and in view of these facts a verdict of death by misadventure must be brought'.[58] The parish priest Fr John Considine visited the dying woman and sent word to the police at Gort, who arrived at the scene; however, when asked by the priest to take the dying woman's statement the officer allegedly refused.[59]

On 20 December 1920, Laurence MacDonagh was shot dead during a naval search operation on Inishmore, the largest of the Aran Islands.[60] Three navy vessels landed simultaneously, with disembarking troops systematically searching homes, creating pandemonium among the local population who hid out among the island's many rocks and caves. MacDonagh was shot dead while fleeing his home. He was unarmed and shot in the back with the authorities claiming that he had been 'shot dead while trying to escape'.[61]

A republican ambush in the Headford district in January 1921 illustrates the ferocity of reprisals against civilians with no republican connection. On 19 January, Volunteers ambushed a lorry of Auxiliaries at Kilroe, situated four miles from Headford town.[62] Crown Forces subsequently flooded into the north Galway countryside killing four farmers' sons and burning eight houses, including the parochial house of the parish priest. Lorries roamed the narrow roads firing indiscriminately with civilians wounded in the villages of Kilconly, Sylane and Glenamaddy.[63] Crown Forces dismounted at a farmhouse, one mile from Headford and shot dead Thomas Collins, aged 21.[64] The Auxiliaries returned to the area over the following days and killed three more young men. William Walsh, aged 30, of Clydagh, Headford, was taken from his kitchen and shot dead in his yard.[65] An hour later, another farmer's son, Michael Hoade, was taken from his house near Caherlistrane, badly beaten and shot.[66] James Kirwan, aged 22, from Ballinastack, was shot dead after Crown Forces chased him through the fields.[67] Revenge for the Kilroe attack continued for some time, and on 3 March, Thomas Mullen, aged 29, of Killavoher, Clonberne, was arrested, beaten, shot dead and his body dumped a few miles from where he was working.[68] Like the previous victims, he had been doing a day's labour for a local farmer and had no republican connections. It was believed his brothers were Volunteers and it may be for this reason he was killed.[69]

Having a distinguished military career did not protect John Joe MacDonnell from the rage of the police. Following a republican attack that killed two policemen in Clifden on the night of 16 March 1920, at least sixteen houses were burned by Crown Forces and hundreds of young men arrested. A civilian ex-serviceman, MacDonnell was shot dead after calling to the police station to appeal for help in dousing the flames engulfing his father's hotel.[70] MacDonnell was a retired military officer and his killing while appealing to the police for help was particularly brutal.

Targeted assassination

The Crown Forces carried out a series of brutal assassinations that shocked the community and severely disrupted the Volunteers from late 1920 onwards. These killings highlight the superior intelligence and ruthless nature of the Crown Forces and had a devastating effect on republican morale. These targeted killings of republicans and civilians incorrectly believed to be republicans, were concealed by police authorities in their reports to Dublin Castle. The RIC Inspector for Galway West Riding recorded a series of killings carried out by republicans throughout 1920 and 1921. Despite the elaborate motives contained in reports, an array of evidence suggests Crown Forces carried out the killings with blame attributed to the Volunteers to deflect attention. Nine killings across the county bore strong similarities and were carried out by professional and competent assassins, acting with stealth and local knowledge.

On the evening of 17 September, Joseph Athy, aged 22, was shot dead and his workmate Patrick Burke was wounded, by unknown gunmen as they travelled home from work near Oranmore; survivors reported seeing gunmen in army fatigues fleeing the scene.[71] Athy was from a well-known republican family and the attack took place four weeks after a republican ambush in the district on 21 August. The killing was a direct response to the ambush and the killing 'evened the score' for the Crown Forces.

On 2 October, John O'Hanlon, aged 34, secretary of the Turloughmore Sinn Féin club, was shot dead by men who arrived at his home in the middle of the night.[72] O'Hanlon's body was found in a nearby field. The RIC Inspector for West Galway subsequently reported that he had been 'shot while trying to escape'.[73] O'Hanlon received a republican funeral and his death appears unrelated to any previous attack in the district.

The next killing took place on the night of 19 October, when well-known Sinn Féin representative Michael Walsh was taken from his family business at the Old Malt Pub on High Street in Galway town by a group of partially disguised men. Walsh was marched toward the Long Walk where he was shot and his body thrown into Galway Bay.[74] He was a popular local character and was not regarded as a militarily significant figure; the public nature of his execution was particularly shocking.

Four days after the killing of Michael Walsh, another publican, Thomas Egan, who was not an active republican, was shot dead near Athenry when four partially disguised men entered his home.[75] Egan's pub was the centre of the local community and was situated close to where landlord Frank Shawe-Taylor had been killed by agrarian agitators the previous March. The Crown Forces denied involvement in the killing, claiming it was carried out by disgruntled locals who feared Egan was going to go to the authorities with information relating to the killing of Shawe-Taylor.[76] The obviously concocted account of events was risible and there was little doubt in the community about who was responsible. Egan was given a large funeral and the outpouring of grief in the community, and conviction among the Egan family that Crown Forces were responsible contradicts the notion that he was killed as an informer.

The Crown Forces killed senior republican Joseph Howley in early December 1920. Howley had been in hiding since police burned his house in the aftermath of the Oranmore ambush in which a policeman was killed on 21 August 1920. Howley was killed at Broadstone railway station in Dublin as he alighted in the company of several other Galway republicans on 9 December.[77] He was approached on the platform by several men in plain clothes and shot dead.[78] His death deprived the movement of one of its key officers and republicans blamed members of the local RIC for tracking Howley's movements in order to have him killed.

This distinct pattern of killings continued into the New Year, and on the night of 20 February 1921, Volunteer John Geoghegan, a 26-year-old Sinn Féin district councillor from Moycullen in south Connemara, was taken from his bed by unknown men and shot dead.[79] His body was dumped at the back of his home and a notice pinned to his chest that read, 'yours faithfully, M. Collins'. The community believed the killing was the work of the Crown Forces and the family stated that the killers had Irish accents and wore policemen's caps.[80] The County Inspector of the RIC subsequently gave his killing one line in his monthly report, stating merely that 'a leading IRA officer was shot'.[81] His death may have been a further reprisal for the killing of P.W. Joyce and Geoghegan's commander Micheál Ó Droighneáin recalled:

> John Geoghegan was a wonderful man, the most unselfish I ever came across. It was he I sent to Dublin in connection with the Joyce letters; it was he I sent across the Corrib for a priest. I had given him orders not to sleep at home, but his answer to me was 'if they come looking for me and I am not there, they will shoot one of my brothers, and I cannot allow that to happen!'[82]

Killings of a similar nature continued as the year progressed, and on the 6 April, Volunteer Patrick Cloonan, a 27-year-old farmer from Maree, was taken from his bed by a group of disguised men and shot dead.[83] He had been on the run for several months and was staying at the house of his aunt at Ballinacloughty, Oranmore. The killers reportedly went straight to his bedroom and his body was found on the seashore near Tawin Island. Despite a republican funeral and a commemoration, the RIC recorded he had been killed by the Volunteers as 'he was at one time an advanced Sinn Féiner, but latterly it was reported that he was endeavouring to cut away from the movement and go to America. It is believed that some of the Sinn Féiners thought he was about to give them away before he left and therefore killed him.'[84] Cloonan was the third Volunteer from the Oranmore district to be killed since the Volunteers had attacked the police in the district in September 1920.

The killing of Patrick Molloy may also have been linked to an earlier republican attack at Kilroe in January 1921. On 30 April, Molloy, a farmer's son aged 26, was taken from his home a short distance from the original site of the ambush and shot dead. His body was labelled with a placard, 'Reported Informer, Convicted Spy: Others Beware, IRA'.[85] The County Inspector of the RIC provided an elaborate fiction, noting that local people were behind the killing and 'the real motive would appear to be retaliation for a previous killing which Molloy is believed to have committed in connection with a land dispute'.[86] Like other similar killings, the victim's family, the community, the local clergy and the Volunteers had no doubt that the Crown Forces killed Molloy.[87]

Several killings during this period had no obvious explanation and may have been cases of mistaken identity. Hugh Tully and Christopher Folan were killed in their homes in identical fashion in Galway town on the night of 11 May 1921. Like the previous killings, the assassins wore disguises and arrived at night.[88] In the case of Christopher Folan, however, the assassins made a number of errors. According to his family, the men arrived at the Folan home at O'Donohue Terrace, near Eyre Square, wearing waterproofs and driving goggles and asked for James Folan. James was Christopher's brother and had recently been released from Galway jail for republican activity. James was not at home and the killers took his two brothers into a room and shot them both, with Christopher dying from his wounds.[89] A short time later, disguised men made their way to a second house in the area and asked for Hugh Tully.[90] Tully, a railway worker who had no involvement in politics, came to the door and was shot in the head. He had survived an earlier attack when police broke into a house he shared with Volunteer Seán Broderick on 9 September 1920. The County Inspector of the RIC recorded that the men had been killed by republicans and the motive for the Folan killing was 'fear of the Sinn Féin party that Folan might give information'; in the case of Tully, it was claimed 'he was on good terms with the police and was probably suspected of giving information'.[91] As in previous killings, the RIC report of events were an obvious fabrication and the community accorded both victims large funerals attended by nationalists and leading republicans alike with condemnations of the police issued by clergy and local newspapers.

A week after the double killing in Galway town, Thomas McKeever, a shop assistant in Dunmore in the north of the county was killed in a fashion similar to the previous victims. McKeever was taken from his lodgings by disguised assassins who shot him and left his body in a nearby field. He was a native of Cork and had no connection with politics; however, the County Inspector of the RIC recorded that the dead man was a 'Sinn Féiner and alleged to be giving information'.[92] Once again, the killing was made to look like the work of republicans and the body labelled 'Convicted Spy – Traitors Beware'. As in previous cases, witnesses recalled seeing three men in waterproofs and goggles acting strangely and the *Connacht Tribune* noted that the deceased man lived an abstinent life and had no enemies in the area.[93] The parish priest publicly refuted the police account of events and declared that McKeever was uninvolved in republican activities and denounced the Crown Forces as murderers.[94]

With the exception of Joseph Howley, all eleven victims of these attacks were killed at night, by small groups of men who acted with stealth, and all of the killings, except that of O'Hanlon, were attributed to republicans or local people by the RIC. Many of the bodies were labelled as spies in an attempt to deflect attention away from the real killers. The perpetrators wore disguises with witnesses reporting that they wore long coats with the collars turned up and driving goggles or caps pushed low over their faces to disguise their identities.

Killed in custody

The Crown Forces killed several senior republicans while in custody. Michael Moran led the north Galway Volunteers during their early attacks on the Castlehacket and Castlegrove barracks and at Gallagh Hill where two RIC were killed. Following the Gallagh ambush, Moran's home was fired into by Crown Forces and the Volunteers placed a guard to protect his family.[95] Moran had been on the run since the ambush when he was picked up by the police in November. An armed escort was taking him from Eglinton Street barracks to Earls Island Barracks in Galway town on November 24 when he was shot dead, with the authorities subsequently claiming he was 'shot while trying to escape'.[96] Volunteer Michael Higgins, who fought with Moran, recalled 'a fine cool determined leader, and a great loss to the Volunteers'.[97] The removal of Moran led to a period of disorganisation and decline in the movement in the north of the county and it was an obvious retaliation for the Gallagh attack.

The killing of Volunteers Patrick and Harry Loughnane were the most brutal of the period with the brothers subjected to extensive torture before their deaths. The Loughnanes were picked up by the Auxiliaries at their family farm in the Shanaglish district of Beagh in south Galway on 27 November 1920. The local Volunteers had carried out the Castledaly ambush several weeks earlier in which Harry and Patrick had taken part and in which a policeman was killed. The brothers were tortured and their badly mutilated bodies found nearly three weeks later in a shallow pool of water at Umbriste, two miles from Ardrahan. They had their hands and legs broken, were missing fingers, had been set alight and had hand grenades exploded in their mouths.[98] Such was the violence that photographs of their mutilated corpses were widely distributed lest it be claimed that the level of violence was exaggerated.

The Crown Forces eventually captured one of the republican leaders involved in the ambush at Kilroe in January 1921 when they arrested Volunteer officer Louis Darcy at Oranmore train station on 23 March 1921.[99] Darcy was on his way to Dublin to meet Volunteer GHQ to resolve a dispute over the allocation of arms.[100] A student, he was a committed and competent Volunteer and had been on the run since explosives were found at his home at Clydagh, Headford. Like his comrade Michael Moran, he was officially listed as being 'shot while trying to escape'.[101] He was a charismatic leader and his memory was celebrated in ballads and poems that became popular in his native district.[102]

Volunteer operations frequently went wrong and in one particularly gruesome incident, William Freeney, a Volunteer from Derrydonnell, Athenry, was burned to death while carrying out an arson attack with his comrades at the Athenry Tennis and Croquet Club on 30 June 1920. The club was a popular social venue for the landed gentry, including leading military officers, and following the Truce, Freeney received a large republican funeral. He was a former prisoner and a committed Volunteer and his remains were only recovered in the shell of the building after the Volunteers had left the scene.

Ex-servicemen and violence

Ex-servicemen who had fought in the War were frequently the victims of an Ireland fundamentally changed from that which so many had been encouraged by nationalist leaders to leave. As Jane Leonard has outlined, 'they brought with them the scars of the war experience, whether physical or psychological. They attempted to restore family life and to find work. But in many important respects, the Irish homecoming was different from that in Britain … Irish veterans returned home to a country not at peace, but where a different war was raging.'[103]

There were a number of attacks on ex-servicemen in Galway during the period and many more would have gone unreported. In January 1920, an ex-serviceman was shot in the legs in Oranmore following warnings to resign from his job as a postman, which he had resumed after disbandment.[104] In November 1920, men broke into the home of an ex-serviceman named Fahey in Galway town, beating him badly and breaking his front teeth.[105] An ex-serviceman, W.H. Dryden, was kidnapped by three armed men in the town on 9 December and taken to the village of Moycullen where he was told he was going to be drowned for collaborating with the Crown Forces.[106] He managed to escape and was picked up by the RIC.[107]

Along with William Joyce, previously discussed, three alleged informers, all Catholics, were killed by republicans during the period, two of whom were ex-servicemen. Patrick Thornton was killed by a group of men at Loughaunbeg, near Spiddal in west Galway on 4 February 1920, and Tom Morris was killed near Kinvara in south Galway on 2 April 1921. Thornton had fought in the First World War with the Connaught Rangers and was invalided in November 1915. He worked in England for a number of years before returning to Galway in 1919. He was beaten and shot by a group of men outside a public house. Four men were charged with his killing but it is unclear if they were Volunteers.[108] The police noted that he was unpopular in the area as 'he was of a bullying disposition' and 'he and his brothers were opposed to Sinn Féin'.[109] Thornton's killing bears the hallmarks of an impromptu drunken attack rather than a premeditated execution, and while he was clearly hostile to local republicans, the label of informer may have served to justify his death.

Thomas Morris, aged 57, was a native of Loughcurra, Kinvara, in south Galway. He was a policeman in Waterford before joining the Royal Irish Fusiliers. After the War, he returned to live with his sister to convalesce. He was shot dead on 2 April 1921 after being taken from his sister's home by the Volunteers. His body was found blindfolded and a notice hung around his neck claiming he was a convicted spy.[110] Volunteer Michael Hynes recalled that his captors refused to bring a priest to hear an act of contrition from Morris 'in case he would intercede'.[111] The *Connacht Tribune* claimed he had been unpopular in the district and had been under threat for some time.[112] Morris was known to socialise with the Crown Forces and this marked him out as an obvious target; his house had previously been ransacked and he had temporarily fled the district. Giving evidence at the military inquest into his death, his sister stated, 'it was thought at the time that he was a spy'.[113]

Although there were rural districts with few active Volunteer companies, fraternising with the Crown Forces marked out some ex-servicemen as transgressors of what was considered acceptable conduct. In the case of both Morris and Thornton, it was possibly their drinking habits, more than any other factor, that singled them out as targets for retribution. Ex-servicemen were more likely than others in the rural community to defy local conventions, as many sought the comradeship they experienced in the War. Men who remained at home and were in tune with the tenor of local feeling were more reticent to socialise with police, and in the case of Tom Morris, it may have been the lack of company to drink with which ultimately led to his death. The role of alcohol was also a factor in the behaviour of Patrick Thornton and police noted his bullying attitude towards republicans. Both men had been invalided out of the military, had small but steady pensions, a lot of time on their hands and a mutual contempt for local republicans.

One other suspected informer was killed by republicans in north Galway in a similar fashion to Morris and Joyce though he was not an ex-serviceman. The body of Thomas Hannon, aged 21, a Catholic civilian who worked for a local landowner, C.D. O'Rourke, was found by schoolchildren on 27 April in the Clonberne district. A notice was pinned on his body, 'Convicted Spy IRA'.[114] He had been taken by armed men from the North Galway flying column on the afternoon of the 26 April and locals reported hearing shots being fired later that day. Volunteer John P. McCormack later recalled:

> I remember that about 11 a.m. Miss O'Rourke and a man called Hannon rode into our positions on horseback. They were called on to halt. Miss O'Rourke did so but Hannon rode on. He was captured and brought back to the gate lodge, where he was held prisoner all day with others who had come into our positions. Our party was armed with about fourteen rifles and twenty-four shotguns. I was placed as guard over Hannon for part of the day and given orders to guard him carefully as he was accused of spying. I think he was court martialled that day. Volunteer Patrick Walsh and I took him to one of the priests of Clonberne parish before he was executed. He was executed immediately after having been attended by the priest.[115]

The degree of antipathy between ex-servicemen and republicans and negative attitudes towards ex-serviceman within the wider community can be exaggerated. As Paul Taylor has argued, the degree of suspicion and hostility toward ex-servicemen by some republicans during the independence struggle should not be extrapolated into a caricature of an Ireland where they played the role of traitors in a changed society. Taylor points out, 'the ex-servicemen were not a homogenous group, either when volunteering or upon their return. They came from all walks of Irish society and were not exceptional in their loyalty to Britain; the reasons for which many volunteered, to secure home rule and fight for small nations, reflected popular opinion.'[116] During the independence struggle, the vast majority of ex-servicemen in Galway simply went about rebuilding their lives and did their best to cope, unmolested by republicans or other elements.

Political support for ex-servicemen was considerable and, even after January 1921, when Sinn Féin won considerable support on the Galway Urban District Council, the council remained active on the welfare of ex-servicemen, taking a number of steps to promote housing and employment opportunities for demobilised soldiers. The council considered a letter from the local Discharged Soldiers' Association in November 1919 asking that their members get preference of employment in connection with housing schemes.[117] While they did not implicitly state they were in favour of such a policy, the council promoted a number of schemes to directly provide housing and employment to ex-servicemen. They had hoped to provide direct employment by employing ex-soldiers exclusively on the erection of a new pier at Salthill; however, the plan was scuppered when no funds could be found to run the scheme.[118] In February 1921, the council passed a motion stating, 'the committee considers that every facility be given for the purpose of assisting the proposed scheme for erecting houses for ex-servicemen'.[119] A scheme of grant-in-aid to Claddagh fishermen whose boats and equipment were in need of repair following their return from the War received the council's backing in March 1919. The council also proposed opening a motor engineering department in the town for fishermen who had served in the army and navy and the Ministry of Reconstruction advised that their proposals were being examined by the Congested Districts Board (CDB).[120]

The tendency to view ex-servicemen as passive victims of republican violence is too simplistic.[121] The Galway branch of the Ex-Servicemen and Sailors' Federation had a considerable membership in Galway town, and some were adamant about what needed to be done to defeat the Volunteers. At a meeting of ex-servicemen in the town in March 1921, M.J. Hennon, general secretary of the Legion of Irish Ex-Servicemen, told his audience to loud applause, 'If the government cleared out of the country, it would be governed to the satisfaction of all Irish men by the ex-servicemen. Let the government clear out and the ex-servicemen will deal with the people who are kicking up trouble in the country. It may be talk, but you [ex-servicemen] could do it if you had co-operation behind you.'[122] Such militant rhetoric concealed a considerable degree of bluff but statements were frequently explicit in their contempt for the Volunteers. Ex-servicemen's associations did not disguise their political sympathies and appeared to have little fear of retribution. It is likely that Hennon's reported remarks represented a moderated version of the proceedings that a responsible newspaper editor was willing to print. At a meeting of ex-servicemen in Galway town in October 1920, the president of the Galway branch told members that grants totalling £18,225 for ex-servicemen had been obtained by their energies but 'impressed upon the men, the necessity of careful consideration before expressing an opinion'.[123]

Ex-servicemen were prominent at the funerals of members of the Crown Forces throughout the period. Following the Ballyturin ambush, near Kilchreest in May of 1921, Divisional Inspector Cruise publicly forwarded a letter of thanks to Mr Montgomery, the honorary secretary of the Galway Ex-Soldiers Federation, noting 'he desired to return thanks through you, to the ex-servicemen who turned out in such great numbers at the funerals yesterday'.[124] Large crowds attended ex-servicemen's celebrations and good humour and order characterised parades and social occasions.[125] In November 1920, at the height of 'the terror', the Galway Ex-Servicemen's Association held their annual armistice parade in front of large crowds of cheering supporters who lined the route in a heavy rainstorm.[126] A band and flag bearers from the 6th Dragoon Guard entered the University quadrangle and forced seventy students and their professors to recite God Save the Queen and three students who refused to remove their hats were publicly flogged.[127] Notices had been placed around the town earlier in the week warning shops to stay shut, 'in memory of the gallant lads who fell for the sake of dear old England and the RIC who were killed by their own countrymen … Anybody that disobeys this order will have no roof over their heads in 24 hours.'[128] Following the procession, 400 ex-servicemen and their families were entertained at a reception at Earls Island army barracks. J.F. Goulding of the Galway Ex-Sailors and Soldier's Federation wrote an open letter to the *Connacht Tribune* claiming that, 'in no other town in the country, could there be a response as was given to the appeal to local people to turn out for the parade'.[129]

Branches of the 'Comrades of the Great War' association, founded to perpetuate the spirit of comradeship that began in the trenches, existed in Galway, along with a very active branch of the Ex-Soldiers and Sailors Federation. Antipathy between republicans and ex-servicemen mirrored the antagonism between nationalists and republicans with both sides engaging in opportunistic violence, with skirmishing rarely going beyond brawling and street fighting in which alcohol was often a factor. In the first months of 1921, however, anti-Sinn Féin literature was posted around Loughrea and Tuam with slogans including, 'Up the Rebels = To Hell with Ireland's Prosperity'.[130]

Violence and the countryside

The brutal logic of state reprisals was initially highly effective in stifling the Volunteers in Galway but the Crown Forces were never fully able to prevent a determined cadre of young fighters from re-emerging in early 1921. As the violence of the independence struggle escalated, the Volunteers faced considerable local opposition, however, and conservative nationalist opinion frequently blamed republicans for the reprisals of the Crown Forces. The condemnation of the Church may have had a limited effect on younger fighters, but to their parents' generation and the wider community, such condemnations were significant. Speaking in Tuam Cathedral, Archbishop

Gilmartin apportioned the blame for the violence of the Crown Forces on both the police and republicans and told his congregation, 'armed resistance to the existing government is unlawful; firstly because there is no chance of success, secondly, the evils of such a course would be much greater than the evils it would try and remedy'.[131] In February 1921, Dr O'Dea, Bishop of Galway, expressed concern for the salvation of the souls of republicans, lest 'they be lost in consequence of the dangers of the recent struggle. We can all see how strong temptations are at present, especially temptations to take life, to injure person or property or take or keep what belongs to others. Yet if men yield to these temptations they fall into sin … so that they may become lost souls.'[132] Archbishop Gilmartin later warned the Volunteers that they had no mandate for their actions from the Irish people and 'secret organisations may prove to be a most dangerous snare that may easily entail excommunication: continue to listen to those who are officially charged with salvation of your souls'.[133] Denouncing the 'downright terrorism' committed in his diocese by the Crown Forces, he castigated:

> The doctrine of hatred, assiduously fostered by politicians during the war has found its last refuge and worst manifestations here. Things have been done in the name of the law which are disgrace to anyone professing the most attenuated form of Christianity, things which, for downright barbarity, have not been exceeded by the Turks or the Red Indians on the war path. The root cause is the British government.[134]

The first six months of 1920 gave rise to a false confidence within the Galway Volunteers that the arrival of the Black and Tans fundamentally shattered. The Crown Forces' campaign, while counter-productive in the long term, in terms of public opinion, was extremely successful in the short term, in hampering the Volunteers' campaign. The Crown Forces were considerably more violent in Galway than elsewhere in Connacht but just why there were so many reprisals in the county is unclear.[135] Joost Augusteijn has highlighted the important role the behaviour of the Crown Forces had on public opinion and noted that 'the poor image of the Crown Forces and in particular the Black and Tans and Auxiliaries, was of course, created by effective Sinn Féin propaganda'.[136] Augusteijn concludes that, while perceptions of British misrule were an important motivation for republican fighters, this image of the Crown Forces was 'fostered by the growing body of historical writing, which painted a very romantic image of an unscrupulous Britain violently oppressing an independent Ireland'.[137] The evidence of this study suggests that far from being passive receivers of republican propaganda, rural communities feared and loathed the Crown Forces due to their sustained campaign of extreme violence against republicans and civilians alike.[138]

The Crown Forces were highly successful in detaining republican suspects and the Brigadier General of the 5th Division reported to his superiors in early December 1920 that practically all known republican leaders in the Galway Brigade area, not currently on the run, had been arrested in the previous six weeks.[139] Active officers, who survived the period, did so by staying on the run and the financial burden for their families of having their homesteads burned was enormous. The war against the Volunteers by the Crown Forces was one of assassination. A significant number of senior republican officers were killed including, Michael Moran, Joseph Howley, Joseph Athy, John O'Hanlon, Louis Darcy, Patrick and Harry Loughnane, Michael Walsh, Patrick Cloonan and John Geoghegan. All of these republican leaders were shot in or near their homes, or while in custody. Only Seán Mulvoy, who was shot dead by an Auxiliary in Galway town, can said to have been 'killed in action' with the vast majority of casualties 'killed while trying to escape'. In contrast to the intelligence operations of the Crown Forces, republican intelligence was haphazard. While one notable informer, Patrick W. Joyce, was revealed through intelligence networks, there were simply not enough reliable channels of formal intelligence and the Volunteers continued to rely on casual sources to gain sporadic information.

The police in Galway acted on intelligence about their victims' whereabouts and, as previously discussed, republicans believed there was collaboration with the local RIC, who possessed crucial knowledge about republican targets. Why civilians such as Thomas McKeever of Dunmore or Hugh Tully of Galway were taken from their beds and shot dead remains unclear. Exactly who was responsible for the killing of civilians will likely remain a mystery; however, regular RIC were clearly crucial in the provision of accurate local knowledge in attacks most likely carried out by the Auxiliaries and Black and Tans. The Crown Forces fought a most effective campaign of terror that instilled paranoia among the community and republicans alike. In this respect, while the killing of republicans stifled the Volunteers, the killing of random civilians was equally effective in generating a climate of fear that eroded support for republican attacks in rural communities lest the community face the certain wrath of state-sanctioned killers.

CHAPTER 7

War of Independence III: Communal Conflict, 1918–22

Few European states in the modern era have been impervious to ethnic conflict; however, even in divided societies, communal conflict cannot be reduced to the common denominator of ethnic or religious ties and there are generally a range of issues involved including class resentment and historical grievance.[1] The experience of the southern Protestant community during the years 1918–23 was undoubtedly negative and accelerated the pre-existing trend of migration to Britain and further afield. In this respect, Donald L. Horowitz has noted that in periods of political upheaval, ethnic tension is often at the root of violence that results in the appropriation of resources and the flight of large numbers of people.[2]

The disestablishment of the Church of Ireland in 1871 was the first in a series of grave blows to the prestige of the Anglican community in Ireland as incremental changes towards increasingly democratic government began an unassailable encroachment upon the privileges of the minority community. In the early decades of the twentieth century, the Anglican community, despite their small numbers, possessed disproportionate economic and social influence. T.P. O'Neill has argued, 'their [the Anglican Community's] system had existed for so long that they feared any upset to it. Institutions like the Bank of Ireland had been almost exclusively theirs. Promotion opened to wider sections of the community would upset existing balances.'[3] As Miriam Moffitt has pointed out, in terms of popular nationalist movements such as the Land League and the United Irish League (UIL), Protestants in the twenty-six counties were faced with an inherent dilemma: 'was it in their best interests to support their Catholic neighbours, showing solidarity within their social class, or were they better served by aligning themselves with landlords, thereby demonstrating a religious cohesion?'[4] As Moffitt has argued, the four decades before the revolution represented a series of humiliations for the Church of Ireland and Protestants were less likely to be drawn to the agendas of the nationalist movement; 'in distancing themselves from nationalist movements, they operated in line with accepted mores of their social and religious communities'.[5] A similar scenario presented itself during the revolutionary period, and as T. P. O'Neill has pointed out, in relation to the revival of nationalist opinion following the 1916 Rising, 'They [Anglicans] had little or no part in the resurgence which followed: in the rise of Sinn Féin, in the War of Independence, in the founding of Dáil Éireann.'[6]

In periods of social and political upheaval, group identity is heightened as competition for scare values and material goods propels people increasingly to view themselves as members of distinct groups whose interests conflict with those of perceived rival groups, and factors such as historical dispossession fuel the resurgence of lingering resentment. The revolutionary period was one of deep uncertainty for Protestants in the twenty-six counties and social and political upheaval contributed to Protestant flight. Enda Delaney has noted that, during the years 1911–26, the Anglican community in the twenty-six counties fell by 34 per cent, the Presbyterian community by 29 per cent and the Methodist community by 35 per cent.[7] While part of this trend can be explained by the uncertainty surrounding the establishment of the Free State and the withdrawal of the British military and sections of the old civil service, violence, or more pertinently, the fear of violence among the Protestant community cannot be ignored as a contributing factor.

The degree to which sectarianism motivated the republican movement remains one of the most controversial aspects of the Irish revolution. As we have seen, while agrarian unrest was inherently facilitated by political upheaval, uncertainty facilitated the legitimisation of sectarian resentment with a study of west Cork leading Peter Hart to conclude that sectarianism was 'embedded in the vocabulary and syntax of the revolution'.[8] In relation of the West of Ireland, Hart has asserted that a campaign of ethnic cleansing took place in many parts of the country, including the east Galway countryside. Noting the 'dreary steeples of Ballinasloe', he concluded, 'as revolutionary violence spiralled upwards, more and more of its victims were civilians and more and more of them were Protestant'.[9] Hart's conclusions have proven controversial, however, and Brian Hanley has asserted, 'there was no attempt at "genocide" perpetrated against Protestants during the Irish Revolution, nor any "ethnic cleansing" and these terms should be banished from serious discussion on the matter'.[10]

Hart's assertion in relation to ethnic cleansing in Galway is highly problematic. The vast majority of the Protestant community was not intimidated during the period and there is no evidence of any systematic attempt at persecution of any social group. The Volunteers did not target the Protestant community and the three alleged informers who were shot, Patrick Joyce, Tom Morris and Thomas Hannon were Catholics. There was undoubtedly a resurgence of sectarian ill feeling among elements of the Catholic community; however, sectarian resentment was fomented by a combination of historical and economic resentment over access to land and resources. In Ballinasloe town and its hinterland, including the estate of Lord Ashtown at Woodlawn, Aughrim, Ahascragh and Kilconnell, some Protestants were the subject of intimidation that resulted in families leaving the district. Intimidation was a function of the wider breakdown of law and order and a fracturing of the authority of the Volunteers after the conclusion of the War of Independence. In this respect, sectarian harassment was carried out by members of the wider community rather than active Volunteer units. The nature of the resentment against certain Protestant families in these districts needs to be coherently examined and the complexity of the motives behind attacks identified if we are to avoid simplistic interpretations of complex historical grievances.

A people apart: the Protestant community

As outlined in Table 6, Protestant flight from County Galway had been ongoing since the 1860s and the decline of the minority community was well established in the decades before the rise of militant republicanism. From a figure of 8,202 members of the Church of Ireland in 1861, less than half that number, just 3,544 members, lived in the county by 1911. Decline was relatively steady over the previous fifty years with a reduction of 735 in the decade between 1861 and 1871 and 605 between 1871 and 1881. Protestant flight increased dramatically during the 1880s, however, with a decline of 1,522 between 1881 and 1891, before stabilising to a level of 938 between 1891 and 1901 and 858 between 1901 and 1911.[11]

Small numbers of isolated Protestant families were scattered across the county with more substantial Protestant communities concentrated in the hinterland between Ballinasloe and Portumna and in the towns of Galway and Ballinasloe, and to a lesser extent, Tuam. Anglicans constituted the overwhelming majority of the Protestant community with only 495 Presbyterians and 152 Methodists on the 1911 census. The much smaller Presbyterian community declined at a far less dramatic rate than Anglicans during the same period, from a figure of 581 in 1861 to 495 in 1911, a drop of less than a hundred members over a fifty-year period. As we shall see, the smaller rate of decline among Presbyterians reflected their role in the mercantile sector and the professions,

TABLE 6
Religious affiliations in Galway, 1861–1911

	Catholics	Anglicans	Presbyterians	Methodists
1861	263,187	8,202	881	406
1871	241,181	7,487	615	319
1881	234,088	6,862	642	324
1891	208,364	5,340	628	271
1901	187,220	4,402	616	186
1911	177,920	3,544	495	152

Source: Table XXIX: Comparative View of the Number and Percentage of Persons Belonging to Each Religious Profession in the County of Galway as Constituted at Each Census from 1861 to 1911: *Census Returns for Ireland, 1911, Showing Area … Province of Connaught, County of Galway,* p. 163, H.C., 1913 (Cd.; 6052, 6052-I, 6052-II, 6052-III, 6052-IV, 6052-V), cxvii, p.1.

which, unlike the larger Anglican community, were relatively unaffected by changes to the land tenure system brought about by decades of land reform. There were only a very small number of Presbyterian farmers listed in the 1911 census figures and the degree to which they retained strong links with counties of origin other than Galway is remarkable. Of the eighteen Presbyterian farmers listed, only two were actually born in Galway with the majority born in either Ulster or Scotland.[12]

The origins and economic profile of the small Protestant communities in Galway emerged from distinct historical processes. In terms of urban Protestants, there was a small but long-established Protestant community in Galway town. This largely Anglican community was well integrated in the town's civil and social establishment, in contrast to the Protestant community of more recent origin in Ballinasloe, which was a mixture of Presbyterians and Anglicans, largely of northern origin who tended to be involved in the mercantile sector and the professions. In contrast to the Anglican community in Galway town, rural Protestant families were, to a significant extent, socially outside the common culture of the wider Catholic community and tended to be centred around the big houses and landed estates of established Protestant land-owning families. The rural Protestant community represented a privileged minority of large landowners of long standing, their employees and those who leased land from them.[13]

Established Protestant landowning families in Galway such as the Le Poer Trenchs of Woodlawn, the Lopdells of Athenry, the Shawe-Taylors of

Ardrahan and Athenry, the Dillons and Mahons of Ahascragh and the Dalys of Raford were viewed unsympathetically in the popular affections of the wider community. This established group was bolstered after 1850 by a small but influential tier of landowners who bought large estates from the encumbered estates courts including, the Berridges of Ballynahinch and the Waithmans of Merlin Park.[14] Many of the older Galway families, such as the Dalys, the Brownes and the Blakes, constituted wide networks of related families who owned land in various parts of the county, and despite the vast changes wrought by decades of land reform, were still a considerable economic force. Among this diverse group, Protestant landed families who held strong unionist views, such as the Le Poer Trenchs of Woodlawn, the Dillons of Clonbrock and the Mahons of Ahascragh were traditionally reluctant to employ Catholics in their households. In 1911, the most prominent unionist family in the county, the Dillons of Clonbrock, employed eleven servants in their household, all of whom were Protestant and none of whom were born in Galway.[15] Protestant landowners in Galway were often forced to go to considerable lengths to find suitable Protestant employees and William Henry Mahon's cook was from Strabane, his chauffeur was Scottish and his gardener was from Wicklow.[16]

Lord Ashtown of Woodlawn was particularly resented by the Catholic community for importing Protestant workers onto his estate in place of Catholic families who he sacked during an earlier dispute.[17] Hostility to Protestant workers on his estate during the period 1920–3 was fuelled by lingering economic grievance rather than specifically religious and political resentment.[18] There was a relatively large self-contained community of migrant Protestant workers working on his estate in 1911 with sixty-one members of the Anglican and Presbyterian community living in Woodlawn.[19] Ashtown's four gamekeepers were Protestants from Cork, Offaly, Cavan and Wales;[20] likewise, his fourteen household servants were Anglicans, six of whom were English and three of whom were from Ulster;[21] the Woodlawn post office was run by a Protestant family, the Sheirsons, and prized jobs as grooms, stewards and herdsmen were held by Protestants from England and other parts of Ireland.

The steady decline in the Anglican community over the previous fifty years was reflected in the dwindling congregations in rural Anglican parishes. The Ballymacward Anglican parish in north-east Galway had twenty-three vestrymen in 1873, including three of the county's most prominent landowners, Thomas Mahon, Earl Clancarty and Charles Persse, yet, by 1903 the register of vestrymen had declined to half of the 1873 level with only twelve members.[22] Ten years later, the parish had only three registered vestrymen and from 1913 to 1920, just three families constituted the congregation. This demographic trend continued into the opening decades of the twentieth century, and in the rural Kilmacduagh parish in south-west Galway, there were twenty baptisms between 1900 and 1909, but only twelve between 1910 and 1919, comprising the Spink, Vereker, Leggett, Spragg and Magge families, all of whom lived on the Lough Cutra estate.[23]

The relatively high-profile nature of the Anglican community did not generate significant overt hostility in Galway town. In contrast to the rural Anglican community centred around big houses, the longstanding urban Protestant community was well integrated into the wider community, and despite their relatively small numbers, they occupied prominent positions of civil authority. In 1911, Thomas Lawson was the manager of the Bank of Ireland; William Binns was the Council's chief engineer; Walter Seymour was secretary of the Urban Council; Joseph Young was a member of the Board of Guardians and a leading employer; Leslie Edmunds was chief inspector for the Congested Districts Board (CDB); Charles Radford was chief officer of the Coast Guard; George Brownell was principal light keeper for the Commission of Public Lights; James MacCullagh was medical inspector for the Local Government Board; and William Cornwall held the principal position in the Post Office.[24]

Catholic businesses dominated the mercantile sector of Galway town but there were a number of prominent Protestant-owned businesses including, Dillon's Jewellers, Young's mineral water plant and Moon's department store. The senior ranks of the military and police were dominated by members of the Church of Ireland, and during the War of Independence, the county's successive Royal Irish Constabulary (RIC) County Inspectors, George Bennet Heard, George Bedell Ruttledge, George Lewis Hildebrand and Richard Francis Cruise were all Anglicans. Renmore barracks was the home of the Connaught Rangers and leading officers Colonel H. D. Chaimer and H.C. Bowles were high-profile figures in the upper tiers of the social life of the town.

The demographic decline experienced by rural Protestant communities during the period was replicated in urban parishes, but was somewhat less dramatic, reflecting the professional, commercial and civic occupations of urban Protestants, who were less affected by the dramatic changes to the land tenure system. The congregation at St Nicholas's Parish in Galway town was declining for several decades before independence, and while there were 121 baptisms between 1900 and 1909, this declined to just 83 between 1910 and 1919, with only 30 born between 1920 and 1930.[25] The professions listed for the fathers of the eighty-three children baptised in St Nicholas's, from 1910 to 1919, offer a profile of the Anglican community in Galway town.[26] Of the fifty-nine heads of families listed, the most common professions were the military, navy and police.[27] Ten members of the RIC were represented, six of whom were constables, along with three sergeants and one RIC pensioner. In terms of the military, there were thirteen members of the navy and army represented, the majority of whom were sergeants in the Connaught Rangers. In terms of the social profile of the remaining members of the congregation, the small number of unskilled or manual workers is notable.

Outside Galway town, the most significant concentration of Galway Protestants was in Ballinasloe town with 227 members of the Church of Ireland, ninety-five Presbyterians and forty-three Methodists registered as living in the urban electoral district in the 1911 census.[28] Ballinasloe was a typical 'garrison town' and the major employer was the county asylum that employed over 140 people. A similar connection with counties of origin outside Galway is apparent in the case of Ballinasloe Protestants and of the Church of Ireland population living in the urban electoral district; 121, or just over half the community, were born outside the county.[29] A similar picture of migration into the town is evident within the Presbyterian community with fifty-five, or well over half the community, born outside Galway. In the Methodist community, the pattern is repeated with twenty-one of the forty-three members on the 1911 census recorded as being born outside Galway.[30] While the Church of Ireland community tended to migrate from a range of counties, the Presbyterian community tended to migrate from the north and from Scotland, with ten Presbyterians born in County Monaghan alone.

In 1911, Protestants occupied positions of influence in Ballinasloe. Edward Rothwell was clerk of the Petty Sessions, Elliot Armstrong was Justice of the Peace and James Elder was chairman of the Board of Guardians. One significant difference between the Protestant communities in Ballinasloe and Galway town was the large number of merchants and those involved in trade in Ballinasloe. The commercial life of the town included large Protestant firms and the combined drapers, grocers and furniture stores of the Rothwell, Elder, Nixon and Moffett families were among the largest retail outlets in the west of Ireland. Of these prominent business owners, James Nixon, who owned a drapery business, was a Methodist and originally from Cavan and Joseph Moffett, also a draper, was a Presbyterian from Monaghan.[31]

The 1911 census lists over seventy Protestants working in merchant businesses in Ballinasloe town, including owners and employees of drapers, general stores, grocers, bakers, dress makers, bootmakers, chemists and others, including the post office, which employed Protestants only. Of this group, only twenty-three listed their county of origin as Galway, with the largest group, eighteen, listing a county of origin in Ulster. When one analyses the counties of origin of a group of thirty employers or senior employees involved in trade in the town, only ten were born in Galway with the majority of the remainder born in Ulster, Britain or the midlands. When one examines the census returns of the forty-three younger employees working in these businesses, a similar pattern is revealed. Of this larger group of forty-three employees, only thirteen were born in Galway, and a similar spread of counties of origin as amongst their employers is evident, with young apprentices, assistants and managers coming from the north of Ireland, Leitrim and the midlands for jobs in firms owned by co-religionists. We can conclude from this data that Protestant merchants and traders in Ballinasloe, the majority of whom had moved to the town to go into business, brought young employees from their own counties of origin for highly sought after positions in trade. As we shall see, economic resentment was to be an important factor in generating hostility towards the Protestant community during the lawlessness that erupted later in the period.

Protestants and politics

Political unionism in Galway during the revolutionary period was elitist, ineffectual and resolutely Anglican.[32] The Galway branch of the Irish Unionist Alliance was revived in 1911 during the impending resolution of the Home Rule Bill but only one public meeting was organised.[33] The meeting was held in the Railway Hotel in Eyre Square and was attended by Protestant landowners from the east of the county and arranged in response to the leadership of the Unionist Alliance's memorandum that all county boards organise at least one public demonstration against Home Rule.[34] The movement was technically active from 1911 until 1914, but became dormant again for five years before being temporarily revived in 1919.[35] Active membership was confined to an elite coterie of the county's landed families with Lord Clonbrock, W.J. Waithman and W.H. Mahon acting as chairman, vice-chairman and secretary. The association met irregularly, with fewer than ten members attending occasional private meetings in the Railway Hotel, Athenry. The Galway Landowners Association held its meetings alongside the Irish Unionist Alliance (IUA) gatherings, as most members of the former group were also members of the latter.[36]

The Galway Unionist Alliance remained secretive due to the hostility their efforts aroused among the broader community and this extended to keeping the names of members and local subscribers private. In terms of broadening the appeal of the movement, the IUA in Galway made little effort to recruit and no obvious attempt was made to enlist the Protestant farming community in the Ballinasloe district or the considerable Protestant urban professional community in the towns of Ballinasloe, Tuam and Galway. The exception to this trend was their initial courting of Church of Ireland ministers, twelve of whom were contacted by W.H. Mahon in 1912 to elicit support for the revival of the Association.[37] Throughout the period, there were only two prominent Catholic members of the organisation. Sir Henry Grattan Bellew failed to renew his membership after the initial revival of the movement in 1912. James McDermott was active throughout the period and was discussed as a potential delegate to the national organisation in 1914 with Lord Clonbrock promoting his candidacy on the basis that 'it would be an advantage to get an R.C. [Roman Catholic] to do it'.[38] The movement's dismal attempt to generate funds through an annual subscription proved an embarrassment, with Clonbrock informing his colleagues in 1911, 'with the exception of the first ten members, I'm afraid no subscriptions will be available'.[39]

The organisation's initial activity centred around the distribution of an anti-Home Rule pledge which the IUA asked all county committees to facilitate. The Galway executive duly wrote to the county's leading Protestant's asking for their support. Most landowners were unwilling to ask their workmen to sign the petition and James O'Hara wrote that several Protestants in his district were afraid to sign the pledge, 'in case they might suffer for doing so'.[40] Seymour Ellis wrote, 'I regret I cannot sign the memorial, as I live in an isolated part of the country and for fifty years my family and I have suffered so very much because of our political opinions and those of the majority of the people did not always agree, that it may be better now that I should not take part in politics when the consequences would be further persecution.'[41] Lord Gough of Lough Cutra told the committee, 'It would be as much as their life would be worth to sign anything ... this is a hopeless corner of the world, one can only keep going by not raising controversial questions.'[42] James MacDermott, the organisation's only prominent Catholic, wrote, 'the people are utter cowards'.[43]

A small loyalist constituency existed on the fringes of the broader Protestant community and the Marquis Clanricarde's land agent, Edward Shaw-Tener, noted that the introduction of northern planters on his estate had 'added between farmers and employees over forty unionist voters to the loyal population'.[44] One of these men, James Jackson, advised the association, 'this [home rule crisis] will not end without the guns and the sooner the better'.[45] The Clanricarde planters were brought to Galway by their landlord at the end of the nineteenth century from Ulster. Of the twenty-eight planters who remained on the estate in 1908, all bar one were Protestants.[46] The association wrote to their members asking if there was any possibility of a violent backlash against

Protestants in their districts in the advent of Home Rule not being passed, and of the eighteen respondents, only two expressed fears about retaliation.[47] Mahon's enquiries to all members regarding the advisability of the creation of a Protestant volunteer force and the importation of arms to protect Protestants was rejected by all but two respondents.[48]

Economic resentment over Protestant domination of the commercial life in the town of Ballinasloe became a catalyst for latent sectarianism to develop into intimidation during the War of Independence and the conscription crisis proved to be the trigger. In May 1918, the Ballinasloe Board of Guardians debated the statement of the Presbyterian Assembly of Ireland in 1918 which had supported a degree of conscription for Ireland and a resolution condemning the local Protestant community for their perceived support for their Church leaders' stance was passed.[49] Several statements from nationalist representatives reflected deep hostility towards local Protestants and the community was publicly threatened with retaliation should conscription be enforced. A councillor informed the Board of Guardians:

> You have people at home in Ballinasloe refusing to sign against conscription. And in fact, advocating that the conscription Act should be enforced. I have it on the utmost reliable authority that the majority of Ballinasloe Presbyterians are supporting conscription. They are only fifteen families altogether but little or much, they made well by their connection with the Ballinasloe people. We will know what to say and what to do when the time comes.

> Every single one of these families has thrived, got rich and was protected and trusted in every way by the people of Ballinasloe. They were treated as our own brothers and here is their gratitude and compensation. I think we ought to strongly condemn the Ballinasloe Presbyterians as well as the Belfast people. They have motor cars, land and horses now which they had not when they first got here ... We should know who is for us and who is against us. The time will come when we will defeat this crisis and we will be able to show those people what way and manner we look on their conduct. The records of the conscription pledge should be kept, so afterwards we will know who's who.[50]

Following the conscription crisis, resentment appears to have died down and there is no evidence that any intimidation took place in the district. For nationalists of all hues, loyalist violence in Belfast, Lurgan and Banbridge in July

1920, however, gave added impetus to the ongoing 'Belfast boycott' with local committees formed and public meetings held across the country to respond to the northern crisis. Protestant communities in the twenty-six counties came under pressure to show their support for the beleaguered Catholic community in the north-east publicly. The boycott posed a dilemma for Protestant communities outside the north-east with many public bodies publicly calling for Protestant traders and merchants to condemn the violence and cease trading with their Belfast co-religionists.[51] Much of the condemnation by Protestant traders, clergymen and politicians emanated from a mixture of genuine distaste for loyalist violence and practical considerations for their own vulnerability.

At the Galway urban council in August 1920, a motion was proposed that the town's employers should be asked to sack their Protestant workers in retaliation for the Belfast riots; however, the proposal was dismissed and a resolution supporting the Belfast boycott was endorsed.[52] The following month the urban council called upon all traders in the town to refuse to handle goods from Belfast should they arrive in the city and the Volunteers expelled a representative from a Belfast drapery firm in early September. A labour representative suggested that the Urban District Council should not trade with local Protestants who had made no protest against the loyalist violence, but his suggestion was over-ruled by a Sinn Féin representative who 'depreciated this attitude as an imitation of the northern savagery which they should take every precaution to guard against'.[53]

In September 1920, a member of the Tuam Board of Guardians asked, 'why the Protestants of the west, who never got insult from a Catholic majority because of creed, did not speak out and condemn the actions of their co-religionists in the north. The Protestants of the west are absolutely silent.'[54] In response, Edmund Hill wrote to the *Connacht Tribune* suggesting that 'the Protestants of Galway come together and publicly denounce the sectarian acts being carried out in Belfast'.[55] The paper welcomed the sentiments, noting that 'there is little likelihood that anything of this nature will ever blight the lives of people who have always lived on good terms with one another'. The Protestant community responded to Hill's suggestion, and at a subsequent meeting of various Protestant denominations, a resolution was passed 'condemning the victimisation and intimidation of Roman Catholics that is taking place at the current time in the north of Ireland and no provocation caused by other outrages could justify such a policy. At all times the most friendly relationship and goodwill have been extended to us by the Roman Catholic community in this town and district. Religious intoleration is unknown in this part of Ireland.'[56] In Ballinasloe, the local Protestant community also responded and

James Elder presided at a meeting in Ballinasloe to devise a means of helping Belfast Catholics who had been driven from their homes and a subscription fund set up.[57] Sectarian tension remained bubbling under the surface and erupted into street fighting in August 1920 with rival groups of young men clashing on the streets. The Sinn Féin-backed *Galway Express* subsequently gloated, 'the orange ascendancy gang have showed their bigotry by cursing the Pope in the streets, some today have a colour other than orange on their skulls'.[58]

The collapse of deference

The Protestant experience of revolution cannot be analysed in isolation from the wave of agrarianism that swept the county in the first half of 1920. As agrarian unrest persisted, it posed serious questions for the republican leadership as the movement increasingly sought to assume the mantle of legitimate protectors of law and order. With a number of prominent Protestant landowners among the largest graziers in east Galway, Protestants were disproportionately the victims of agrarian campaigns; however, those targeted were overwhelmingly Catholics and nationalist.

Land arbitration courts had been active since early 1918; however, they were incapable of coping with the sheer scale of unrest. Volunteer John Feehan recalled, 'Wholesale sheep stealing was prevalent throughout Connemara at this time and the RIC were taking no action. We made a roundup of the Twelve Pins with a force of Volunteers and farmers concerned, and collected the sheep into one area where the farmers could collect their stolen sheep.'[59] Volunteer Thomas Mannion recalled that in North Galway, 'Some disputes between neighbours never went into the courts but were settled by the Volunteers. Such cases still hold good. The people then had a very great regard for the sincerity of the Volunteers and sank their small differences out of respect for them.'[60] Volunteer Patrick Glynn noted, 'We always endeavoured to get disputing parties to settle their difference between themselves, telling them that if they failed to reach agreement to come back again. They usually reached agreement. We were not inclined to fine anybody. We tried to act sensibly and reasonably in those cases and to get the opposing parties to do likewise.'[61] Volunteer Thomas Keely recalled that in south Galway, 'many of the cases of agrarian trouble were settled by the Volunteers, apart from the Dáil Éireann courts. Cases occurred in which people, taking advantage of the troubled state of the country broke down farm fences with a view to getting portions of land. The volunteers investigated those cases, found the parties responsible for breaking down the fences and made them repair them.'[62]

The tenants on the Blake estate at Menlo had been agitating for the division of the estate demense for some time when James Ward was shot dead at the gate lodge, where he was employed as a herdsman, on 6 February 1920.[63] The agitation over the Menlo Woods encapsulated the complexities that land agitation could generate for the republican movement. For some time, Menlo Demesne had been the subject of a violent agitation to force Thomas Blake to sell his land to the Estates Commissioners. Following the shooting of Ward, it was reported that, 'feeling against him was imputed to his continued employment with the landlord, whose retention of the land is held to be an injustice'.[64] Members of the Volunteers in the Castlegar district may have been involved in the agitation and Brian Molloy was one of Galway's most committed Volunteer officers. His Volunteer company in Castlegar was one of the best organised and most committed in the county, and while the agitation was ongoing, Molloy and his men carried out attacks on the police at Oranmore and Loughgeorge. The agitation became problematic for Sinn Féin in 1920 when the Galway Council purchased part of the demesne. When a delegation from the council arrived in Menlo they were greeted by angry agitators armed with ash plants who made their feelings abundantly clear that the land should be divided among the tenants rather than the council. In a dramatic change of heart, a decision was taken at a meeting of the Galway Urban Council in April 1920 not to proceed with the purchase, and William Flaherty, a former labour representative, commented, 'buy it today and get a bullet tomorrow'.[65] The fact that the Menlo case wasn't brought before a Sinn Féin court even though the agitation involved their members, illustrates the power a strong local republican leader could command.

The problem in establishing culpability was also an issue in the killing of Athenry landlord, Frank Shawe-Taylor, shot dead on the morning of 3 March 1920. As discussed previously, Shawe-Taylor had been at the centre of a long running boycott to compel him to sell his farm. He was shot at point-blank range as he sat in his car, with the road in front of his estate blocked with a felled tree. As in the Menlo killing, several men were arrested but subsequently released due to lack of evidence.[66] The Volunteers were not all agrarian agitators and vice versa, but overlaps existed in the Athenry district and neither the Volunteers nor Sinn Féin made a public condemnation of the killing.

In the north of the county, Martin Cullinane, a small farmer, was killed when armed men with blackened faces raided the home of a neighbour at Ardskamore, Corofin, on the night of 4 March 1920.[67] Cullinane was shot by a group of up to fifteen intruders who were searching his house for a shotgun they believed was concealed. Volunteer Dick Conway recalled that in his district of Sylane in north Galway in 1919, of the twenty shotguns collected by the Volunteers 'only one was handed over in good grace'.[68] Noting that twenty-two houses were raided and fifteen shotguns taken by masked men in the Loughrea, Athenry and Portumna areas in January 1920, the police had 'no doubt that the raids were organised by Frank Fahy MP, who was down here previous to the raids. They all took place in his division.'[69] The Volunteers asked people to voluntarily hand over arms to them, rather than the police and the accuracy of the Volunteers' intelligence is borne out by the fact that, in fifteen of the twenty-two homes visited, they successfully retrieved weapons.[70]

In the early months of 1920, agitation was concentrated in the southeast of the county and centred on the Kilconnell–Ahascragh–Woodlawn districts. Over previous months, the *Galway Express* claimed that 300,000 acres had been cleared of stock with 30,000 sheep and cattle dispersed, while the paper printed a list of twenty-nine landowners who had been targeted.[71] Over the previous weeks, deputations of tenant farmers visited many of the major landowners in the district including William Persse at Kilchreest, Charles O'Hara-Trench at Clonfert and Lord Ashtown at Woodlawn, asking them to give up grazing lands to the Estates Commissioners.[72] At the end of March, all of Lord Ashtown's stock, located in the countryside around the village of Kilconnell, was cleared in one night in a vast drive that saw many animals painted in the national colours. By early April, with the annual yearly auctions for land approaching, all but one of Lord Ashtown's graziers had reportedly agreed to sell up their interest in their holdings, leaving the landlord with no one to lease land to.[73]

In early April, amid the renewed wave of unrest, an extraordinary conference of landowners and tenants' representatives was held in Hayden's Hotel in Ballinasloe. The impetus for the conference was the popular belief that much of the land owned by the CDB in southeast Galway was going to be used by the government to resettle ex-soldiers who had fought in the War.[74] The people, the *Galway Express* claimed, saw that peaceful means were useless and 'moderate persuasion' needed to be applied.[75] From the tenants' perspective, the conference was a success with thirteen landowners coming to agreements with a solicitor who negotiated on their behalf. The success of the conference demonstrated the crucial juncture that had been reached in the east Galway countryside and neither the republican movement nor the police were capable of impeding it.

The April conference agreed on a range of issues concerning mechanisms to resolve and administer disputes, which Sinn Féin would administer and the Volunteers enforce. Issues of court procedure, fees and expenses were codified and an organisational structure for the county agreed. A more sophisticated arbitration system emerged based on the ten poor law divisions in the county, with fifteen arbitrators selected for every division and at least one priest to be included on each.[76] A quorum of three representatives from the panel was deemed necessary and every court was to have jurisdiction over three parishes at a minimum.[77]

From early 1920 onwards, arbitration courts were held in the towns of Portumna, Loughrea and Ballinasloe. The courts were held in hotels and struggled to accommodate the numbers who wished to attend. Sessions were attended by diverse sections of society with landlords, Protestant rectors, former MP William Duffy and professed loyalists, such as the Duc Du Stacpole among those attending. Following the expansion of the courts, police reports testified to their widespread success and acceptance by all sections of the population and they led directly to the collapse of the Crown assizes which ceased to function until the winter of 1920. The Galway assizes collapsed in July and no jurors could be found to deal with cases, as plaintiffs and defendants chose to take their cases to the new Sinn Féin courts.[78]

The wave of agitation that gripped parts of the east of the county for five months receded in May as both large and small farmers began to bring their cases to the arbitration courts. The social control that Sinn Féin sought, and which it looked highly unlikely that it would be able to command, was restored and the party could present itself as legitimate guardians of law and order. From proclaiming 'Hail Russia' just a few months previously, the Sinn Féin controlled *Galway Express* now denounced 'Bolshevism by manly men' as agrarian violence was proclaimed intolerable and treasonable. In an editorial entitled, 'The Lowering of an Ideal', the paper decried, 'the men of the west have wrapped the green flag around them and gone forth to conquer land. We cannot agree that the means used by our young men are honourable in every case.'[79] The Volunteers regularly imprisoned people accused of a range of criminal acts or for perceived acts of social deviance. Theft was the most common reason, and in such cases, men were tried before a republican court and imprisoned in makeshift cells in abandoned houses guarded by the Volunteers.

Settling old scores

Bitterness towards members of the Protestant community escalated into violent hostility following the Volunteers' truce with the Crown Forces in 1921 and was facilitated by the uncertainty which the period between the ending of the War of Independence and the founding of the new state generated. In this context, it was the collapse of both the Volunteers' authority and the disestablishment of the RIC which fostered an unprecedented level of lawlessness that encouraged long-simmering resentments to erupt into violent recrimination. As Fergus Campbell and Terence Dooley have outlined, the level of intimidation of landowners in rural areas across east Galway throughout the years 1920, 1922 and 1923 was considerable.[80] Lawlessness took a number of forms from July 1921 onwards including revenge attacks against ex-members of the RIC, agrarian violence against landlords and large landowners and their employees, and non-political, opportunistic violence including robberies. Hostility towards ordinary members of the Protestant community remained uncoordinated and part of a wider social phenomenon.

There were cases of extreme violence, and in April 1922, Conor O'Malley was killed during a raid on a delivery van carrying eggs in the Skehana district in north Galway. O'Malley was shot dead by five masked assailants and his van burned out. Two female delivery girls were unharmed and the motive for the killing is unclear.[81] Catholic landowner John Blake, of Brooklawn in the north Galway district of Kilconly, was shot and wounded by three assailants in August 1922. He had been the centre of a long-running agrarian dispute to force him to sell his grazing land for division among his tenants.[82] Catholic landowner Walter Joyce was shot dead in similar circumstances near Mountbellew in north Galway on 9 January 1923.[83] Joyce was a justice of the peace and a member of the grand jury. Ordinary people could also become the victims of lawlessness, and a young farmer, John Fahy of Aughrim, was shot dead during the same week as Joyce was killed.[84] As these shootings demonstrate, even at the height of the lawlessness and agrarian violence, one's religion counted for little where land was coveted.

Violence against ex-RIC escalated during the slide into Civil War. On 15 March 1922, two ex-RIC men, Sergeant Gibbons of Westport and Sergeant Gilmartin, Oughterard, along with Patrick Cassidy, a farmer and former official of the CDB from Mayo, were shot dead in a co-ordinated attack carried out by four unknown gunmen at St Brides Home, Galway. Their killers allegedly told their victims to say an act of contrition before shooting them in the head and abdomen.[85] Cassidy was recovering from gunshot wounds after being shot earlier in the month and a third RIC man, Constable Patrick McGloin of Sligo, survived the attacks but sustained severe wounds. During the previous month, an attempt had been made to shoot Sergeant Keane in Prospect Hill, Galway town, with the gunmen wounding his wife after firing through his front door.[86] In June, the homes of a number of former RIC were attacked with gunfire in Loughrea and Athenry, ex-sergeant John Kelly was kidnapped, and a number of men ordered to leave the district.[87] During the same month, all former members of the RIC in Ballinasloe town were visited by masked men with two ex-constables, James Tapley and William Horan, shot and wounded.[88] There were a total of thirty-five claims for compensation by ex-RIC men in Galway, lodged with the British government, for severe distress caused by intimidation from July 1921 onwards with nine police employees from the Ballinasloe district applying for help to relocate abroad.[89]

Growing lawlessness coalesced with escalating political hostility towards the Protestant community in Ballinasloe. In April 1922, a resolution signed by the entire Ballinasloe Rural District Council, comprising both nationalist and republican representatives:

> Desired to bring under the notice of the public … the failure of non-Catholics in Ballinasloe and District to take any action in connection with the atrocities in Belfast; That the non-Catholics here, as in other parts of Ireland, are amongst the most prosperous in the community; It is time a Conference of the leading people of Southern Ireland was held with a view to making an exchange of the Catholic Workers on Belfast for some of the large non-Catholic landowners and businessmen, or as an alternative that families be migrated from Belfast and billeted on non-Catholic families outside the Six County Area, as this seems to be the only remedy to avoid the possible extinction of the Northern Catholics.[90]

The resolution was technically incorrect in asserting that the Protestant community had done nothing to help Catholics in the north and, as has been previously discussed, at least one public meeting was organised by Protestants in the town. In June, the hostility towards the minority community escalated and incidents of low-level violence took place that lasted for several weeks and resulted in a number of Protestant families leaving the district. In relation to the intimidation, the *Church of Ireland Gazette* reported in June:

> The campaign is carried out in the night time by unnamed persons who give no reason for their actions. The system which usually follows is, at first, the dispatch of an anonymous letter giving the recipient so many days or hours to clear out. If this notice is disregarded, bullets are fired at night through his windows, bombs are thrown at his house or his house is burned down … the list of those prescribed is added to constantly and every Protestant is simply waiting for their turn to come.[91]

Shots were fired into several Protestant homes and premises and the *Irish Times* reported that a Mr Salter, a shop manager, Mr Swan, an insurance agent, Mrs Rezin, a widow, Mr Davidson, a railway linesman, and the town's stationmaster, Mr Crawford, were among those targeted.[92] On 19 July, the Protestant church at the nearby village of Ahascragh was damaged in an arson attack. The attacks were vigorously condemned by the Catholic clergy and the chairman of a meeting of local Catholics, Revd P.J. Shanagher, told the *Irish Times*, 'it was the climax to many crimes, including public and private robberies, previously committed in the parish, not one of which would go unavenged by God'.[93] The community responded in Ahascragh and a committee of local Catholics passed a resolution 'that we the Catholic people of Ahascragh, and adjoining parish, hereby express our horror and indignation at the unchristian conduct of unchristian individuals who burned the Ahascragh Protestant Church and we beg to offer our profound sympathy to Revd. Mr Thompson and every member of his congregation, with all of whom we have lived on the most friendly relations'.[94] An anonymous letter to the *Irish Times* from the nearby district of Clonfert subsequently claimed that 'many of us in the west have of late lived the life of the hunted'.[95]

In respect of rural Protestants in the Ballinasloe hinterland, a number of families were targeted during the period. Claiming compensation for intimidation due to his political beliefs, Archdeacon Richard Shannon of Aughrim told the authorities that 'it was well known that Protestants were loyal to the crown'.[96] Likewise, Elizabeth Walshe claimed that in Ballinasloe 'we were well known to be loyalists and helpers of the loyalist cause'.[97] Albert Barrett left Ballinasloe for Canada 'as men in my position who are loyalists are given fair play and can hold to their principles'.[98] In the Kilconnell district, Edward Thompson claimed 'all the families about, except the few Protestants, were undoubtedly republican and anti-British in sympathy'.[99] As previously discussed, Lord Ashtown was a hate figure for his vitriolic condemnations of the UIL, Sinn Féin and manifestations of Irish nationalism generally. As previously discussed, Ashtown's firing of the Catholic workmen on his estate in 1911 and the importation of Protestant workers created deep resentment in the Kilconnell district.[100] Violence on the Woodlawn estate highlights the mingling of economic, political and sectarian resentment which fomented agrarian violence, and distinguishing between agrarian, sectarian and political motives can be complex. In May 1922, the anti-Treaty IRA took over Ashtown's mansion at Woodlawn. A statement was subsequently issued stating the property was 'confiscated to maintain the victims of the orange gunmen who are homeless and starving. In the absence of other resources for this purpose, the executive council has decided that the unionists and Freemasons of the south and west of

Ireland be compelled to supply the needs of the refugees.'[101] Ashtown had fled the estate several years earlier, and on 7 June, the school he maintained on the estate was burned down.[102] He eventually made twenty-two separate claims for compensation under the 1923 Compensation Act.[103]

The Irish Grants Committee paid compensation for political violence inflicted on people due to their loyalty to the state and it was in the claimants' financial interest, therefore, to depict agrarian intimidation as political in character with a large number of claims rejected for this reason. A number of Protestant families who had taken jobs on the Ashtown estate fled the district during the period. Edward Thompson, who was a labourer on the estate, was awarded £150 after he claimed he had to flee the district after taking in RIC members as lodgers and being subsequently boycotted by Catholic neighbours.[104] Frederick Falkiner claimed he fled the estate after his house was fired into and a threatening letter was delivered to his home. He was unable to sell his stock or the land he was leasing and claimed he was forced to pay a ransom for the release of his brother who had been kidnapped.[105] Falkiner's brother, Richard, also claimed a substantial sum of compensation and detailed a litany of attacks on his property and stock. He stated his house was attacked as 'my opinions were very well known and only loyalists suffered victimisation such as I and my family experienced … What enraged them was two union jacks we had in the sitting room, they tore them up and burnt them.'[106] Lord Ashtown's gamekeeper, William Colgan, successfully claimed £560 and stated republicans told him that the reason he had to leave was that 'he was a north Protestant and would not join the Republican army'.[107] A number of other workers on the estate, including Richard Seale, Elizabeth Wilkinson and May Craig received small amounts in compensation for intimidation and theft.[108]

The Irish Grants Committee was empowered to consider financial claims for compensation from individuals in respect of financial loss arising out of an injury in the sense of a wrongful act directed against the claimant on account of their support of the British government prior to the 11 July 1921, the injury being inflicted in the period between 11 July 1921 to May 1923. While most claims involved amounts of less than £200, a number of substantial payments were made to some of the county's largest landowners: Lord Killanin of Spiddal House received £9,600; Dudley Persse of Roxborough House received £5,496; Thomas Lewin of Castlegrove House received £5,275; Charles Lynch Staunton of Clydagh House received £4,500; James Greathead of Lydican Castle received £4,175; Mary Wallscourt of Ardfy Castle received £3,750.[109]

Under the damage to Property Compensation Act 1923, the Free State government also offered compensation to individuals who had suffered at the hands of the revolutionary forces.[110] These claims for damage to property destroyed by the IRA were mainly composed of claims from the owners of big houses and RIC barracks. While many claims were unsuccessful and payments for compensation varied dramatically, the register of claims represents an index of collateral damage inflicted by the IRA during the period. There were 211 claims made for damage to property destroyed in County Galway, compared to 200 for Mayo; 191 for Sligo; 129 for Leitrim; and 61 for Roscommon.[111] The largest claims for compensation in Galway included £22,000 paid to Denis Kirwan for the destruction of Castlehacket House in 1923, over £30,866 paid to Michael H. Burke for the destruction of Ballydugan House near Loughrea in 1922 and £17,000 paid to Lord Killanin for the destruction of Spiddal House in 1923.[112]

A number of claims were made on behalf of Protestant institutions for damage to Church property. The trustees of the Irish Church Missions, an institution dedicated to proselytising Catholics in Connemara, claimed £1,150 for damage to their school and vicarage at Carna and Moyrus, in October and November 1922 respectively, and £6,438 for the destruction of their orphanage at Ballyconree, Clifden in June 1922.[113] The Irish Church Missions were particularly reviled amongst the wider community, and as Miriam Moffitt has explained, the practise known as 'souperism' was widely held in disdain and 'jumpers' were held in particular disregard in west Galway.[114] Revd George Collins claimed £7,500 for the destruction of the Anglican Church at Ahascragh in July 1922 on behalf of the Representative Church Body.[115] The Representative Church Body also claimed £688 for damage to the Anglican Church at Spiddal in July and September 1922 and claims for damage to the Anglican Church at Moyrus in November 1922 were also lodged.[116]

Freemasons were frequently the bogeymen of nationalist and republican rhetoric and while outlandish conspiracy theories abounded, the Freemasons were regarded as a conservative, loyal institution deeply hostile to the forces of the revolution. Alexander Grant received £966 for the destruction of the Masonic hall in Galway in April and in July 1922, and William Lotts received £367 for the destruction of the Masonic Hall at Ballinasloe in July 1922.[117]

Revolution and communal conflict

Amartya Sen has argued that ethnic and religious violence is often 'fomented by the imposition of singular and belligerent identities on gullible people, championed by proficient artisans of terror'.[118] During the revolution in Ireland there was an obvious cultural, economic and political gulf between the Protestant minority and the wider nationalist community. The complexity of motive that generated sectarian hostility reveals multifarious and intensely local, historical grievances over rival claims to access to land and employment, where religion became a function of economic and political resentment and the distinction between political violence, sectarian intimidation, agrarian insurgency and opportunistic crime was frequently blurred.

There was no inherent link between militant republicanism and sectarianism, but an enduring sectarian cleavage between the two communities in Galway was embedded within rural society and the breakdown of civil authority facilitated by the collapse of the RIC and the slide into Civil War facilitated the settling of old scores. In the popular imagination of the poor, Protestants and large landowners could be lumped together as oppressors and revolutionary upheaval provided the opportunity for the poor to turn the tables on their social betters and settle long-standing grudges. In this respect, the southern Protestant experience of revolution conforms to the European experience of migration and social unrest following the First World War. Joshua A. Sanborn has noted that intensely localised murders and 'movements of people' inevitably comprise the 'essence and end' of much broader political conflicts in the immediate aftermath of the First World War.[119]

There are few smooth routes to national independence and identity and political allegiances are always multifaceted and cannot be reduced to simplistic labels. As Donald L. Horowitz has argued, in periods of upheaval, issues of social class often derive their impetus from ethnic or religious aspirations and/or apprehensions and 'even in the most severely divided society, there are also other issues … everywhere there exists buyers and sellers, officials and citizens, co-workers, and members of professions'.[120] The illusion of a singular identity on the part of both the perpetrators and victims of communal violence is not sufficient as an explanation for social unrest, as religion was not an all-encompassing exclusive identity and a failure to distinguish between class antagonism, sectarian resentment and opportunistic criminality ignores the variety of motivations behind inherently complex events. Sectarianism was a function of economic and social resentment, as Sen has argued; identity is always robustly plural and there are a great variety of categories to which people belong. In this respect, even well integrated communities that enjoy good community relations can be the 'very same community in which bricks are thrown through the windows of immigrants who move into the area from elsewhere'.[121]

Protestant flight from Galway had been ongoing since the late nineteenth century and constituted a well-established trend long before the rise of militant republicanism. The Protestant experience of revolution in Galway was undoubtedly negative and contributed to the high level of emigration from within the Protestant community during the early decades of independence.[122] However, the plight of Protestants in the west was in no sense comparable to the violence inflicted upon the Catholic minority in the north-east of Ireland. It was certainly a frightening time to be a Protestant in parts of the countryside but these attacks should not be exaggerated and claims of ethnic cleansing are unsustainable.

Forced to be Free?: Violence, Banditry and the Revolution

Remembering and un-remembering

During the revolution in Ireland the inherent tendency for formative national events to be interpreted from profoundly local perspectives cannot be underestimated. In April 1966, a small plaque, erected to the memory of Liam Mellows and his comrades who took part in the 1916 Rising, was destroyed in an explosion at Limepark, south Galway.[1] It is unclear who was responsible for the explosion, just days before the plaque was due to be unveiled by a Fianna Fail veteran of the Rebellion. The destruction of the monument served as a stark reminder that even with the passing of half a century, the revolution remained a contentious topic. Earlier in the year, the *Connacht Tribune* published a series of vitriolic letters questioning the patriotic merits of the insurgents.[2] The reputation of one local leader, in particular, was attacked, and in turn vigorously defended, with claims and counter claims of fascist and communist sympathies on the part of nationalists and republicans respectively.

Philosopher Paul Ricoeur has explored the reciprocal relationship between remembering and forgetting that can profoundly alter the perception of historical experience and the production of historical narrative.[3] At times of great historical moment, an excess of remembering of some events, at the expense of an excess of forgetting about others can greatly influence the collective consciousness of a nation. In the years following the foundation of the Irish State, the need to forget aspects of the revolutionary era became paramount to the evolution of an imagined, functional and collective historical narrative. In this respect, Ella O'Dwyer has argued that the irony of the historiographical debates that have surrounded the narrative of violent republicanism 'lie in the realisation that the suppression of the historical narrative which fostered the annihilation of the rebel voice also facilitates the death of the conservative response'.[4] While subsequent generations superimposed a retrospective romance onto the independence struggle, the hostility that the growth of the physical force movement generated within the nationalist community was jettisoned from popular and historical memory. The period began as an era of great hope for the nationalist community, yet, ended in the disappointment, acrimony and retribution of the Civil War. The intense hatreds the Civil War engendered blighted politics for decades and compounded mutual antagonisms, lingering suspicions and deep resentments that the War of Independence had nurtured. With the coming of independence, nationalists were faced with the task of accommodating a level of antagonism towards republicanism with the collective demand for a heroic national ethno-genesis. The only adequate solution was communal silence that permitted the complexities of the revolution to be quietly jettisoned.

Historian Heather Laird has highlighted the problems non-nationalist organisations, such as groups of rural poor who coveted their neighbours' land, present for the historiography of post-colonial states when the activities of such groups have not been absorbed into the logic of the new state.[5] The experience of broadly defined social groups, such as the southern Protestant minority, frequently fall out of the domain of conventional history as the problematic questions they present for consolatory interpretations of national history negate the value of objective remembering. There are many facets to historical 'un-remembering'; however, it is the Volunteers' path from perceived delinquency to local heroes that presents fundamental questions about how the period has been re-interpreted in the popular consciousness.

While official memory became constrained and manipulated by an imperviousness to historical reality, the inauthentic can still be punctured by historical investigation. In this respect, local and familial memory of the period was frequently more critical, nuanced and sophisticated than historians might acknowledge. Most families who played central roles in the revolution continued to remember the past, but all too frequently, it was within tightly knit circles based on familial bonds and shared experience. The caricature of the national revolution that emerged in official history, however, should not be replaced with an equally simplistic interpretation fixated upon the legitimacy of political violence in modern Ireland.[6] Republicanism during the revolutionary period was not an expression of irrationalism or a conduit for anarchy and the Volunteers did not live their lives as if they were works of art or feel compelled to construct a consoling image of themselves as the emancipators of an ancient civilisation.[7] Their goals were infinitely rational and their campaign reflective of the dynamics of an impatient generation of idealists for whom the Ireland of their parents was no longer enough.

In comparison to more active republican areas in Munster, the Volunteers in Galway were often disorganised and frequently incompetent; nonetheless, they succeeded in posing a significant threat to the Crown Forces in rural districts due to the commitment of a hard-core of young rural men and women. Although their attempts to attack the Royal Irish Constabulary (RIC) were frequently unsuccessful, they could not have survived without the support of considerable sections of the rural community. One of the principal tasks the revolutionaries faced during the independence struggle was persuading their community to turn away from their long-standing political institutions and take a potentially disastrous chance on a younger and unproven political leadership. Republicans were never entirely successful in winning over rural communities to all aspects of their campaign and only in retrospect were they deemed 'the army of the people'. In reality, they remained the army of some of the people, some of the time. As Brian Hughes has noted, defiance of the republican campaign from within the nationalist community was far more widespread during the period than traditionally depicted: 'defiance also came in a wide range of acts of independent informing: denouncing the IRA, refusal to pay a levy, refusal to pay rates to a republican collector, refusal to obey a boycott, attending British institutions and so forth'.[8]

The independence struggle was a war of young rural men and women and Stephen Gwynn, MP for Galway town, observed at first hand the generational dimension to the revolution:

> Such men as these [veterans of the original Land War] who had been in jail half a dozen times for their part in the fight, were incapable of believing that the country would ever turn from them, or refuse to accept their guidance. Yet, already, in 1905, there was a generation, to whom the story of the Land War of the eighties and their whole tradition was only a story, of which they were tired. They were weary also of being put down by their elders, who told them that they had never known what it was to do a hard day's work for Ireland.[9]

Despite their overwhelming success in the 1918 General Election and the rise of the Volunteers, republicans were not accepted as a legitimate political force by many nationalists and the three main nationalist newspapers in Galway remained implacably opposed to Sinn Féin throughout the period. Writing in his political memoir in 1919, William O'Malley, former MP for West Galway, described the results of the 1918 General Election as 'the treachery and ingratitude of a people'.[10] O'Malley was adamant that many republicans sprang from 'the English garrison – that is the parties that got all the government jobs, from a judgeship to a police inspector, they were the sons of policemen, land agents, grass farmers or land grabbers'.[11] While O'Malley's recollections were indelibly coloured by his personal bitterness, he was far from a lone voice in his contempt for the new political establishment.

A narrow focus on the republican military campaign obscures the significance of the movement's broader achievements. The acceptance by a significant section of the people, grudging or otherwise, of the republican counter-state involving republican policing, arbitration courts, active service units and public representation in a society where violence over land was an enduring phenomenon represented the movement's greatest achievement. Agrarian violence ultimately gave both republicans and their nationalist opponents an opportunity to reconcile themselves with the mass of ordinary people. The land arbitration courts and the republican police provided an opportunity for more conservative groups to play a moderating role in the new movement. Without losing face, former United Irish League (UIL) members could support the new forces of 'law and order' in early 1918 and again in 1920. From being abruptly shut out of the rapidly evolving political discourse, nationalist representatives, such as former MP William Duffy, attended arbitration courts and made favourable comments on their findings. One of Sinn Féin's greatest opponents, Thomas Kenny of the *Connacht Tribune*, gave ample coverage to the court's findings and highlighted their effectiveness in quelling agrarian violence.

Republicans' defence of the rights of property reflected their commitment to preserving the political achievements of the revolution, and in this respect, Sinn Féin became increasingly indistinguishable from their predecessors in the UIL. The republican boycott of the police and court system became so successful that the Volunteers were able to present themselves as the legitimate upholders of law and order, assuring conservative nationalists that the revolution would not involve radical social change. To condemn the political direction of the revolution as a missed opportunity for social revolution, however, represents a misunderstanding of the essentially conservative nature of rural Ireland and an over-estimation of the capacity and desire to affect fundamental change among ordinary republicans.

Revolution and banditry

Resistance to the state during the period 1913–22 did not run solely along the lines of republicanism and historian David Fitzpatrick has highlighted the continuity between the IPP's harnessing of agrarian violence and the manipulation of the same phenomenon by Sinn Féin, who effectively assumed the role of broker between the state and the people in April 1918. The small tenant agitations, though viewed by elites as typical of an anarchic peasantry, represented a continuum of struggle against the social inequality inherent in the dominant land tenure system in areas where the grazing system predominated. A range of unsavoury incidents sheltered under the cloak of agrarian emancipation; nonetheless, the campaigns against petty landlordism were also a claim to nationhood, albeit masked in under-articulated social grievance.

If subsequent generations of historians have failed to agree on the intersection between land hunger and political mobilisation, the authorities in Galway were similarly divided on the consequences of land purchase. RIC District Inspector Clayton believed the policy of the Congested Districts Board (CDB) was directly responsible for rural unrest in the county as 'some of the most worthless and disloyal have received farms from the CDB in preference to the worthy and loyal. This policy has had a bad affect.'[12] In contrast, District Inspector Ruttledge believed the redistribution of large estates had a positive effect in terms of unrest as 'when a man gets his land, he settles down and there is no one more conservative than an Irish small farmer. The day of the paid politician and agitator in this country will be over when the people have the land in their hands.'[13] When questioned about larger farmers and their lack of participation in the 1916 Rising in Galway, District Inspector Ruttledge told the Rebellion Commission, 'they don't care to lose money. I don't think the farmers were ever better off. They are not too willing to be disturbed, that is so, the farming classes are never too willing to be disturbed.'[14]

The police inspectors' seemingly rival analyses, however, were not necessarily contradictory and the sheer scale of land transferred by the state from landlord to tenant in Galway was both a result of, and a stimulus for, agrarian violence. In the countryside, violence worked but this should not be extrapolated into a particular potential for violence among the land-hungry rural poor, as in Galway both the urban and rural poor ultimately became a brake on revolution. The rural agrarian collectivities' compulsion towards violence, their essentially diffuse and individualistic struggles, their impenetrability and localism all militated against the formation of broader, co-ordinated, disciplined, associational movement such as the Volunteers. These disparate struggles could not ultimately be welded to a national movement encompassing broad social support, and in this regard, historian Eric Hobsbawm has noted the problems rural proletarian movements face in forming national movements and concluded that such agitations inevitably remain scattered and regional.[15] Thus, for the rural poor during the revolutionary era, political confrontation could be quite non-revolutionary and many rejected joining the Volunteers, endeavouring to achieve their economic independence by engaging in violent agrarianism.

Despite having benefitted from the wave of agrarian agitation in early 1918, Sinn Féin leaders came to perceive agrarianism as the lawlessness of a greedy tenantry and the language of republican condemnation in the summer of 1920 mimicked that of the authorities. Many small farmers had nothing to lose and everything to gain by agrarian violence, and unlike their urban counterparts, were keenly aware of the transforming potential of violence. While agrarianism played a key role in the initial appeal of Sinn Féin, there was little popular ideological identification with, or even a general cognisance of socialist ideology among rural republicans. The Sinn Féin newspaper, the *Galway Express*, consistently presented the republican cause in pragmatic, rather than ideological terms. In this respect, declaring support for the co-operative and labour movements, while condemning the merchant classes in general, represented a populist appeal for support from the mass of ordinary people who could be roused by an appeal to perennial class resentments.

Eric Hobsbawm has noted that social and economic banditry in a revolutionary scenario ultimately 'become ambiguous, doubtful and short'.[16] Agrarianism challenged the established order and became a potential incubator of revolt, yet such activity ultimately came into conflict with the broader associational demands of political revolution.[17] In this respect, the 'little world' of the poor with its overlapping kinship bonds conforms to models of peasant organisation worldwide, with the poor, as Hobsbawm has noted, belonging primarily to the local, rather than the national.[18]

Winners and losers

Revolutions, like all periods of social and political upheaval inevitably generate winners and losers. The Civil War was to cast the Volunteers into a scenario they never envisaged and it was a disaster for the young men and women who had led the revolution. Some former republican fighters inevitably made lucrative political careers on both sides of the political divide that defined the Free State; however, for every fighter that became a TD, there were hundreds more veterans who had to emigrate to Boston, New York or Chicago. Galway's old political elite, routed so thoroughly by their republican opponents in 1918, made a significant electoral comeback in the 1920s. The republican movement's most implacable opponent, Máirtín Mór McDonogh, was elected to Dáil Éireann in June 1927. Re-elected again in September 1927, he lost his seat in 1932 but regained it again in 1933. William Duffy and James Cosgrave, both of whom were defeated by republicans in the 1918 General Election, were among the small number of IPP members to be successfully elected as both MPs and TDs. Cosgrave, who had been MP for South Galway, was returned as an independent in the 1923 General Election but lost his seat in 1927. He later became a local representative for Fianna Fail. Duffy was returned to Dáil Éireann for the Irish Centre Party in 1927.[19] Shortly before his death in December 1948, he wrote with characteristic flourish to the *Irish Times* of the indignity that he and many of his old political colleagues were exposed to following the ascendency of Sinn Féin:

> For the past twenty years, the priceless work of the Party is scarcely mentioned, except with scoff or jibe … It is well that there is a home, a beautiful and lasting home, where quantities and qualities are accurately measured, that poor ex-members of parliament can aspire to after leaving this world of unreality, for then they will be judged on merit.[20]

The 1916 Rising remained one of few episodes that Galway veterans could recall with some degree of unity, yet, the fate of the Galway leadership told its own story. Liam Mellows, whose attempt to foment revolt in Galway in 1916 was thwarted by a combination of bad luck and inexperience, was executed by the Free State on 8 December 1922. In the General Election held earlier in the year, he garnered just over 10 per cent of the vote in Galway, finishing last of eight candidates standing in the county. His execution was a reprisal for an earlier shooting by the anti-Treaty IRA in which Galway TD, Pádraic Ó Máille, was shot in the spine and his comrade Sean Hales killed. In 1949, Mellows' mother, Sarah, wrote to Fr Tom Burke of Castlegar asking for financial help. She had suffered a breakdown in health and requested 'the loan of a few pounds for a month or so', as her burial insurance had lapsed and she was concerned she would lose her cover. She was struggling to get by on her state pension and a small group of old comrades were helping with her rent. 'Few are my friends and visitors these days,' she wrote, 'so this sickness is a poor thing and an added expense.' The letter signed off 'very lonely without anyone to speak to …'[21]

The fate of the Galway leader of Cumann na mBan, Julia Mary Morrissey, was equally tragic. Morrissey, like most of her Cumann na mBan comrades, rejected the Treaty and supported the anti-Treaty IRA. She subsequently suffered chronic ill-health and was confined to an asylum for several decades before her death in 1974. The Military Service Pension Board sent pension forms on three occasions; however, when they were not returned correctly, she received no compensation, and without close family, she died in obscurity and her grave was unmarked.

The absence of obvious glory characterised the experience of the men and women who fought for independence in the west of Ireland and the realities of revolution left families divided by emigration, ill-health and imprisonment. In this respect, their experience mirrored that of many veterans of the First World War. Both sides of this seeming divide were motivated by positive intentions and endured hardship and grief; however, both groups believed they were building a new Ireland that would be fundamentally better. Young people gave their lives for a vision of the future without a precise definition of exactly what that new Ireland would look like. They were led on by others, and in most cases, did their best to fulfil the dream of an Ireland they believed to be worth struggling for. A small number of prominent figures made political careers from their involvement and many more were genuinely appreciated by their communities; however, in many cases, casualties and veterans of both the War and the independence struggle were not remembered beyond their own families and the ideas they fought for were forgotten.

Endnotes

Introduction

1   Donald L. Horrowitz, *Ethnic Groups in Conflict* (California: University of California Press, 1985).

2   Desmond Ryan, *Seán Treacy and the 3rd Tipperary Brigade* (Tralee: The Kerryman, 1945), p. 5.

3   Dan Breen, *My Fight for Irish Freedom* (Dublin: Talbot Press, 1924); Tom Barry, *Guerrilla Days in Ireland* (Tralee: Anvil Books, 1964).

4   For two conflicting assessments of the achievements of a single brigade see Jim Maher, *The Flying Column, West Kilkenny, 1916–1921* (Dublin: Geography Publications, 1987) and Ernie O'Malley's account of the same brigade in *On Another Man's Wound* (London: Anvil Books, 1936), pp. 221–35.

5   See in particular, Peadar O'Donnell, *There Will Be Another Day* (Dublin: Dolmen, 1963); Ernie O'Malley, *Army Without Banners, Adventures of an Irish Volunteer* (Boston: Four Square, 1937); O'Malley, *On Another Man's Wound*; Liam Mellows, *Notes from Mountjoy Jail* (London: Irish Communist Group, 1925).

6   O'Donnell, *There Will Be Another Day*, p. 12.

7   Mellows, *Notes from Mountjoy Jail*, p. 9.

8   Richard English and Cormac O'Malley (eds), *Prisoners: The Civil War Letters of Ernie O'Malley* (Dublin: Poolbeg, 1991), p. 36.

9   See in particular, F.S.L. Lyons, *Culture and Anarchy in Ireland, 1890–1939* (Oxford: OUP, 1979); William Irwin Thompson, *The Imagination of an Insurrection, Dublin Easter 1916* (Oxford: OUP, 1967).

10 Erhard Rumpf, A.C. Hepburn, *Nationalism and Socialism in Twentieth Century Ireland* (Liverpool: LUP, 1977).

11 David Fitzpatrick, 'The Geography of Irish Nationalism', *Past & Present*, 78 (1978), pp. 113–44.

12 David Fitzpatrick, *Politics and Irish Life 1913–1921: Provincial Experience of War and Revolution* (Dublin: Gill & Macmillan, 1978).

13 See in particular, Joost Augusteijn, 'Accounting for the Emergence of Violent Activism Among Irish Revolutionaries, 1916–21', *Irish Historical Studies*, xxxi (May 2007), pp. 237–45; David Fitzpatrick (ed.), *Revolution? Ireland 1917–1923* (Dublin: Trinity History Workshop, 1990); Tom Garvin, *The Evolution of Irish Nationalist Politics* (Dublin: Gill & MacMillan, 1981); Charles Townshend, 'The Irish Republican Army and the Development of Guerrilla Warfare, 1916–21', *English Historical*

Review, xciv (1979), pp. 318–45; Charles Townshend, *Political Violence in Ireland: Government and Resistance Since 1948* (Oxford: OUP, 1983).

14 Peter Hart, *The IRA and Its Enemies: Violence and Community in Cork, 1916–1923* (Oxford: OUP, 1998); Peter Hart, *The IRA at War, 1916–1923* (Oxford: OUP, 2003); Marie Coleman, *County Longford and the Irish Revolution, 1910–1923* (Dublin: Irish Academic Press, 2003); Joost Augusteijn, *From Public Defiance to Guerrilla Warfare: the Experience of Ordinary Volunteers in the Irish War of Independence, 1916–1921* (Dublin: Irish Academic Press, 1996); Michael Farry, *The Aftermath of Revolution: Sligo, 1921–23* (Dublin: UCD Press, 2000).

15 See in particular, John Horne (ed.), *Our War, Ireland and the Great War* (Dublin: RIA, 2008).

16 David Fitzpatrick, 'Review: Fergus Campbell, "Land & Revolution, Politics in the West of Ireland, 1898–1921"', *American Historical Review*, cxii (2007), pp. 281–2.

17 Fergus Campbell, *Land & Revolution: Politics in the West of Ireland, 1898–1921* (Oxford: OUP, 2005).

18 Table XXXVII – showing the number of persons who spoke Irish only and Irish and English in each county district in the County of Galway, *Census Returns for Ireland, 1911, showing area, houses, and population; also the ages, civil or conjugal condition, occupations, birthplaces, religions, and education of the people Province of Connaught*, p. 224, H.C., *1913* (Cd. 6052, 6052-I, 6052-II, 6052-III, 6052-IV, 6052-V), cxvii, p.1.

19 Patrick Moylett Memoir, IE UCDAD P78, UCD Archives, p. 26.

20 *Tenth report of the Royal Commission appointed to inquire into and report upon the operation of the Acts dealing with Congestion in Ireland: evidence and documents: Appendix to the Tenth Report: Minutes of Evidence Taken in Counties Galway and Roscommon, 18*[th] *September to 4*[th] *October 1907*, H.C., 1908 (Cd. 4007), xvii, Digest of Evidence, Patrick McDonagh, p. xxix.

21 *Ibid.*, Digest of Evidence, Reverend Mark Conroy, p. xxvii.

22 *Ibid.*, Digest of Evidence, Reverend B. McAndrew, p. xx.

23 *Ibid.*, Digest of Evidence, Mr Peter J. O'Malley, p. vii

24 *Ibid.*, Digest of Evidence, Reverend James Kelly, p. xiii.

25 *Ibid.*, Digest of Evidence, Reverend Michael McHugh, p. xx.

26 *Ibid.*, Digest of Evidence, Mr Joseph Kelly, p. xxvi.

27 *Ibid.*, Digest of Evidence, Mr Joseph Kelly, p. xxvi

28 *Ibid.*, Digest of Evidence, Henry A. Burke, p. v.

29 'Table VI – Area in 1911 and houses and population in 1891, 1901 and 1911 in each County district and district electoral division comprised therein in the County of Galway', *Census Returns for Ireland, 1911* …

30 Máirtín Ó Cadhain, 'The Year 1912', *The Road to Brightcity: Short Stories Translated by Eoghan Ó Tuairisc* (Dublin: Poolbeg Press, 1981), p. 31.

31 John Cunningham, *'A town tormented by the sea:' Galway 1790–1914* (Dublin: Geography Publications, 2004), p. 1.

32 Burton E. Stevenson, *The Charm of Ireland* (London: B.F. Stevens & Brown, 1914), pp. 292–318.

33 Cunningham, 'A town tormented by the sea', p. 3. See also, Jackie Ui Chionna, He Was
    Galway, Mártín Mór McDonogh (Dublin: Four Courts Press, 2016).
34 Table IX – showing the number and net tonnage of vessels that arrived and departed
    with cargoes and in ballast, from and to foreign countries and British possessions, and
    coastwise, at each port, in Ireland in the year 1913, Report on the Banking, Railway, and
    Shipping Statistics of Ireland for 1914–June, p. 28, H.C., 1916 (Cd. 7675), lxxx, p. 237.
35 Cunningham, 'A town tormented by the sea', p. 189.
36 Máirtín Ó Cadhain, 'The Gnarled And Stony Clods Of Townland's Tip', The Road
    to Brightcity: Short Stories Translated by Eoghan Ó Tuairisc, p. 80.
37 Ó Cadhain, 'The Road to Brightcity', The Road to Brightcity, p. 64.
38 Census Returns for Ireland, 1911 …
39 Tenth report of the Royal Commission appointed to inquire into and report upon the
    operation of the Acts dealing with Congestion in Ireland: evidence and documents: …
    The Evidence of Reverend Macken, pp. xlv.
40 See Liam Kennedy, 'Farmers, Traders and Agricultural Politics in Pre-Independence
    Ireland', in Samuel Clark, James Donnelly Jnr (eds), Irish Peasants: Violence and
    Political Unrest, 1780–1914 (Dublin: Gill & Macmillan, 1998), pp. 339–73.
41 Eleventh Report of the Royal Commission Appointed to Inquire Into and Report Upon
    the Operation of the Acts Dealing with Congestion in Ireland; Digest of Evidence, 1908,
    H.C., 1908 (Cd. 4089), xlii, p. 587. The Evidence of Peter O'Malley, p. vii.
42 Emigration Statistics for Ireland, 1915, p. 4.
43 Table XLI – showing emigration from the County of Galway during each year from
    1 May 1851 to 31 March 1911: Census returns for Ireland, 1911…
44 Report and Tables Relating to Irish Migratory Agricultural and Other Labourers for
    1915, p. 4, H.C., 1916 (Cd. 8386), xxxii, p. 815.
45 Ibid., p. 5.
46 Ibid., p. 7
47 Plummer Flippen Jones, Shamrock Land, A Ramble Through Ireland (New York:
    1908), pp. 147–74.
48 Tenth report of the Royal Commission appointed to inquire into and report upon the
    operation of the Acts dealing with Congestion in Ireland: evidence and documents …
    Evidence of J.J. Ward, p. lxiii.
49 Ibid.
50 East Galway Democrat, 28 July 1914.
51 Ibid.
52 Irish Times, 25 May 1912.
53 Irish Times, 14 December 1912.

Chapter 1

1   Tony Varley, 'A Region of Sturdy Smallholders? Western Nationalists and Agrarian
    Politics during the First World War', Journal of the Galway Archaeological and
    Historical Society, 55 (2003), pp. 140.

2   Fergus Campbell, *Land & Revolution: Politics in the West of Ireland 1898–1921* (Oxford: OUP, 2005); Fergus Campbell, 'The Social Dynamics of Nationalist Politics in the West of Ireland, 1898–1918', *Past and Present*, 184 (2004), pp. 175–209.

3   Eric Hobsbawm, 'Peasants and Politics', *Uncommon People, Resistance, Rebellion and Jazz* (New York: Weidenfeld & Nicolson, 1998), pp. 146–66; Charles Tilly, *The Rebellious Century, 1830–1930* (London: J.M. Dent, 1975); George Rude, *The Crowd in History: A Study of Popular Disturbance in France and England, 1730–1848* (New York: Serif, 1964).

4   Campbell, *Land and Revolution*, p. 224.

5   CI monthly report, west Galway, November 1914, CO 904/95.

6   Campbell, *Land and Revolution*, p. 175.

7   *Ibid.*, p. 121.

8   Terence Dooley, 'Landlords and the Land Question, 1879–1909', Carla King (ed.), *Famine, Land and Culture in Ireland* (Dublin: UCD Press, 2000), pp. 116–39.

9   Tony Varley, 'Irish Land Reform and the West between the Wars', *Journal of the Galway Archaeological and Historical Society*, 56 (2004), pp. 213–32.

10 *Connacht Tribune*, 27 March 1915, p. 4.

11 Table XIII – Returns of Estates Purchased by The Estates Commissioners During the Period from 1ˢᵗ November, 1903 to 31 March, 1918, *Irish Land Acts, 1903–09: Report of the Estates Commissioners for the year from 1st April, 1917, to 31st March, 1918, and for the period from 1st November, 1903, to 31st March, 1918, with appendix*, p. 28, H.C. 1919 (Cmd.; 29), xxiv, p. 137.

12 Table XXI – Returns giving particulars of Allotment of Untenanted Land Purchased by the Estates Commissioners under the Irish Land Acts, 1903–09 and Vested in Purchasers, up to March, 1918, *Irish Land Acts, 1903–09: Report of the Estates Commissioners ...* p. 44.

13 *Ibid.*

14 Samuel Clark, 'Social Composition of the Land League', *Irish Historical Studies*, 17 (1979), pp. 447–65; *Social Origins of the Irish Land War* (Princeton: PUP, 1979).

15 Campbell, *Land & Revolution*, pp. 8–84.

16 *Agricultural Statistics of Ireland; With Detailed Report for 1914*, vii, H.C., 1916 (Cd. 8266), p. 621.

17 *Ibid.*, p. ix.

18 *Departmental Committee on Agricultural Credit in Ireland. Agricultural Credit in Ireland: Report*, p. 122, H.C., 1914 (Cd. 7375), xiii, p.1.

19 See Patrick Melvin, *Estates and Landed Society in Galway* (Dublin: Edmund Burke, 2010).

20 *Ibid.*

21 'Return Showing the Results of Agitation against the Grazing System in May 1915', Brendan Mac Giolla Choille (ed.), *Intelligence Notes, 1913–1916* (Dublin: Oifig an tSolathair, 1966), pp. 194–5.

22 *Ibid.*

23 Campbell, *Land and Revolution*, pp. 85–166.

24 Terence Dooley, *The Decline of the Big House in Ireland, A Study of the Irish Landed Families, 1860–1960* (Dublin: Wolfhound Press, 2001).

25 Table E – Geographical Distribution of Crime, Annual Average (1908–1912) and Proportion to Population of Indictable Offences, of Persons proceeded against for Drunkenness, and of Suicides in Each County in Ireland, p. xvii, *Criminal and Judicial Statistics for Ireland, 1912*, xvi, H.C., 1913 (Cd. 6916), lxxvi, p. 659.

26 Table 23 – Returns From The Several Counties, Indictable Offences, Nature of Crimes Known To The Police in Each County and County City in 1914, *Criminal and Judicial Statistics for Ireland, 1914*, xv, H.C., 1916 (Cd. 8077, 8006), lxxxii, p. 451.

27 *Connacht Tribune*, 28 March 1914, p. 6.

28 *Connacht Tribune*, 16 January 1915, p. 4.

29 Tilly, *Rebellious Century, 1830–1930*, pp. 17–23.

30 Clark, *Social Origins of the Irish Land War*, pp. 350–71.

31 Anne Coleman, *Riotous Roscommon* (Dublin: Four Courts Press, 1999).

32 For details of the dispute at Colemanstown see, *Connacht Tribune*, 9 October 1915, p. 8. For details of the Moorpark agitation, see *Irish Times*, 20 June 1914.

33 CI monthly report, east Galway, July 1914, CO 904/94.

34 CI monthly report, east Galway, February 1915, CO 904/92.

35 *Connacht Tribune*, 28 August 1915, p. 5.

36 *Irish Times*, 2 June 1914.

37 *Irish Times*, 25 March 1908

38 CI monthly report, east Galway, April 1914, CO 904/93.

39 CI monthly report, east Galway, January 1914, CO 904/92.

40 CI monthly report, east Galway, April 1914, CO 904/93.

41 CI monthly report, east Galway, April 1914, CO 904/93.

42 *Connacht Tribune*, 20 June 1914, p. 6.

43 CI monthly report, east Galway, March 1915, CO 904/96.

44 William Broderick was a steward for Shawe-Taylor. *Connacht Tribune*, 27 March 1915.

45 CI monthly report, east Galway, July 1915, CO 904/97.

46 Patrick Maume, 'Trench, Frederick Oliver 3rd Baron Ashtown', *Dictionary of Irish Biography* (Cambridge: CUP, 2002).

47 *Returns Showing How Farms from which Tenants were Evicted on Certain Specified Estates Since the 1st May 1879 were Occupied at the Time of the Inquiry of the Evicted Tenants Commission; and on the 1st Day of May 1903*, H.C., 1903 (Cd. 173), lvii, p. 505.

48 Clonbrock's correspondence in relation to his role in the Irish Unionist Alliance is available in the Clonbrock Papers, MS 35,781; MS 35,782; MS 35, 784, NLI. For biographical details see, L. Perry Curtis Jnr, 'The Last Gasp of Southern Unionism: Lord Ashtown of Woodlawn', *Eire–Ireland*, 40 (Winter/Fall, 2005), pp. 140–88.

49 'Memorandum of Accounts on the Clanricarde estate, 3 Dec. 1873'; 'Summary of rent on the Clanricarde estate, Feb. 1883', Clanricarde Papers, Harewood Archives, West Yorkshire Archive Service, Leeds.

50 Conor McNamara, 'The Most Bitter Struggle of them all: the Clanricarde Estate and Legislative Reform in Ireland', *Journal of the Galway Archaeological and Historical Society*, 67 (2015), pp. 184–201.

51 See Laurence M. Geary, *The Plan of Campaign, 1886–1891* (Cork: CUP, 1986).

52 *Connacht Tribune*, 25 April 1914, p. 5.

53 *Irish Independent*, 14 April 1916, p. 3.

54 *Ibid.*

55 *Connacht Tribune*, 22 April 1916, p. 4.

56 *Freeman's Journal*, 20 April 1916, p. 4.

57 'No Reduction; No Rent, The Story of Woodford and the Archbishop of Dublin on the Plan of Campaign', *The Pall Mall Gazette Extra*, 30 December 1886.

58 *Returns Showing How Farms from which Tenants were Evicted ...*

59 Miriam Moffitt, *Clanricarde's Planters and Land Agitation in East Galway, 1886–1916, Maynooth Studies in Local History, 97* (Dublin: Four Courts Press, 2011).

60 *Hansard 4* [etc.], 24 March 1904, vol. 132, cc 644–98.

61 *Ibid.*

62 *Ibid.*

63 *Hansard 4* [etc.], 08 July 1907, 177, cc 1183–292.

64 *Eleventh Report of the Royal Commission Appointed to Inquire Into and Report Upon the Operation of the Acts Dealing with Congestion in Ireland; Digest of Evidence*, p. 599, H.C. 1908 (Cd. 4099), xliii, p. 369, Evidence of Martin Finnerty.

65 *Bill to Facilitate the Provision of Land for Certain Evicted Tenants in Ireland, and for Other Purposes Connected Therewith, and to Make Provision with Respect to the Tenure of Office by the Estates Commissioners; Amendment by Commission*, H.C. 1907 (HC.; 258), ii, p. 129.

66 *Hansard 4* [etc.], 08 July 1907, 177, cc 1183–292.

67 *Ibid.*

68 *Hansard 4* [etc.], 06 April, 187, c 899.

69 CI monthly report, east Galway, July 1915, CO 904/97.

70 *Connacht Tribune*, 9 May 1915, p. 3.

71 CI monthly report, east Galway, September 1915, CO 904/98.

72 CI monthly report, east Galway, September 1915, CO 904/98.

73 *Connacht Tribune*, 2 January 1915, p. 3.

74 CI monthly report, east Galway, April 1914, CO 904/93.

75 *Connacht Tribune*, 21 March 1914, p. 6.

76 *Connacht Tribune*, 14 February 1914, p. 7.

77 *Ibid.*

78 CI monthly report, east Galway, February 1914, CO 904/92.

79 *Connacht Tribune*, 11 April 1914, p. 5.

80 CI monthly report, east Galway, April 1914, CO 904/93.

81 *Connacht Tribune*, 16 May 1914, p. 5.

82 CI monthly report, east Galway, August 1914, CO 904/93.

83 CI monthly report, east Galway, January/April 1915, CO 904/96.

84   CI monthly report, east Galway, December 1915, CO 904/98.

85   CI monthly report, east Galway, December 1915, CO 904/98.

86   *Connacht Tribune*, 17 July 1915, p. 6.

87   For details of malicious burnings at Graige Abbey, see *Connacht Tribune*, 15 August 1914, p. 3. For details of the conflict at Creggs, see *Connacht Tribune*, 30 May 1914, p. 8.

88   John Cunningham, *'A town tormented by the sea': Galway 1790–1914* (Dublin: Geography Publications, 2004), pp. 212–25.

89   See Daly of Dunsandle Estate Papers (pre-catalogue material, NLI).

90   Varley, 'A Region of Sturdy Smallholders' p. 127. (Peter Fahy, James Ward, Patrick Lally, Dermot Dempsey, Michael Kennedy, John Broderick, Bernard Ward and Mary Finn were under police protection.) See also, County Inspector RIC monthly confidential report, East Galway, July & August 1914, CO 904/94.

91   CI monthly report, Galway, June 1915, CO 904/93.

92   William Naughton, *The Priest's Boy: A Story of Irish Country Life* (Dublin, 1913).

93   CI monthly report, east Galway, February 1914, CO 904/92.

94   CI monthly report, east Galway, February 1914, CO 904/92.

95   CI monthly report, east Galway, March 1914, CO 904/92.

96   CI monthly report, east Galway, May 1914, CO 904/92.

97   *Connacht Tribune*, 16 May 1914, p. 6.

98   *Ibid.*

99   CI monthly report, east Galway, May 1914, CO 904/97.

100 *Irish Times*, 27 February 1915.

101 CI monthly report, west Galway, February 1915, CO 904/96.

102 CI monthly report, west Galway, February 1915, CO 904/96.

103 *Connacht Tribune*, 13 March 1915, p. 5.

104 *Ibid.*

105 CI monthly report, west Galway, March 1915, CO 904/96.

106 Hobsbawm, 'Peasants and Politics', p. 157.

107 Hobsbawm, 'Peasants and Politics', pp. 146–66.

Chapter 2

1   *Connacht Tribune*, 8 August 1914, p. 4.

2   Michael Wheatley, *Nationalism and the Irish Party: Provincial Ireland, 1910–1916* (Oxford: OUP, 2005), p. 252.

3   Conor McNamara, 'A Shopkeepers' League or a Tenants' League? The Town Tenants Movement in the West of Ireland, 1914–1918', *Studia Hibernica*, 36 (2009–10), pp. 135–60.

4   Conor McNamara, '"The Most Shoneen Town in Ireland", Galway in 1916', *History Ireland*, 19:1 (2011), pp. 34–7.

5   Larry Lardiner, History of the Irish Volunteers in Galway (unpaginated) (BMH, CD 151.3).

6   BMH/WS 373 (John Hosty), p. 4.

7   *Connacht Tribune*, 17 January 1914, p. 4.

8   Brian M. Walker, *Parliamentary Election Results in Ireland, 1801–1922* (Dublin: RIA, 1978), p. 170.

9   *Ibid.*, p. 167.

10   *Ibid.*, pp 162–3.

11   Georgina Clinton, 'William O'Malley', *Dictionary of Irish Biography* (Cambridge: CUP, 2002).

12   William O'Malley, *Glancing Back, 70 Years: Experiences and Reminiscences of a Pressman, Sportsman and Member of Parliament* (London: Wright and Brown, 1933).

13   For details of the Tully grazing dispute, see *Connacht Tribune*, 25 April 1914.

14   CI RIC monthly report, west Galway, January 1914, CO 904/92.

15   O'Malley, *Glancing Back*.

16   *Connacht Tribune*, 12 February 1916, p. 4.

17   Patrick Maume, 'Stephen Gwynn', *Dictionary of Irish Biography* (Cambridge: CUP, 2002).

18   Stephen Gwynn, *The Case for Home Rule* (Dublin: Maunsel, 1911), p. v.

19   Stephen Gwynn, *Experiences of a Literary Man* (London: Thornton Butterworth, 1926), p. 273.

20   Jackie Ui Chionna, *He Was Galway, Máirtín Mór McDonogh, 1860–1934* (Dublin: Four Courts Press, 2016).

21   Liam O'Flaherty, *The House of Gold* (London: Jonathan Cape, 1929), p. 18.

22   John Cunningham, *Labour in the West of Ireland, Working Life and Struggle, 1890–1914* (Belfast: Athol Books, 1995), p. 151.

23   For an interview with O'Halloran, see, Cunningham, *Labour in the West of Ireland*, pp. 187–91.

24   For details of the strike, see, Cunningham, *Labour in the West of Ireland*, pp. 164–73.

25   John Cunningham, *'A town tormented by the sea:' Galway 1790–1914* (Dublin: Geography Publications, 2004), pp. 241–2.

26   *Connacht Tribune*, 9 October 1915, p. 5.

27   *Connacht Tribune*, 24 July 1915, p. 5.

28   Uí Chionna, *He Was Galway*, p. 142.

29   *Connacht Tribune*, 5 January 1916, p. 5.

30   *Connacht Tribune*, 5 January 1916, p. 5.

31   *Ibid.*

32   *Connacht Tribune*, 4 March 1916, p. 4.

33   BMH/WS 1,203 (Patrick Coy), p. 3.

34   *Irish Times*, 2 January 1948.

35   Conor McNamara, 'The Most Bitter Struggle of them all: the Clanricarde Estate and Legislative Reform in Ireland', *Journal of the Galway Archaeological and Historical Society*, 67 (2015), pp. 184–201.

36   *Irish Times*, 7 May 1914.

37   *Tuam Herald*, 26 October 1918, p. 4.

38 For Cosgrave's obituary, see, *Irish Times*, 20 April 1936.

39 Bridget Hourican, 'William Hazleton', *Dictionary of Irish Biography* (Cambridge: CUP, 2002).

40 *Irish Times*, 18 July 1914.

41 *Irish Times*, 18 July 1914.

42 *Hansards*, Military Service Bill, H.C., Deb. 10 April 1918, cc 1475–606.

43 *Report on Recruiting in Ireland* (Cd; 8168), H.C., 1916, p. 3.

44 *Ibid.*, p. 3.

45 Keith Jeffery, 'Obligation: "Irishmen Remember Belgium"', *Ireland and the Great War* (Cambridge: CUP, 2000), pp. 5–36.

46 Inspector General RIC, Monthly Report, August 1914, CO 904/94.

47 *Connacht Tribune*, 3 October 1914, p. 4.

48 *Connacht Tribune*, 8 August 1914, p. 4.

49 I am grateful to John Cunningham, NUIG, for this information.

50 *Tuam Herald*, 26 September 1914, p. 2.

51 *Tuam Herald*, 5 September 1914, p. 4.

52 *Galway Express*, 29 January 1916.

53 For the most accurate figures see, David Fitzpatrick, 'Militarism in Ireland, 1900–1922', in Thomas Bartlett & Keith Jeffery (eds), *A Military History of Ireland* (Cambridge: CUP, 1996), p. 388; Keith Jeffery, *Ireland and the Great War* (Cambridge: CUP, 2000).

54 'Irish soldiers in the first World War: who, where and how many?', *Irish Times*, 2 August 1914.

55 *Report on Recruiting in Ireland* (Cd. 8168), H.C., 1916, p. 3.

56 *Ibid.*, p. 4.

57 Three died in 1919 and there are no details for twenty casualties.

58 David Murphy, *The Irish Brigades, 1685–2006* (Dublin: Four Courts Press, 2007), pp. 188–91; Tom Johnstone, *Orange, Green & Khaki, The Story of the Irish Regiments in the Great War, 1914–18* (Dublin: Gill & MacMillan, 1992).

59 *Connacht Tribune*, 6 December 1913, p. 2.

60 BMH/WS 714 (Thomas Hynes), p. 1.

61 Unpaginated manuscript, Pádraig Ó Fathaigh Papers (MS 21,288, NLI); Typescript Notes by Pádraig Ó Fathaigh (MS 21,289, NLI).

62 See BMH/WS 383 (Revd Thomas Fahy), p. 1.

63 Tony Varley, 'Tom Kenny and the Agrarian Dimension of the Galway Rising', *Farming & Country Life, 1916* (Galway, 2016), p. 23; Tony Varley, 'The Eclipsing of a Radical Agrarian Nationalist: Tom Kenny and the 1916 Rising in County Galway', in Marie Mannion (ed.) *Centenary Reflections on the 1916 Rising, Galway County Perspectives* (Galway: Galway County Council, 2016), pp. 92–113.

64 BMH/WS 342 (Michael Newell), p. 1.

65 BMH/WS 1,379 (Peter Howley), p. 2.

66 BMH/WS 347 (Patrick Callanan), p. 1.

67 'History of the Irish Volunteers in Galway' (unpaginated).

68 *Ibid.*
69 CI monthly report, east Galway and west Galway, May 1914, CO 904/93.
70 Chief Inspector RIC, monthly report, May 1914, CO/904/93.
71 CI monthly report, east Galway, May 1914, CO 904/93.
72 CI monthly report, east Galway, June 1914, CO 904/93.
73 Irish National Volunteers: Order book, Military Inspection Staff, August 1914 to November 1916 (Col. Maurice Moore Papers, MS 9,703, NLI).
74 CI monthly report, east Galway, July 1914, CO 904/94.
75 *Ibid.*
76 CI monthly report, west Galway, August 1914, CO 904/94.
77 *Connacht Tribune*, 4 July 1914, p. 5.
78 *Ibid.*
79 CI monthly report, west Galway, October 1914, CO 904/95.
80 *Ibid.*
81 *Ibid.*
82 For a report of the meeting, see *Connacht Tribune*, 3 October 1914, p. 5. For a literary account of the meeting see Walter Macken, *The Scorching Wind* (London: MacMillan, 1964), pp. 29–34.
83 *Connacht Tribune*, 3 October 1914, p. 5.
84 *Ibid.*
85 *Connacht Tribune*, 3 October 1914, p. 4.
86 BMH/WS 373 (John Hosty), p. 8.
87 *Connacht Tribune*, 17 October 1914, p. 5.
88 BMH/WS 373 (John Hosty), p. 9.
89 BMH/WS 447 (Thomas Courtney), p. 2.
90 BMH/WS 714 (Thomas Hynes), p. 2.
91 BMH/WS 447 (Thomas Courtney), p. 22.
92 CI monthly report, west Galway, February 1915, CO 904/96.
93 *Connacht Tribune*, 13 February 1915, p. 5.
94 *Ibid.*
95 CI monthly report, west Galway, April 1915, CO 904/96.
96 CI monthly report, west Galway, May 1915, CO 904/96.
97 *Ibid.*
98 *Ibid.*
99 *Connacht Tribune*, 14 February 1914, p. 6.
100 *Connacht Tribune*, 10 July 1915, p. 7.
101 For reports on the split see, *Connacht Tribune*, 17 April 1915, 29 June 1915, 10 July 1915, 11 September 1915.
102 'The Story for the 1916 Rising in Galway', reproduced *Connacht Tribune*, 22 January 2016, p. 24.
103 Bridget Ruane, 'Memories of my early years in Cahercrin, Craughwell', *Beginnings Magazine* (Presentation College Athenry, 1982).
104 *Ibid.*

105 *Cumann na mBan, County Galway Dimensions* (Galway County Council, 2016).

106 *Connacht Tribune*, 8 August 1914, p. 6.

107 For details of Mellows' early life see, C. Desmond Greaves, *Liam Mellows and the Irish Revolution* (London: Lawrence and Wishart, 1971), pp. 30–41.

108 BMH/WS 779 (Robert Brennan), p. 46.

109 For this period of Mellows' life see Greaves, *Liam Mellows and the Irish Revolution*, pp. 41–53.

110 Details of Mellows' diary as a Fianna organiser were published in *Irish Freedom*, June 1913.

111 BMH/WS 1,207 (Alfred White), p. 1.

112 BMH/WS 1,207 (Alfred White), p. 7.

113 BMH/WS 187 (Annie Fanning), p. 2.

114 BMH/WS 87 (Bulmer Hobson), p. 2.

115 BMH/WS 779 (Robert Brennan), pp. 45–6.

116 BMH/WS 298 (Ailbhe Ó Monacháin), p. 7.

117 BMH/WS 298 (Ailbhe Ó Monacháin), pp. 11–12.

118 Memorial to Commandant Liam Mellows (Pádraig Ó Fathaigh Papers, MS 21,289, NLI).

119 'I Remember Mellows', handwritten manuscript by Francis Hynes, unpaginated, MS 15,289, NLI.

120 BMH/WS 446 (Frank Hynes), p. 5.

121 'The Story for the 1916 Rising in Galway', reproduced *Connacht Tribune*, 15 January 2016, p. 25.

Chapter 3

1 See Fergus Campbell, 'The Easter Rising in Galway', *History Ireland* (14:2), 2006, pp. 22–5; *Land and Revolution: Nationalist Politics in the West of Ireland 1891–1921* (Oxford: OUP, 2005); C. Desmond Greaves, *Liam Mellows and the Irish Revolution* (London: Lawrence and Wishart, 1971), pp. 85–102; Conor McNamara, 'Liam Mellows and the Irish Revolution', *History Ireland* (19:4) 2011, pp. 36–7.

2 BMH/WS 298 (Ailbhe Ó Monacháin), p. 20.

3 BMH/WS 298 (Ailbhe Ó Monacháin), p. 15.

4 BMH/WS 673 (Michael Fogarty), p. 4.

5 BMH/WS 373 (John Hosty), pp. 12–3.

6 BMH/WS 1,437 (Thomas Nohilly), p. 4.

7 Uinseann MacEoin, *Survivors: The Story of Ireland's Struggle as Told Through Some of her Outstanding People* (Dublin: Argenta Publications, 1980), p. 78.

8 Larry Lardiner, History of the Irish Volunteers in Galway (BMH, CD 151.3).

9 *Ibid.*, p. 10.

10 BMH/WS 347 (Patrick Callanan), p. 6.

11 CI monthly report, east Galway, May 1916, CO 904/61.

12 Greaves, *Liam Mellows and the Irish Revolution*, p. 81.

13   Letter from Anna Fahy to Ailbhe Ó Monacháin, dated 29 June 1932 (Ó Monacháin Papers, BMH CD 151).

14   *Ibid.*

15   Martin Dolan, 'The Story of the 1916 Rising in Galway', published in the *Connacht Tribune* during April 1966, reproduced in *Connacht Tribune*, 5 February 2016, p. 34.

16   *Ibid.*

17   'The Story for the 1916 Rising in Galway', reproduced *Connacht Tribune*, 5 February 2016, p. 35.

18   Mattie Neilan, '1916 Rising in County Galway', *Capuchin Annual* (1967), p. 324.

19   'The Story of the 1916 Rising in Galway', reproduced *Connacht Tribune*, 5 February 2016, p. 35.

20   BMH/WS 446 (Frank Hynes), pp. 12–13.

21   BMH/WS 446 (Frank Hynes), p. 12.

22   BMH/WS 298 (Ailbhe Ó Monacháin), p. 17.

23   'The Story of the 1916 Rising in Galway', reproduced *Connacht Tribune*, 12 February 2016, p. 38.

24   'True Story of the Galway Insurrection', *Gaelic American*, 20 January 1920.

25   BMH/WS 342 (Michael Newell), pp. 6–7.

26   'The Story of the 1916 Rising in Galway', reproduced *Connacht Tribune*, 19 February 2016, p. 44.

27   BMH/WS 298 (Ailbhe Ó Monacháin), p. 20.

28   'True Story of the Galway Insurrection'.

29   'The Story of the 1916 Rising in Galway', reproduced *Connacht Tribune*, 19 February 2016, p. 44.

30   'The Story of the 1916 Rising in Galway', reproduced *Connacht Tribune*, 4 March 2016, p. 44.

31   BMH/WS 1,564 (Michael Kelly), p. 8.

32   *Ibid.*

33   BMH/WS 446 (Frank Hynes), pp. 13–14.

34   'The Story of the 1916 Rising in Galway', reproduced *Connacht Tribune*, 4 March 2016, p. 44.

35   Liam Mellows to Ms Herbert, Troy, New Jersey, dated 10 February 1919 (Uncatalogued material, NLI).

36   'The Story for the 1916 Rising in Galway', reproduced *Connacht Tribune*, 4 March 2016, p. 45. This version of events has been disputed by a relative of one Cumann na mBan participant.

37   Fr Feeney is remembered by a stained-glass window in Glencorrib Church, in the parish of Shrule, Co. Galway. Monsignor Dr Thomas Fahy (1887–1973) was educated at Esker National School and St Joseph's College, Garbally, and was appointed Professor of Classics in UCG in 1927.

38   BMH/WS 1,564 (Michael Kelly), pp. 9–10.

39   BMH/WS 383 (Reverend Thomas Fahy), pp. 3–4.

40   BMH/WS 447 (Frank Hynes), p. 16.

41   The most accurate list of participants in the Galway Rebellion is to be found in, Gerry Cloonan, *Galway Rising Centenary Commemoration, 1916–2016* (Craughwell, 2016).

42   *Connacht Tribune*, 29 April 1916, p. 3.

43   *Ibid.*

44   *Ibid.*

45   *Ibid.*

46   *Ibid.*

47   *Ibid.*

48   *Ibid.*

49   *Ibid.*

50   *Ibid.*

51   *Galway Express*, 29 April 1916.

52   *Ibid.*

53   *Ibid.*

54   Joseph Kilbride to Office of Chief Secretary regarding Easter Rising in Galway (5611/7872, CSORP, NA).

55   BMH/WS 714 (Thomas Hynes), p. 4.

56   BMH/WS 447 (Thomas Courtney), p. 10

57   BMH/WS 406 (Frank Hardiman), p. 5.

58   BMH/WS 373 (John Hosty), p. 14.

59   BMH/WS 374 (Micheal Ó Droighnéain), p. 7.

60   *Galway Express*, 29 April 1916.

61   *Connacht Tribune*, 29 April 1916, p. 3.

62   *Galway Express*, 6 May 1916.

63   *The Sayonara, The Guillemot, The Gloucester, The Laburnum* and *The Snowdrop*.

64   *Connacht Tribune*, 29 April 1916, p. 4.

65   *Connacht Tribune*, 20 May 1916, p. 2.

66   *Tuam Herald*, 20 May 1916, p. 2.

67   *Tuam Herald*, 20 May 1916, p. 4.

68   *Galway Express*, 6 May 1916.

69   *Tuam Herald*, 20 May 1916, p. 4.

70   *Tuam Herald*, 20 May 1916, p. 2.

71   *Galway Express*, 13 May 1916.

72   Bridie Lane (MSP34REF20331); Delia Hynes (MSP34REF57882).

73   I am grateful to Luke Callinan for this information.

74   *Connacht Tribune*, 20 May 1916, p. 3.

75   For details on Steinberger see, Rosaleen O'Neill, 'Modern Languages', in Thomas Boylan, Tadhg Foley (eds), *From Queen's College to National University: Essays on the Academic History of QCG/UCG/NUI, Galway* (Dublin: Four Courts Press, 1999), pp. 360–83.

76   *UCG Student Annual, 1916–17*, p. 44–5.

77   Mary Anne Vaughan, 'Finding Constable Whelan: an incident from 1916', *Ossory,*

Laois and Leinster, 4 (2010), pp. 231–5.

78 'Statement of DI Heard at Inquest into death of Constable Patrick Whelan', GS 15/01, GCCA.

79 See *Irish Times,* 28 July 1922; 1 August 1922.

80 *Freeman's Journal,* 27 July 1922, p. 5; *Irish Times,* 28 July 1922; 1 August 1922.

81 *Connacht Tribune,* 29 July 1922, p. 10.

82 'Letterfrack/Leenane, Landing of arms at', POL2, NUIGA.

83 Details of deportations were reproduced in the *Sinn Féin Rebellion Handbook* (Dublin, 1916), pp. 62–9.

84 BMH/WS 1,564 (Michael Kelly), p. 11.

85 BMH/WS 342 (Michael Newell), p, 9.

86 Thomas B. Cleary to his wife Mary, Athenry, dated 12 June 1916 (Cleary Papers, private collection).

87 Dublin Castle Special Branch Personality Files (Thomas Ruane, CO/904/214/388, TNA).

88 BMH/WS 1,138 (Gilbert Morrissey), p. 2.

89 For details of Mellows' time on the run after the Rising, see BMH/WS 446 (Frank Hynes), pp. 18–29.

90 BMH/WS 585 (Frank Robbins), p. 115.

91 BMH/WS 405 (Patrick Callanan), p. 5.

92 BMH/WS 909 (Sidney Czira, 'John Brennan'), p. 37.

93 Greaves, *Liam Mellows and the Irish Revolution,* p. 222.

94 BMH/WS 909 (Sidney Czira, 'John Brennan'), p. 44.

95 *Ibid.*

96 Liam Mellows to Joseph McGarrity dated 9 January 1920 (MS 17,628/8, McGarrity Papers, NLI).

97 BMH/WS 909 (Sidney Czira, 'John Brennan'), p. 38.

98 *Ibid.*

99 BMH/WS 585 (Frank Robbins), p. 146.

100 *Ibid.,* p. 146.

101 BMH/WS 585 (Frank Robbins), pp. 123–4.

102 BMH/WS 298 (Ailbhe Ó Monacháin), p. 15.

103 'The Story of the 1916 Rising in Galway', reproduced *Connacht Tribune,* 15 January 2016, p. 24.

Chapter 4

1 *Connacht Tribune,* 26 June 1920, p. 6.

2 Fergus Campbell, *Land & Revolution: Politics in the West of Ireland 1891–1921* (Oxford: OUP, 2005); Fergus Campbell, 'The Social Dynamics of Nationalist Politics in the West of Ireland, 1898–1918', *Past and Present,* 184 (2004), pp. 175–209; Tony Varley, 'Agrarian Crime and Social Control: Sinn Féin and the Land Question in the West of Ireland in 1920', *Whose Law and Order? Aspects of Crime and Social*

Control in Ireland (Belfast: Sociological Association of Ireland, 1998).

3   Richard Mulcahy, 'The Irish Volunteer Convention, 26 October, 1917', *Capuchin Annual* (1967), pp. 400–10.

4   *Ibid.*, p. 404.

5   Michael Laffan, *The Resurrection of Ireland, The Sinn Féin Party, 1916–1923* (Cambridge: CUP, 1999), pp. 116–21; Darrell Figgis, *Recollections of the Irish War* (Dublin: E. Benn, 1927), pp. 172–7.

6   Brian M. Walker, *Parliamentary Election Results in Ireland, 1801–1922* (Dublin: RIA, 1978), pp. 188–9.

7   CI monthly report, west Galway, April 1917, CO 904/102.

8   CI monthly report, east Galway, December 1917, CO 904/104.

9   Terence Dooley, *The Land for the People: The Land Question in Independent Ireland* (Dublin: UCD Press, 2004), p. 32.

10   See Paul Bew, 'Sinn Féin, Agrarian Radicalism and the War of Independence, 1919–1921', D. George Boyce (ed.), *The Revolution in Ireland, 1879–1923* (Dublin: Gill & MacMillan, 1988), pp 217–36; Terence Dooley, *The Decline of the Big House in Ireland* (Dublin: Wolfhound Press, 2001), pp. 171–208; David Fitzpatrick, *Politics and Irish Life: 1913–1921, Provincial Experience of War and Revolution* (Dublin, Gill & Macmillan, 1978), pp. 61–9; Ernest Rumpf, A.C. Hepburn, *Nationalism and Socialism in Twentieth Century Ireland* (Liverpool: LUP, 1977), pp. 50–7.

11   CI monthly report, east Galway, November 1917, CO 904/104.

12   CI monthly report, west & east Galway, December 1917, CO 904/104.

13   CI monthly report, west Galway, July 1917, CO 904/103.

14   CI monthly report, west Galway, December 1917, CO 904/ 104.

15   CI monthly report, east Galway, May 1917, CO 904/106.

16   CI monthly report, east Galway, January 1917, CO 904/102.

17   CI monthly report, west Galway, May 1917, CO 904/103.

18   CI monthly report, west Galway, May 1917, CO 904/103.

19   CI monthly report, west Galway, April 1917, CO 904/102.

20   Seán Ó Tuairisg, *An Mine: Sléacht agus Ár i gCois Fharraige* (Gaillimh: Cló Iar-Chonnacht, 2017).

21   For details of the 2017 centenary commemoration, see, *Connacht Tribune*, 2 June 2017, pp. 34–6.

22   *East Galway Democrat*, 8 September 1917.

23   *East Galway Democrat*, 7 July 1917.

24   *East Galway Democrat*, 7 July 1917.

25   *Connacht Tribune*, 6 April 1918, p. 5.

26   *East Galway Democrat*, 30 November 1918.

27   *East Galway Democrat*, 28 April 1917.

28   *East Galway Democrat*, 23 June 1917.

29   *East Galway Democrat*, 8 September 1917.

30   *Tuam Herald*, 14 December 1918, p. 2.

31   *Ibid.*

32 *Connacht Tribune*, 17 November 1917, p. 3.
33 *Connacht Tribune*, 10 November 1917, p. 5.
34 *Connacht Tribune*, 1 December 1917, p. 3.
35 *Connacht Tribune*, 24 November 1917, p. 5.
36 *Ibid.*
37 *Connacht Tribune*, 12 January 1918, p. 3.
38 *Connacht Tribune*, 6 April 1918, p. 5.
39 *Connacht Tribune*, 13 July 1918, p. 3.
40 CI monthly report, west Galway, February 1918, CO 904/105.
41 *Connacht Tribune*, 2 February 1918, p. 3.
42 *Ibid.*
43 *Connacht Tribune*, 19 January 1918, p. 3.
44 *Connacht Tribune*, 12 January 1918, p. 3.
45 *Connacht Tribune*, 26 January 1918, p. 3.
46 *Ibid.*
47 *Connacht Tribune*, 5 January 1918, p. 2; 19 January 1918, p. 3; 26 January 1918, p. 3.
48 CI monthly report, east Galway, February 1918, CO 904/105.
49 CI monthly report, west Galway, April 1917, CO 904/102.
50 CI monthly report, east Galway, April 1918, CO 904/105.
51 CI monthly report, west Galway, January 1918, CO 904/105.
52 *Freeman's Journal*, 20 February 1918, p. 2.
53 *Connacht Tribune*, 2 March 1918, p. 3.
54 Richard Mulcahy, 'Conscription and the General Headquarters Staff', *Capuchin Annual* (1968), p. 384.
55 *Ibid.*
56 *Freeman's Journal*, 22 February 1918, p. 5.
57 CI monthly report, east Galway, June 1918, CO 904/106.
58 For a discussion of the workings of the Sinn Féin Courts, see Mary Kotsonouris, *Retreat From Revolution, Dáil Courts, 1920–24* (Dublin: Irish Academic Press, 1993); Mary Kotsonouris, *The Winding up of the Dáil Courts, 1922–1925: An Obvious Duty* (Dublin: Four Courts Press, 2004); Heather Laird, *Subversive Law in Ireland, 1879–1920: From Unwritten Law to the Dáil Courts* (Dublin: Four Courts Press, 2005).
59 *Galway Express*, 23 March 1918.
60 Laffan, *The Resurrection of Ireland*, p. 134.
61 CI monthly report, west Galway, July 1917, CO 904/106.
62 CI monthly report, east Galway, September 1917, CO 904/110.
63 Mulcahy, 'Conscription and the General Headquarters Staff', p. 383; Pauric Travers, 'The Priests in Politics: The Case of Conscription', *idem*, in Oliver MacDonagh, T.W. Mandle (eds), *Irish Nationalism and Culture, 1750–1950* (London, 1983), pp. 161–81.
64 Quoted in Mulcahy, 'Conscription and the General Headquarters Staff', p. 390.
65 BMH/WS 1,219 (Sean O'Neill), pp. 72–3.

66   *Tuam Herald*, 20 April 1918, p. 2.

67   *Tuam Herald*, 13 April 1918, p. 2.

68   *Tuam Herald*, 20 April 1918, p. 4.

69   *Ibid.*

70   CI monthly report, east Galway, May 1918, CO 904/106.

71   Quoted in Tomás Ó Fiaich, 'The Irish Bishops and the Conscription Issue, 1918', *The Capuchin Annual* (1968), p. 353.

72   *Tuam Herald*, 27 April 1918, p. 2.

73   *Ibid.*

74   *Irish Times*, 5 July 1915.

75   *Tuam Herald*, 25 May 1918, p. 3.

76   *Tuam Herald*, 27 April 1918, p. 2.

77   Seán Ó Luing, 'The German Plot, 1918', *Capuchin Annual* (1968), pp. 377–81.

78   CI monthly report, west Galway, February 1917, CO 904/102.

79   CI monthly report, west Galway, January 1917, CO 904/102.

80   David Foxton, *Revolutionary Lawyers: Sinn Féin and Crown Courts in Ireland and Britain, 1916–1923* (Dublin: Four Courts Press, 2008), pp. 148–53.

81   *Galway Express*, 1 June 1918, p. 2.

82   *Galway Express*, 22 June 1918, p. 3.

83   *Galway Express*, 17 August 1918, p. 2.

84   Diarmaid Ferriter, Lawrence William White, 'Fahy, Francis Patrick', *Dictionary of Irish Biography* (Cambridge: CUP, 2002).

85   Anne Dolan, 'Ó Máille, Pádraig', *Dictionary of Irish Biography* (Cambridge: CUP, 2002).

86   *Galway Express*, 5 January 1918, p. 1.

87   *Galway Express*, 26 January 1918, p. 2.

88   *Ibid.*

89   *Galway Express*, 2 February 1918, p. 3.

90   *Galway Express*, 6 April 1918, p. 4.

91   *Galway Express*, 6 July 1918, p. 3.

92   *Ibid.*

93   *Galway Express*, 31 August 1918, p. 2.

94   *Galway Express*, 2 March 1918, p. 1.

95   *Galway Express*, 9 March 1918, p. 3.

96   *Ibid.*

97   *Galway Express*, 6 April 1918, p. 1.

98   *Galway Express*, 2 March 1918, p. 1.

99   *Galway Express*, 23 March 1918, p. 4.

100 *Ibid.*

101 *Galway Express*, 25 May 1918, p. 4.

102 *Galway Express*, 3 August 1918, p. 4.

103 *Galway Express*, 26 October 1918, p. 2.

104 *Galway Express*, 26 October 1918, p. 2.

105 *Connacht Tribune*, 12 October 1918, p. 4.

106 CI monthly report, east & west Galway, November 1918, CO 904/107.

107 BMH/WS 1,219 (Sean O'Neill), p. 46.

108 CI monthly report, east Galway, November 1918, CO 904/107.

109 BMH/WS 1,202 (Martin O'Regan), p. 4.

110 *Connacht Tribune*, 7 December 1918, p. 5.

111 *Connacht Tribune*, 14 December 1918, p. 2.

112 Walker, *Parliamentary Election Results in Ireland*, pp. 185–91.

113 For Duffy's response see *Connacht Tribune*, 28 December 1918, p. 3.

114 *Connacht Tribune*, 14 December 1918, p. 7.

115 *Tuam Herald*, 4 January 1919, p. 2.

116 Fergus Campbell, 'The Social Dynamics of Nationalist Politics in the West of Ireland, 1898–1918', *Past and Present*, 184 (2004), pp. 175–209.

117 Tony Varley, 'A Region of Sturdy Smallholders? Western Nationalists and Agrarian Politics during the First World War', *Journal of the Galway Archaeological and Historical Society*, 55 (2003), p. 141.

Chapter 5

1 Joost Augusteijn, 'Motivation: Why did they Fight for Ireland? The Motivation of Volunteers in the Revolution' in Augusteijn (ed.) *The Irish Revolution 1913–1923* (London: Palgrave, 2002), pp. 103–20; Ernest Rumpf & Anthony Hepburn, *Nationalism and Socialism in Twentieth Century Ireland* (Liverpool: LUP, 1977); David Fitzpatrick, 'The Geography of Irish Nationalism', *Past and Present*, 78 (1978), pp. 113–44; David Fitzpatrick, *Politics and Irish Life 1913–1921, Provincial Experience of War and Revolution* (Dublin: Gill & Macmillan, 1977); Peter Hart, 'The Geography of Revolution in Ireland, 1917–1923', *Past and Present*, 154 (1997), pp. 142–73; Peter Hart, *The IRA and its Enemies, Violence and Community in Cork, 1916–1923* (Oxford: OUP, 1998); Peter Hart, *The IRA at War, 1916–1923* (Oxford: OUP, 2003); Marie Coleman, *County Longford and the Irish Revolution, 1910–1923* (Dublin: Irish Academic Press, 2003); Joost Augusteijn, *From Defiance to Guerrilla Warfare, the Experience of Ordinary Volunteers in the Irish War of Independence 1916–1921* (Dublin: Irish Academic Press, 1996); 'Accounting for the Emergence of Violent Activism among Irish Revolutionaries, 1916–21', *Irish Historical Studies*, 139 (May 2007), pp. 327–44; Tom Garvin, *The Evolution of Irish Nationalist Politics* (Dublin: Gill & MacMillan, 1981); Charles Townshend, 'The Irish Republican Army and the Development of Guerrilla Warfare, 1916–21', *English Historical Review*, xciv (1979), pp. 318–45; Charles Townshend, *Political Violence in Ireland: Government and Resistance Since 1948* (Oxford: OUP, 1983).

2 BMH/WS, 1,682 (Margaret Broderick-Nicholson), p. 5.

3 CI monthly report, west Galway, July 1920, CO 904/112.

4 BMH/WS 1,756 (Seamus Murphy).

5 BMH/WS 1,612 (P.J. McDonnell), p. 14.

6   BMH/WS, 673 (Michael Fogarty), p. 9.

7   BMH/WS 1,219 (Sean O'Neill), p. 95.

8   BMH/WS 453 (George Staunton), p. 6.

9   BMH/WS 1,717 (Peter Greene), p. 5.

10 BMH/WS 1,202 (Martin O'Regan), p. 8.

11 Dorothy Macardle, *The Irish Republic* (Dublin: Irish Press Ltd, 1937), p. 964.

12 *Connacht Tribune*, 17 January 1920; BMH/WS 1,201 (John Conway), pp. 6–10; BMH/WS 1,247 (Michael Higgins), pp. 3–8.

13 BMH/WS 1,201 (John Conway), p. 4.

14 *Ibid.*, p. 8.

15 BMH/WS 1,320 (Michael J.Ryan), p. 15.

16 BMH/WS 1,018 (Martin Fahy), p. 6.

17 *Irish Times*, 26 May 1920; *Connacht Tribune*, 29 May 1920.

18 BMH/WS 714 (Thomas Hynes), p. 16.

19 BMH/WS 1,677 (Seán Broderick), p. 3.

20 For a list of those who took part in the Bookeen attack, see BMH/WS 1,124 (Daniel Kearns), p. 12.

21 *Irish Times*, 5 July 1920.

22 BMH/WS 448 (Patrick Callanan), p. 10.

23 *Connacht Tribune*, 24 July 1920.

24 For details of the attacks see BMH/WS 1,183 (Thomas Wilson), pp. 9–11; BMH/WS 1,246 (Michael Cleary), pp. 6–8; BMH/WS 673 (Michael Fogarty), pp. 11–13.

25 *Connacht Tribune*, 24 July 1920; *Irish Times*, 22 July 1920.

26 *Connacht Tribune*, 27 November 1920; *Irish Independent*, 26 November 1920.

27 *Irish Independent*, 23 August 1920.

28 BMH/WS 698 (Thomas Sweeney Newell), p. 2.

29 *Irish Times*, 23 August 1920; *Connacht Tribune*, 4 September 1920; *Irish Independent*, 23 August 1920.

30 *Freeman's Journal*, 18 September 1920; *Irish Independent*, 18 September 1920; *Irish Times*, 18 September 1920.

31 *Irish Times*, 6 December 1920; *Connacht Tribune*, 11 December 1921.

32 *Irish Times*, 2 November 1920; *Connacht Tribune*, 6 November 1920; *Irish Independent*, 2 November 1920; BMH/WS 1,033 (Patrick Glynn), pp 11–12; BMH/WS 1,007 (Daniel Ryan), pp. 7–9. BMH/WS 1,008 (Martin Fahy), pp. 13–15.

33 BMH/WS 1,007 (Daniel Ryan), p. 8.

34 *Freeman's Journal*, 5 November 1920; *Connacht Tribune*, 6, 13 November 1920; *Irish Times*, 20 November 1920.

35 *Irish Times*, 3 November 1920.

36 *Connacht Tribune*, 6 November 1920.

37 BMH/WS 1,137 (Patrick Connaughton), p. 11.

38 CI monthly report, west Galway, November 1920, CO 904/113.

39 CI monthly report, west Galway, December 1920, CO 904/113.

40 CI monthly report, west Galway, March 1921, CO 904/114.

41   BMH/WS 453 (George Staunton), p. 13.

42   BMH/WS 1,612 (P.J. McDonnell), p. 30.

43   BMH/WS 1,692 (John Feehan), p. 32.

44   BMH/WS 1,612 (P.J. McDonnell), p. 31.

45   *Ibid.*, p. 27

46   *Ibid.*, p. 32.

47   BMH/WS 1,692 (John Feehan), p. 33.

48   *Irish Times*, 19, 21 March 1921; *Irish Independent*, 18 March 1921; *Connacht Tribune*, 19 March 1921.

49   BMH/WS 1,692 (John Feehan), p. 33.

50   *Ibid.*, p. 35.

51   *Irish Times*, 19 March 1921; *Connacht Tribune*, 19 March 1921.

52   BMH/WS 1,692 (John Feehan), p. 37.

53   *Irish Times*, 8 April 1921.

54   'Jack Feehan', Notebooks of Ernie O'Malley (P17b, 113, UCDA).

55   *Irish Independent*, 8 April 1921.

56   BMH/WS 453 (George Staunton), p. 14.

57   BMH/WS 1,612 (P.J. McDonnell), p. 42.

58   BMH/WS 453 (George Staunton), p. 15.

59   BMH/WS 1,612 (P.J. McDonnell), p. 46.

60   BMH/WS 453 (George Staunton), p. 16.

61   BMH/WS 1,692 (John Feehan), p. 46.

62   *Ibid.*

63   *Irish Times*, 25 April 1921; *Connacht Tribune*, 26 April 1921.

64   BMH/WS 1,612 (P.J. McDonnell), p. 45.

65   *Ibid.*, p. 49.

66   BMH/WS 1,692 (John Feehan), p. 52.

67   *Ibid.*, p. 60.

68   *Ibid.*, p. 69.

69   *Ibid.*, p. 74.

70   *Ibid.*, p. 85.

71   For accounts of the activities of the column see, BMH/WS 1,437 (Thomas Nohilly), pp. 13–21; BMH/WS 1,408 (Thomas Mannion), pp. 7–18; BMH/WS 1,489 (Patrick Dunleavy), pp. 11–25; BMH 1,425 (Patrick Treacy), pp. 4–16.

72   BMH/WS 1,425 (Patrick Treacy), p. 6.

73   *Irish Times*, 7 June 1921; *Tuam Herald*, 11 June 1921.

74   BMH/WS 1,437 (Thomas Nohilly), p. 14.

75   BMH/WS 1,408 (Thomas Mannion), p. 13.

76   BMH/WS 1,425 (Patrick Treacy), p. 9.

77   BMH/WS 1,408 (Thomas Mannion), p. 13.

78   BMH/WS 1,425 (Patrick Treacy), p. 9.

79   *Irish Times*, 29 June 1921; *Tuam Herald*, 2 July 1921.

80   BMH/WS 1,437 (Thomas Nohilly), p. 20.

81   BMH/WS 1,408 (Thomas Mannion), p. 16.
82   BMH/WS 1,425 (Patrick Treacy), p. 15.
83   BMH/WS 1,007 (Daniel Ryan), p. 13.
84   BMH/WS 11,033 (Patrick Glynn), pp. 13–14.
85   BMH/WS 11,033 (Patrick Glynn), p. 15.
86   BMH/WS 1,007 (Daniel Ryan), p. 15.
87   BMH/WS 1,491 (Thomas Keely), p. 8.
88   BMH/WS 1,033 (Patrick Glynn), p. 5.
89   BMH/WS 1,007 (Daniel Ryan), p. 17.
90   *Ibid.*, p. 26.
91   BMH/WS 1,491 (Thomas Keely), p. 10.
92   BMH/WS 11,033 (Patrick Glynn), p. 16.
93   *Irish Times*, 17, 18 May 1921.
94   BMH/WS 1,007 (Daniel Ryan), p. 20.
95   BMH/WS 11,033 (Patrick Glynn), p. 18.
96   *Ibid.*
97   *Irish Times*, 23 May 1921.
98   BMH/WS 1,492 (Thomas Keely), p. 10.
99   Timothy G. McMahon (ed.), *Pádraig Ó Fathaigh's War of Independence: Recollections of a Galway Gaelic Leaguer* (Cork: CUP, 2000), p. 75.
100   BMH/WS 11,033 (Patrick Glynn), p. 18.
101   *Ibid.*, p. 20.
102   BMH/WS 1,612 (P.J. McDonnell), p. 82.
103   BMH/WS 1,007 (Daniel Ryan), p. 23.
104   BMH/WS 1,061 (Laurence Flynn), p. 15.
105   Brian Hughes, *Defying the IRA? Intimidation, Coercion, and Communities during the Irish Revolution* (Liverpool: LUP, 2016), p. 205.
106   *Irish Times*, 21 March 1921.
107   *Tuam Herald*, 12 March 1921.

Chapter 6

1   John Borgonovo, Gabriel Doherty, 'Smoking Gun: RIC Reprisals, Summer 1920', *History Ireland* (March/April, 2009), pp. 36–9.
2   W.J. Lowe, 'Who were the Black and Tans?', *History Ireland*, 2:3 (Autumn, 2004), pp. 47–51.
3   Charles Townshend, *The British Campaign in Ireland, 1919–21, The Development of Political and Military Policies* (Oxford: OUP, 1973), p. 201.
4   John Borgonovo, Gabriel Doherty, 'Smoking Gun? RIC Reprisals, Summer 1920' *History Ireland*, 17:2 (March/April 2009), pp. 36–9.
5   Review, Padraig Yeates, 'The Black and Tans: British Police and Auxiliaries in the Irish War of Independence', D.M. Leeson, *History Ireland*, 20:1 (Jan/Feb 2012), p. 65.
6   D.M. Leeson, *The Black and Tans: British Police and Auxiliaries in the Irish War of*

Independence (Oxford: OUP, 2012), pp. 39–67.

7   The 5th Division was comprised of Cavalry, Royal Artillery, Royal Engineers, Royal Corps of Signals, 13th Infantry Brigade, 14th Infantry Brigade, Royal Army Service Corps, Royal Army Medical Corps, Royal Army Ordinance Corp, Royal Army Veterinary Corp, Corp of Military Police and the Royal Army Chaplain Department. HQ 5th Division, Location of Troops, WO 35/93A/2, TNA.

8   HQ 5th Division, Location of Troops, WO 35/93A/2, TNA.

9   HQ 5th Division, Location of Troops, WO 35/93A/2, TNA.

10   Patrick Lynch, 'Terror in West Limerick', in J. M. MacCarthy (ed.), *Limerick's Fighting Story, from 1916 to the Truce with Britain* (Dublin: Anvil Books, 1949), pp. 226–44.

11   John O'Hanlon, Turloughmore, 2 November 1920; Michael Moran, Tuam, 24 November 1920; Harry and Patrick Loughnane, Beagh, 27 November 1920; Laurence MacDonagh, Inishmore, 22 December 1920; J.J. McDonnell, Clifden, 16 March 1921; Louis Darcy, Headford, 24 March 1921.

12   See Appendix for full details of attacks and reprisals.

13   *Freeman's Journal*, 18 November 1920, p. 5.

14   Lennox Robinson (ed.) *Lady Gregory's Journals, 1916–1930* (New York: Macmillan, 1947), entry for 20 November 1920.

15   *Irish Times*, 28 September 1920.

16   *Freeman's Journal*, 19 October 1920, p. 3.

17   *Freeman's Journal*, 19 October 1920, p. 3.

18   *Connacht Tribune*, 31 October 1920.

19   *Irish Times*, 6 November 1920.

20   *Irish Times*, 6 November 1920.

21   'Hostile Acts Or Outrages', 5th Division War Diary (WO 35/93A, TNA).

22   *Tuam Herald*, 26 March 1921.

23   *Tuam Herald*, 12 March 1921.

24   *Tuam Herald*, 11 June 1921.

25   Courts Martial of Civilians (ACT-BRO, WO 35/121, TNA).

26   *Connacht Tribune*, 3 April, 1 May, 10 July 1920.

27   *Connacht Tribune*, 27 November 1920.

28   *Tuam Herald*, 8 January 1921.

29   *Connacht Tribune*, 4 December 1920.

30   *Connacht Tribune*, 12 March 1920.

31   *Connacht Tribune*, 5 March 1921.

32   *Irish Times*, 11, 13, 15 September 1920; *Connacht Tribune*, 11, 18, 25 September 1920; *Irish Independent*, 7, 11, 20, 27 September 1920.

33   *Irish Times*, 10 September 1920, *Connacht Tribune*, 11 September 1921, 18 September 1921; *Irish Independent*, 16 September 1920. He is variously referred to as Krum, Krumm, Crom, Crumm and Crum.

34   BMH/WS 1,107 (Louis O'Dea), p. 1; BMH/WS 714 (Thomas Hynes), pp 21–4.

35   *Connacht Tribune*, 11, 18 September 1920.

36   *Ibid.*

37   *Connacht Tribune*, 2 October 1920.

38   *Ibid.*

39   *Freeman's Journal*, 16 September 1920, p. 6.

40   *Irish Times*, 15 September 1920.

41   *Connacht Tribune*, 17 September 1920.

42   *Connacht Tribune*, 11 September 1920.

43   *Irish Independent*, 18 November 1920; *Irish Times*, 18 October 1920; *Connacht Tribune*, 23 October 1920.

44   BMH/WS 1,729 (Joseph Togher), pp. 4–5.

45   BMH/WS 1,718 (Micheal Ó Droighneáin), p. 18.

46   *Ibid.*

47   *Ibid.*, p. 20.

48   CI monthly report, west Galway, October 1920, CO 904/113.

49   *Freeman's Journal*, 18 October 1920, p. 4.

50   *Connacht Tribune*, 20 November 1920.

51   *Freeman's Journal*, 18 October 1920, p. 4.

52   BMH/WS, 1,718 (Micheál Ó Droighneáin), p. 25.

53   *Ibid.*, p. 24.

54   BMH/WS 1,729 (Joseph Togher), p. 8.

55   Patrick Maume, 'William Brooke Joyce (Lord Haw Haw)', *Dictionary of Irish Biography* (Cambridge: CUP, 2002).

56   *Freeman's Journal*, 5 November 1920, p. 6; *Connacht Tribune*, 6, 13 November 1920; *Irish Times*, 20 November 1920.

57   *Irish Times*, 3 November 1920.

58   *Connacht Tribune*, 6 November 1920.

59   *Freeman's Journal*, 5 November 1920, p. 6.

60   *Irish Times*, 21 December 1920, 1 January 1921; *Connacht Tribune*, 1 January 1921; *Irish Independent*, 22 December 1920.

61   *Irish Times*, 22 December 1920.

62   *Irish Times*, 19, 24 January 1921.

63   *Connacht Tribune*, 22 January 1921.

64   *Ibid.*; *Irish Times*, 20 January 1921.

65   *Connacht Tribune*, 29 January 1921; *Irish Independent*, 25 January 1921.

66   *Ibid.*

67   *Ibid.*

68   *Freeman's Journal*, 4 March 1921; *Irish Independent*, 5 March 1921; *Connacht Tribune*, 12 March 1921.

69   BMH/WS, 1,408 (Thomas Mannion), p. 16.

70   *Irish Times*, 19 March 1921; *Connacht Tribune*, 19 March 1921.

71   *Freeman's Journal*, 18 September 1920, p. 5; *Irish Independent*, 18 September 1920; *Irish Times*, 18 September 1920.

72   *Freeman's Journal*, 5 October 1920, p. 5; *Connacht Tribune*, 9 October 1921; *Irish*

Independent, 5 October 1920.

73 CI monthly report, west Galway, October 1920, CO 904/113.

74 *Irish Times*, 21 October 1920; *Connacht Tribune*, 23 October 1920; *Irish Independent*, 21, 27 October 1920.

75 *Irish Independent*, 26 October 1920; *Irish Times*, 26 October 1920; *Connacht Tribune*, 30 October 1920.

76 CI monthly report, west Galway, October 1920, CO 904/113.

77 *Irish Times*, 6 December 1920; *Connacht Tribune*, 11 December 1921.

78 BMH/WS, 1,408 (Thomas Mannion).

79 *Irish Times*, 21, 25 February 1921; *Connacht Tribune*, 26 February 1921; *Irish Independent*, 25 February 1921.

80 See *Irish Times*, 21, 25 February 1921.

81 CI monthly report, west Galway, February 1921, CO 904/114.

82 BMH/WS, 1,718 (Micheál Ó Droighneáin), p. 30.

83 *Irish Times*, 7, 8 April 1921.

84 CI monthly report, west Galway, April 1921, CO 904/115.

85 *Irish Times*, 2, 3 May 1921; *Connacht Tribune*, 7 May 1921.

86 CI monthly report, west Galway, May 1921, CO 904/115.

87 *Connacht Tribune*, 7 May 1921.

88 *Freeman's Journal*, 12 May 1921, p. 4; *Irish Times*, 12 May 1921; *Irish Independent*, 12, 13, 14 May 1921.

89 *Freeman's Journal*, 12 May 1921, p. 4.

90 *Ibid.*

91 CI monthly report, west Galway, May 1921, CO 904/115.

92 *Ibid.*

93 *Connacht Tribune*, 28 May 1921.

94 BMH/WS 1,408 (Thomas Mannion), p. 16; *Connacht Tribune*, 28 May 1921.

95 BMH/WS, 1,320 (Michael J. Ryan), p. 17.

96 *Connacht Tribune*, 27 November 1920; *Irish Independent*, 26 November 1920.

97 BMH/WS, 1,247 (Michael Higgins), p. 9.

98 Papers relating to the deaths of the Loughnane Brothers (Pol 4/7, NUIGA); *Connacht Tribune*, 11 December 1920; *Irish Independent*, 7 December 1920; *Irish Times*, 7 December 1920.

99 *Irish Times*, 28 March 1921.

100 BMH/WS 714 (Thomas Hynes), p. 14.

101 *Irish Times*, 26, 28 March 1921; *Irish Independent*, 28 March 1921.

102 'The Daring Louis Darcy', also known as 'The Lament for Louis Darcy' composed by John Henihan was recorded by members of the Keane family, Caherlistrane.

103 Jane Leonard, 'Survivors' in John Horne (ed.), *Our War: Ireland and the Great War* (Dublin: IAP, 2008), p. 211.

104 *Irish Times*, 1 May 1920.

105 Hostile Acts or Outrages (HQ 5th Division, WO 35/93A/2, TNA).

106 *Ibid.*

107 *Tuam Herald*, 1 January 1921.
108 William Feeney; Patrick Feeney, John Folan and William Feeney were charged with his murder. *Connacht Tribune*, 7, 14 February 1920.
109 *Irish Times*, 5 February 1920; CI monthly report, west Galway, February 1920, CO 904/111.
110 BMH/WS 1,173 (Michael Hynes).
111 *Ibid.*
112 *Connacht Tribune*, 9 April 1921.
113 *Tuam Herald*, 9 April 1921.
114 *Irish Independent*, 28 April 1921, p. 5.
115 BMH/WS 1,400 (John P. McCormack), p. 7.
116 Paul Taylor, *Heroes or Traitors?: Experiences of Southern Irish Soldiers Returning from the Great War 1919–1939* (Liverpool: LUP, 2012), p. 15.
117 Minutes of the Galway Urban District Council, 23 November 1919 (NUIGA).
118 Minutes of the Galway Urban District Council, 10 July 1919, 11 August 1919.
119 Minutes of the Galway Urban District Council, 23 February 1921.
120 Minutes of the Galway Urban District Council, 3 April 1919, 8 May 1919.
121 Jane Leonard, 'Getting them at Last: The IRA and Ex-servicemen', David Fitzpatrick (ed.), *Revolution: Ireland 1917–1923* (Dublin: Trinity History Workshop, 1990), pp. 118–29.
122 *Connacht Tribune*, 19 March 1921.
123 *Connacht Tribune*, 16 October 1920.
124 *Connacht Tribune*, 21 May 1921.
125 See *Irish Times*, 26 July 1919.
126 *Connacht Tribune*, 13 November 1920.
127 *Connacht Tribune*, 20 November 1920.
128 *Connacht Tribune*, 13 November 1920.
129 *Connacht Tribune*, 11 December 1920.
130 *Connacht Tribune*, 21 January 1921; *Tuam Herald*, 5 February 1920.
131 *Tuam Herald*, 1 January 1921.
132 *Tuam Herald*, 12 February 1921.
133 *Ibid.*
134 *Ibid.*
135 Conor McNamara, 'The War of Independence in Connacht', in John Crowley, Michael Murphy, Donal Ó Drisceoil (eds), *Atlas of the Irish Revolution* (Cork: Cork University Press, 2017), pp. 600–07.
136 Joost Augusteijn, 'Motivation: "Why Did They Fight for Ireland", The Motivation of Volunteers in the Revolution', in Augusteijn (ed.), *The Irish Revolution 1913–1923* (London: Palgrave, 2002), p. 106.
137 *Ibid.*, p. 109.
138 General Administration of the Army in Ireland (WO 35, TNA).
139 HQ 5th Division (WO 35/93, A/2, TNA).

Chapter 7

1 Donald L. Horowitz, *Ethnic Groups in Conflict* (California: CUP, 1985), pp. 3–55.

2 *Ibid.*, p. 12.

3 T.P. O'Neill, 'Political Life: 1870–1921', in Michael Hurley (ed.), *Irish Anglicanism 1869–1969, Essays on the Role of Anglicanism in Irish Life* (Dublin: Allen Figgis, 1970), p. 108.

4 Miriam Moffitt, 'Protestant Tenant Farmers and the Land League in North Connacht' in Conor McNamara, Carla King (eds) *The West of Ireland: New Perspectives on the Nineteenth Century* (Dublin: History Press, 2011), p. 93.

5 *Ibid*, p. 95.

6 O'Neill, 'Political Life: 1870–1921', p. 106.

7 Enda Delaney, *Demography, State and Society: Irish Migration to Britain, 1921–1971* (Liverpool: LUP, 2000), p. 71.

8 Peter Hart, *The IRA at War, 1916–1923* (Oxford: OUP, 2003), p. 240.

9 *Ibid.*, p. 234.

10 Brian Hanley, 'Fear and Loathing at Coolacrease', *History Ireland* (January/February 2008), p. 6.

11 Table XXIX: Comparative View of the Number and Percentage of Persons Belonging to Each Religious Profession in the County of Galway as Constituted at Cach Census from 1861 to 1911: *Census Returns for Ireland, 1911, Showing Area … Province of Connaught, County of Galway,* p. 163, H.C., *1913* (Cd. 6052, 6052-I, 6052-II, 6052-III, 6052-IV, 6052-V), cxvii, p.1.

12 Alexander Boden, Robert Ronaldson, Andrew Mitchell, John Coban, Alexander Knox, John Lowry, Colen Metheun, Edwin Farrington, James Hutchinson, William Spratt, John Kidd, Elizabeth Thomas, John Sanderson, Charles Young, David Craig, James Graham. Based on returns taken from the Irish Census 1911 online.

13 Moffitt, 'Protestant Tenant Farmers and the Land League in North Connacht'.

14 See Pádraig G. Lane, 'The Encumbered Estates Court and Galway Land Ownership, 1849–1858', in Gerard Moran (ed.), *Galway, History and Society: Interdisciplinary Essays on the History of an Irish County* (Dublin: Geography Press, 1996), pp. 395–418.

15 Richard Pharr, Arthur McLean, John Thompson, Frederick Hilton, Isabella Ramsey, Minnie Smith, Annie Hood, Dorothy Rushton, Ethel McGann, Mabel Cooke, Charles Ormsby. Based on returns taken from the Irish census 1911 online.

16 Correspondence of Lady Mahon, 1925–28 (Mahon Papers, MS 47,903/4, NLI).

17 Patrick Maume, 'Trench, Frederick Oliver 3rd Baron Ashtown', *Dictionary of Irish Biography* (Cambridge: CUP, 2002).

18 L. Perry Curtis, 'The Last Gasp of Southern Unionism: Lord Ashtown of Woodlawn', *Éire-Ireland*, 40:3–4, pp. 140–88.

19 This figure includes 33 members of the Church of Ireland, 18 Presbyterians, 9 members of the Church of England, 1 member of the Church of Scotland. Based on returns taken from the Irish census 1911 online.

20   Griffith Jones from Wales, Joseph Nash from Cork, Robert Wyse from Offaly and
     Walter Graham from Cavan. Based on returns taken from the Irish census 1911
     online.

21   William Clancy, Ethel Reynolds, Charles Crowley, William Lispcom, Anne
     Sambrook, Margaret Haughton, Jane Beasley, Jemima Patterson, Isabella Johnston,
     Marcy Clements, Emily Lockley, Elizabeth Graham, Sarah Hooey. Based on returns
     taken from the Irish census 1911 online.

22   Ballymacward Vestry Book, 1891–1940, RCB Library.

23   There were only six baptisms between 1920 and 1929 and only ten baptisms in the
     parish between 1930 and 1955. Register of Births, Kilmacduagh, 1874–1967, RCB
     Library.

24   Based on returns taken from the Irish Census 1911 online.

25   Register of Births, St Nicholas Parish, Galway, RCB Library. The congregation
     remained stable after independence; however, with a decline in baptisms to just one
     between 1930 and 1939 compared to the thirty baptisms over the previous decade.

26   Register of Births, St Nicholas Parish, Galway.

27   See Appendix for Professions of fifty-nine heads of families from the Saint Nicholas
     Anglican Parish Register, Galway town, 1910–1919.

28   Figures based on returns from the 1911 census online for County Galway.

29   *Ibid.*

30   *Ibid.*

31   *Ibid.*

32   Internal Memorandum and Notes on the Composition of the Membership and
     Organising Committee of the Galway Branch of the Irish Unionist Alliance (Mahon
     Papers, MS 47,874/2, NLI).

33   For reports of county meetings of the Irish unionist Alliance during the Home Rule
     crisis see: Sligo branch, *Irish Times*, 18 May 1912; Roscommon branch, *Irish Times*,
     9 May 1913; Clare branch, *Irish Times*, 24 October 1913.

34   Irish Unionist Alliance, Annual Reports (Mahon Papers, MS 47,874/1, NLI).

35   Minute Books for the County Galway Irish Unionist Alliance, 1911–18 (Mahon
     Papers, MS 47,874/5, NLI).

36   Letter from Lord Clonbrock to W.J. Waithman, dated 22 May 1912 (Mahon Papers,
     MS 47,874/6, NLI).

37   Correspondence of the Galway Branch of the Irish Unionist Alliance, 1912 (Mahon
     Papers, MS 47,874/7-10, NLI).

38   Lord Clonbrock to W.J. Waithman, dated 7 September 1911 (Mahon Papers, MS
     47,874/4, NLI).

39   Lord Clonbrock to W.J. Waithman, dated 7 October 1911 (Mahon Papers, MS
     47,874/4, NLI).

40   James O'Hara of Lenaboy to the CGIUA, dated 17 September 1912 (Mahon Papers,
     MS 47,874 / 7-10, NLI).

41   Seymour Ellis of Claremorris to the CGIUA, dated 28 September 1912 (Mahon
     Papers, MS 47,874/7-10, NLI).

42   Lord Gough to the CGIUA, dated 22 August 1912 (Mahon Papers, MS 47,874/7-10, NLI).

43   James MacDermott to the CGIUA, dated 12 September 1912 (Mahon Papers, MS 47,874/7-10, NLI).

44   Edward Shaw-Tener to the CGIUA, dated 12 November 1913 (Mahon Papers, MS 47,874/13-16, NLI).

45   James Jackson of Portumna to the CGIUA, dated 31 May 1913 (Mahon Papers, MS 47,874/13-1, NLI).

46   'Appendix B, Planter farms in 1908–9', Miriam Moffitt, *Clanricarde's Planters and Land Agitation in East Galway, 1886–1916* (Dublin: Four Courts Press, 2011), p. 62.

47   Correspondence of the Galway Branch of the Irish Unionist Alliance, 1914 (Mahon Papers, MS 47,874/17, NLI).

48   *Ibid.*

49   *Connacht Tribune*, 8 May 1918.

50   *Ibid.*

51   *Freeman's Journal*, 14 September 1920.

52   *Galway Express*, 14 August 1920.

53   *Freeman's Journal*, 7 September 1920.

54   *Connacht Tribune*, 11 September 1920.

55   *Connacht Tribune*, 11 September 1920.

56   *Connacht Tribune*, 9 September 1920.

57   *Connacht Tribune*, 21 June 1913, 18 September 1920.

58   *Galway Express*, 17 November 1920.

59   BMH/WS, 1,692 (John Feehan), p. 10.

60   BMH/WS 1,408 (Thomas Mannion), p. 6.

61   BMH/WS 1,033 (Patrick Glynn), pp. 3–4.

62   BMH/WS 1,491 (Thomas Keely), p. 3.

63   *Irish Times*, 6 February 1920.

64   *Galway Express*, 14 February 1920; see also *Connacht Tribune*, 10 July 1920, p. 2.

65   *Galway Express*, 10 April 1920, *Irish Times*, 17 April 1920.

66   *Connacht Tribune*, 6 March 1920, p. 5.

67   *Irish Times*, 6 March 1920.

68   BMH/WS 1,201(Dick Conway), p. 3.

69   CI monthly report, east Galway, January 1920, CO 904/111.

70   CI monthly report, east Galway, January 1920, CO 904/111.

71   *Galway Express*, 10 April 1920.

72   *Galway Express*, 28 April 1920.

73   *Galway Express*, 10 April 1920.

74   *Ibid.*

75   *Ibid.*

76   For a discussion of the workings of the Sinn Féin Courts, see Mary Kotsonouris, *Retreat From Revolution, Dáil Courts, 1920–24* (Dublin: Irish Academic Press, 1994);

Mary Kotsonouris, *The Winding Up of the Dáil Courts, 1922–1925: An Obvious Duty* (Dublin: Four Courts Press, 2004).

77   *Galway Express*, 10 April 1920.

78   *Connacht Tribune*, 24 July 1920, p. 6.

79   *Galway Express*, 3 May 1920.

80   Fergus Campbell, *Land and Revolution, Nationalist Politics in the West of Ireland, 1891–1921* (Oxford: OUP, 2005), pp. 226–85; Terence Dooley, *Decline of the Big House in Ireland, A Study of Irish Landed Families, 1860–1960* (Dublin: Wolfhound Press, 2001).

81   *Irish Times*, 26, 27 April 1922.

82   *Irish Times*, 22 August 1922.

83   *Irish Times*, 12 January 1922.

84   *Irish Times*, 10 January 1922.

85   *Irish Times*, 25 March 1922.

86   *Irish Times*, 9 March 1922.

87   *Irish Times*, 17 June 1922.

88   *Irish Times*, 3 June 1922.

89   The files relating to policemen from the Ballinasloe district are: CO 762/26/16 (Bernard Conway); CO 762/118/16 (Kathleen Fitzgerald); CO 762/26/3 (Michael Fitzgerald); CO 762/163/1 (Patrick Keating); CO 762/159/4 (Patrick Larkin); CO 762/123/13 (Patrick Lee); CO 762/47/10 (Sarah Louis); CO 762/48/11 (John Scanlon); CO 762/35/2 (John Tapley), IGC, TNA.

90   *East Galway Democrat*, 19 April 1922.

91   *Church of Ireland Gazette*, 16 June 1922.

92   *Irish Times*, 16 June 1922.

93   *Irish Times*, 25 July 1922.

94   *Irish Times*, 26 July 1922.

95   *Irish Times*, 26 July 1922.

96   CO 762/103/11 (Revd Richard Shannon) IGC, TNA.

97   CO 762/17/17 (Elizabeth Walsh), IGC, TNA.

98   CO 762/12/13 (Albert Barrett), IGC, TNA.

99   CO 762/151/9 (Edward Thompson), IGC, TNA.

100   Curtis, 'The Last gasp of Southern Unionism: Lord Ashtown of Woodlawn'.

101   *Irish Times*, 13 May 1922.

102   CO 762/15/10 (Lord Ashtown), IGC, TNA.

103   Claim numbers: 282-303 (Lord Ashtown), 2D/62/60-69, NA.

104   CO 762/151/9 (Edward Thompson), IGC, TNA.

105   CO 762/183/11, D989/B/9 (Frederick Falkiner), IGC, TNA.

106   CO 762/142/6, D989/B/3/9 (Richard Falkiner), IGC, TNA.

107   CO 762/133/12 (William Colgan), IGC, TNA.

108   CO 762/91/17 (May Craig); CO 762/18/1 (Elizabeth Wilkinson); CO 762/196/24 (Richard Seale), IGC, TNA.

109   CO 762/112/3 (James Greathead); CO 762/55/1 (Lord Killanin); CO 762/43/1 (Thomas Lewin); CO 762/166/22 (Charles Lynch-Staunton); CO 762/65/15

(Dudley Persse); CO 762/115/12 (Mary Wallscourt); IGC, TNA.

110 Damage to Property Compensation Act 1923; Registration of Claims, 2D/62/60-69, NA.

111 *Ibid.*

112 Claim 308 (Michael Henry Burke); Claim 249 (Denis B. Kirwan); Claim 626 (Lord Killanin); Damage to Property Compensation Act 1923; Registration of Claims, 2D/62/60-69, NA.

113 Claim 625, 670 (Charles George Purtis); Claim 950 (Irish Church Missions), 2D/62/60-69, NA.

114 Miriam Moffitt, *Soupers and Jumpers: The Protestant Missions in Connemara, 1848–1937* (Dublin: Four Courts Press, 2008), pp. 159–73.

115 Claim 510 (Revd George Collins), 2D/62/60–69, NA.

116 Claim 591, 592 (Irish Church Body); Claim 593 (Irish Church Body), 2D/62/60-69, NA. It's not clear if claim 593 was paid.

117 Claim 752 (Alexander Grant); Claim 823 (William T. Lotts), 2D/62/60-69, NA.

118 Amartya Sen, *Identity and Violence: The Illusion of Identity* (London: Allen Lane, 2006), p. 2.

119 Joshua A. Sanborn, 'Unsettling the Empire: Violent Migrations and Social Disaster in Russia During World War I', *The Journal of Modern History*, 77:2 (June 2005), p. 290.

120 Horrowitz, *Ethnic Groups in Conflict*, p. 7.

121 *Ibid*, p. 2.

122 Delaney, *Demography, State and Society: Irish Migration to Britain, 1921–1971*, pp. 69–83.

Conclusion

1 *Connacht Tribune*, 23 April 1966.

2 *Connacht Tribune*, 2, 9 April 1966.

3 Paul Ricoeur, *Memory, History, Forgetting* (Chicago: UCP, 2004).

4 Ella O'Dwyer, *The Rising of the Moon, The Language of Power* (London: Pluto Press, 2003), p. 51.

5 Heather Laird, *Subversive Law in Ireland, 1879–1920: From Unwritten Law to Dáil Courts* (Dublin: Four Courts, 2005), p. 121.

6 See Declan Kiberd, 'The Elephant of Revolutionary Forgetfulness', in Máirín Ní Dhonnchádha, Theo Dorgan (eds), *Revising the Rising* (Derry: Field Day, 1991), pp. 1–20.

7 See William Irwin Thompson, *The Imagination of an Insurrection; Dublin Easter 1916* (Oxford: OUP, 1982); F.S.L. Lyons, *Culture and Anarchy in Ireland, 1890–1939* (London: Clarendon Press, 1979), p. 11.

8 Brian Hughes, *Defying the IRA? Intimidation, Coercion, and Communities during the Irish Revolution* (Liverpool: LUP, 2016), p. 207.

9 Stephen Gwynn, *The Irish Situation* (London: Jonathan Cape, 1921), p. 11.

10   William O'Malley, *Glancing Back: 70 years' Experiences and Reminiscences of Pressman, Sportsman and Member of Parliament* (London: Wright, 1933), pp. 138.

11   *Ibid.*, p. 134.

12   CI monthly confidential report, east Galway, October 1917, CO 904/104.

13   CI monthly confidential report, west Galway, January 1917, CO 904/102.

14   *The Royal Commission on the Rebellion in Ireland: Minutes of Evidence and Appendix of Documents.* H.C. [1916] (Cd. 1813), p. 77.

15   'Peasants and Politics', in Eric Hobsbawm (ed.), *Uncommon People, Resistance, Rebellion and Jazz* (New York: The New Press, 1998), p. 157.

16   'Bandits and Revolution', in Eric Hobsbawm (ed.), *Bandits* (London: Abacus, 1969), pp. 106–20.

17   *Ibid.*, pp. 106–20.

18   See Hobsbawm, 'Peasants and Politics'.

19   *Irish Times*, 2 January 1948.

20   *Ibid.*

21   'Sarah Mellows to Fr Tom Burke', Papers of Margaret and Father Tom Burke, Castlegar, P30/34, UCDA.

Appendix

Casualties of violence in County Galway, January 1920–July 1921

Name	Date	Location	Status	Perpetrator
Patrick Thornton	04/02/1920	Spiddal	Civilian	Republicans
James Ward	06/02/1920	Menlo	Civilian	Agrarian
Frank Shawe-Taylor	02/03/1920	Athenry	Civilian	Agrarian
Martin Cullinane	04/03/1920	Corofin	Civilian	IRA
Robert Bishop	06/05/1920	Athenry	Crown Forces	Accident
Herbert Thompson	30/06/1920	Galway town	Crown Forces	Accident
Con. James Burke	19/07/1920	Gallagh	RIC	IRA
Con. Patrick Carey	19/07/1920	Gallagh	RIC	IRA
Con. Martin Foley	21/08/1920	Oranmore	RIC	IRA
Pt. Edward Krum	09/09/1920	Galway town	Crown Forces	IRA
Vol. Sean Mulvoy	09/09/1920	Galway town	IRA	Crown Forces
Vol. Seamus Quirke	09/09/1920	Galway town	IRA	Crown Forces
Vol. Joseph Athy	17/09/1920	Oranmore	IRA	Crown Forces
A.M. Atkins	17/09/1920	Galway town	Crown Forces	Accident
Vol. John O'Hanlon	02/10/1920	Turloughmore	Republican	Crown Forces
Patrick Joyce	16/10/1920	Galway town	Civilian	IRA
Vol. Michael Walsh	20/10/1920	Galway town	Republican	Crown Forces
Thomas Egan	24/10/1920	Athenry	Civilian	Crown Forces
Con. Timothy Horan	30/10/1920	Castledaly	RIC	IRA
Eileen Quinn	01/11/1920	Kiltartan	Civilian	Crown Forces
Fr. Michael Griffin	14/11/1920	Galway town	Civilian	Crown Forces
Vol. Michael Moran	24/11/1920	Galway	IRA	Crown Forces
Vol. H. Loughnane	27/11/1920	Beagh	IRA	Crown Forces
Vol. Pat Loughnane	27/11/1920	Beagh	IRA	Crown Forces

Vol. Joseph Howley	09/12/1920	Dublin	IRA	Crown Forces
Laurence MacDónagh	20/12/1920	Inishmore	Civilian	Crown Forces
Patrick Walsh	01/01/1921	Galway	Civilian	In custody
Michael Mullins	01/01/1921	Galway	Civilian	In custody
Thomas Collins	19/01/1921	Headford	Civilian	Crown Forces
James Kirwan	22/01/1921	Tuam	Civilian	Crown Forces
William Walsh	22/01/1921	Headford	Civilian	Crown Forces
Michael Hoade	22/01/1921	Caherlistrane	Civilian	Crown Forces
Vol. John Geoghegan	20/02/1921	Moycullen	IRA	Crown Forces
Thomas Mullen	03/03/1921	Clonberne	Civilian	Crown Forces
Con. Chas. Reynolds	16/03/1921	Clifden	RIC	IRA
Con. Thom. Sweeney	16/03/1921	Clifden	RIC	IRA
J.J. McDonnell	16/03/1921	Clifden	Civilian	Crown Forces
Vol. Louis Darcy	24/03/1921	Oranmore	IRA	Crown Forces
Tom Morris	02/04/1921	Kinvara	Civilian	IRA
Vol. Patrick Cloonan	06/04/1921	Kilcolgan	IRA	Crown Forces
Con. William Pearson	06/04/1921	Screebe	RIC	IRA
Con. John Boylan	23/04/1921	Kilmilkin	RIC	IRA
Thomas Hannon	26/04/1921	Clonberne	Civilian	IRA
Patrick Molloy	30/04/1921	Kilroe	Civilian	Crown Forces
Hugh Tully	12/05/1921	Galway town	Civilian	Crown Forces
Christopher Folan	12/05/1921	Galway town	Civilian	Crown Forces
Capt. Cecil Blake D.I.	15/05/1921	Gort	RIC	IRA
Capt. F. Cornwallis	15/05/1921	Gort	Crown Forces	IRA
Eliza Blake	15/05/1921	Gort	Civilian	IRA
Con. John Kearney	15/05/1921	Gort	RIC	Crown Forces
Lieut. Rob. McCreery	15/05/1921	Gort	Crown Forces	IRA
Thomas McKeever	20/05/1921	Dunmore	Civilian	Crown Forces
Ser. James Murren	27/06/1921	Milltown	RIC	IRA
Con. Edgar Day	27/06/1921	Milltown	RIC	IRA
Vol. Bill Freeney	30/06/1921	Athenry	IRA	Accident
Mathias Kelly	12/07/1921	Spiddal	Crown Forces	Accident

West Connemara Flying Column, 1921

Commanded by P.J. McDonnell and including John (Jack) Feehan, Martin Connolly, Colm Ó Gaora, James King, George Staunton, Thomas Coyne, William King, Richard Joyce, Michael Joyce, John King, Patrick Wallace, Pádraic Ó Maille, Peter Wallace, John Dundas, John C. King, John S. Connelly, Denis Keane, Stephen Mannion, Thomas Madden, Paul Bartley, William Connelly, Laurence O'Toole, Gerald Bartley, Patrick Keane, Christy Breen, Eámon Ó Maille, Pádraic Ó Nee, Pádraic Geoghegan, Martin Joyce, Charles O'Malley.

Source: BMH/WS 1,612 (P.J. McDonnell), p. 83.

North Galway Flying Column, 1921

Commanded by Thomas Dunleavy (Barnaderg) and including James (Seamus) Moloney, Martin Ryan (Glenamaddy batt), Tim and Patrick Dunleavy (Barnaderg), Thomas Tarmay, Paddy Conway (Caherlistrane), Thomas and Martin Mannion (Dunmore), Thomas Feerick (Milltown), Brian Cunniffe (Kilkerrin), Patrick Treacy (Glenamaddy), Thomas Nohilly (Corofin), Thomas Ryan (Tuam), Jack Knight (Glenamaddy), Peter Brennan (Milltown), Patrick Noonan (Williamastown), Patrick McHugh (Sylane).

Source: BMH/WS 1,425 (Patrick Treacy), p. 5; BMH/WS 1,437 (Thomas Nohilly), p. 16/20.

South Galway Flying Column, 1921

Joseph Stanford (Gort), John Coen (Kilbeacanty), Patrick Glynn (Kilbeacanty), Thomas Keely (Kilbeacanty), Thomas Craven (Belcare), Michael Kelly (Gort), Patrick Houlihan (County Clare), Daniel Ryan (Kilbeacanty), Patrick Glynn (Gort batt). Timothy Reilly, Thomas Reilly, John Keely and Martin Coen, all Kilbeacanty, acted as scouts and Michael Kelly as intelligence officer for the attacks at Ballyturin in May 1921.

Source: BMH/WS 1,007 (Daniel Ryan), p. 26; BMH/WS 1,491 (Thomas Keely), p. 8.

Bibliography

Books/Articles

Joost Augusteijn, *From Public Defiance to Guerrilla Warfare: The Experience of Ordinary Volunteers in the Irish War of Independence, 1916–1921* (Dublin: Irish Academic Press, 1996).

—, 'Motivation: "Why Did They Fight for Ireland", The Motivation of Volunteers in the Revolution', *The Irish Revolution 1913–1923* (London: Palgrave, 2002), pp. 103–20.

—, 'Accounting for the Emergence of Violent Activism Among Irish Revolutionaries, 1916–21', *Irish Historical Studies*, xxxi (May 2007), pp. 237–45.

Tom Barry, *Guerrilla Days in Ireland* (Tralee: Anvil, 1964).

Paul Bew, 'Sinn Féin, Agrarian Radicalism and the War of Independence, 1919–1921', in D. George Boyce (ed.), *The Revolution in Ireland, 1879–1923* (Dublin: Gill & MacMillan, 1988), pp. 217–36.

John Borgonovo, Gabriel Doherty, 'Smoking Gun: RIC Reprisals, Summer 1920', *History Ireland*, (March/April, 2009), pp. 36–9.

Dan Breen, *My Fight for Irish Freedom* (Dublin: Maunsel, 1924).

Fergus Campbell, 'The Social Dynamics of Nationalist Politics in the West of Ireland, 1898–1918', *Past and Present*, 184 (2004), pp. 175–209.

—, *Land & Revolution: Nationalist Politics in the West of Ireland, 1891–1921* (Oxford: OUP, 2005).

—, 'The Easter Rising in Galway', *History Ireland* (14:2), 2006, pp. 22–5.

Samuel Clark, 'Social Composition of the Land League', *Irish Historical Studies*, 17 (1979), pp. 447–65.

—, *Social Origins of the Irish Land War* (Princeton: PUP, 1979).

Georgina Clinton, 'William O'Malley', *Dictionary of Irish Biography* (Cambridge: CUP, 2002).

Gerry Cloonan, *Galway Rising Centenary Commemoration, 1916–2016* (Craughwell: Galway, 2016).

Anne Coleman, *Riotous Roscommon: Maynooth Series in Local History* (Dublin: Four Courts Press, 1999).

Marie Coleman, *County Longford and the Irish Revolution, 1910–1923* (Dublin: Irish Academic Press, 2003).

John Crowley, Michael Murphy, Donal Ó Drisceoil (eds), *Atlas of the Irish Revolution* (Cork: Cork University Press, 2017).

John Cunningham, *Labour in the West of Ireland, Working Life and Struggle, 1890–1914* (Belfast: Athol Books, 1995).

—, *'A town tormented by the sea:' Galway 1790–1914* (Dublin: Geography Publications, 2004).

L. Perry Curtis Jnr, 'The Last Gasp of Southern Unionism: Lord Ashtown of Woodlawn', *Eire–Ireland*, 40 (Winter/Fall, 2005), pp. 140–88.

Enda Delaney, *Demography, State and Society: Irish Migration to Britain, 1921–1971* (Liverpool: LUP, 2000).

Anne Dolan, 'Ó Máille, Pádraic', *Dictionary of Irish Biography* (Cambridge: CUP, 2002).

Martin Dolan, 'The Story of the 1916 Rising in Galway', *Connacht Tribune*, April 1966, reproduced, *Connacht Tribune*, January – April 2016.

Terence Dooley, 'Landlords and the Land Question, 1879–1909', in Carla King (ed.), *Famine, Land and Culture in Ireland* (Dublin: UCD Press, 2000), pp. 116–39.

—, *The Decline of the Big House in Ireland, A Study of the Irish Landed Families, 1860–1960* (Dublin: Wolfhound Press, 2001).

—, *The Land for the People: The Land Question in Independent Ireland* (Dublin: UCD Press, 2004).

Theo Dorgan, Máirín Ní Dhonnchádha (eds), *Revising the Rising* (Derry: Field Day, 1991).

Richard English, Cormac O'Malley (eds), *Prisoners: The Civil War Letters of Ernie O'Malley* (Dublin: Poolbeg Press, 1991).

Michael Farry, *The Aftermath of Revolution: Sligo, 1921–23* (Dublin: UCD Press, 2000).

Diarmaid Ferriter, Lawrence William White, 'Fahy, Francis Patrick', *Dictionary of Irish Biography* (Cambridge: CUP, 2002).

David Fitzpatrick, 'The Geography of Irish Nationalism', *Past & Present*, 78 (1978), pp. 113–44.

—, *Politics and Irish Life 1913–1921: Provincial Experience of War and Revolution* (Dublin: Gill & Macmillan, 1978).

—, (ed.), *Revolution? Ireland 1917–1923* (Dublin: Trinity History Workshop, 1990).

—, 'Irish Farming Families before the First World War', *Comparative Studies in Society and History*, 25:2 (April 1983), pp. 339–74.

Plummer Flippen Jones, *Shamrock Land, A Ramble Through Ireland* (New York: Moffat, Yard & Co, 1908).

David Foxton, *Revolutionary Lawyers: Sinn Féin and Crown Courts in Ireland and Britain, 1916–1923* (Dublin: Four Courts Press, 2008).

Tom Garvin, *The Evolution of Irish Nationalist Politics* (Dublin: Gill & Macmillan, 1981).

Laurence M. Geary, *The Plan of Campaign, 1886–1891* (Cork: CUP, 1986).

C. Desmond Greaves, *Liam Mellows and the Irish Revolution* (London: Lawrence & Wishart, 1971).

Stephen Gwynn, *The Case for Home Rule* (Dublin: Maunsel, 1911).

—, *The Irish Situation* (London: Jonathan Cape, 1921).

—, *Experiences of a Literary Man* (New York: Holt & Co., 1926).

Brian Hanley, 'Fear and Loathing at Coolacrease', *History Ireland* (January/ February 2008), pp. 6–8.

Peter Hart, 'The Geography of Revolution in Ireland, 1917–1923', *Past and Present*, 154 (1997), pp. 142–73;

—, *The IRA and Its Enemies: Violence and Community in Cork, 1916–1923* (Oxford: OUP, 1998).

—, *The IRA at War, 1916–1923* (Oxford: OUP, 2003).

Eric Hobsbawm, *Bandits* (London: Abacus, 1969).

—, *Uncommon People, Resistance, Rebellion and Jazz* (New York: Weidenfeld & Nicolson, 1998), pp. 146–66.

John Horne (ed.), *Our War: Ireland and the Great War* (Dublin: RIA, 2008).

Donald L. Horowitz, *Ethnic Groups in Conflict* (California: CUP, 1985).

Bridget Hourican, 'Hazleton, William', *Dictionary of Irish Biography* (Cambridge: CUP, 2002).

Brian Hughes, *Defying the IRA? Intimidation, Coercion, and Communities during the Irish Revolution* (Liverpool: LUP, 2016).

Keith Jeffery, 'Obligation: "Irishmen Remember Belgium"', *Ireland and the Great War* (Cambridge: CUP, 2000), pp. 5–36.

Tom Johnstone, *Orange, Green & Khaki, The Story of the Irish Regiments in the Great War, 1914–18* (Dublin: Gill & Macmillan, 1992).

Liam Kennedy, 'Farmers, Traders and Agricultural Politics in Pre-Independence Ireland', Samuel Clark, James Donnelly Jnr (eds), *Irish Peasants: Violence and Political Unrest, 1780–1914* (Dublin: Gill & Macmillan, 1998), pp. 339–73.

Mary Kotsonouris, *Retreat From Revolution, Dáil Courts, 1920–24* (Dublin: Irish Academic Press, 1993).

—, *The Winding Up of the Dáil Courts, 1922–1925: An Obvious Duty* (Dublin: Four Courts Press, 2004).

Michael Laffan, *The Resurrection of Ireland, The Sinn Féin Party, 1916–1923* (Cambridge: CUP, 1999), pp. 116–21.

Heather Laird, *Subversive Law in Ireland, 1879–1920: From Unwritten Law to the Dáil Courts* (Dublin: Four Courts Press, 2005).

Jane Leonard, 'Getting them at Last: The IRA and Ex-Servicemen', in David Fitzpatrick (ed.), *Revolution: Ireland 1917–1923* (Dublin: Trinity History Workshop, 1990), pp. 118–29.

D.M. Lesson, *The Black and Tans: British Police and Auxiliaries in the Irish War of Independence, 1920–1921* (Oxford: OUP, 2011).

—, 'Survivors', in John Horne (ed.), *Our War: Ireland and the Great War* (Dublin: RIA, 2008).

W.J. Lowe, 'Who were the Black and Tans?', *History Ireland*, 2:3 (Autumn, 2004), pp. 47–51.

Patrick Lynch, 'Terror in West Limerick', in J.M. MacCarthy (ed.), *Limerick's Fighting Story, From 1916 to the Truce With Britain* (Dublin: Anvil Books, 1949), pp. 226–44.

F.S.L. Lyons, *Culture and Anarchy in Ireland, 1890–1939* (Oxford: OUP, 1979).

Dorothy Macardle, *The Irish Republic* (Dublin: Irish Press Ltd, 1937).

Uinseann MacEoin, *Survivors: The Story of Ireland's Struggle as Told Through Some of her Outstanding People* (Dublin: Argenta Publications, 1980).

Brendan Mac Giolla Choille (ed.), *Intelligence Notes, 1913–1916* (Dublin: Oifig an tSolathair, 1966).

Jim Maher, *The Flying Column, West Kilkenny, 1916–1921* (Dublin: Geography Publications, 1987).

Patrick Maume, 'Trench, Frederick Oliver 3rd Baron Ashtown', *Dictionary of Irish Biography* (Cambridge: CUP, 2002).

—, 'Gwynn, Stephen', *Dictionary of Irish Biography*.

—, 'Joyce, William Brooke (Lord Haw Haw)', *Dictionary of Irish Biography*.

—, 'Trench, Frederick Oliver 3rd Baron Ashtown', *Dictionary of Irish Biography*.

Timothy G. McMahon (ed.), *Pádraig Ó Fathaigh's War of Independence: Recollections of a Galway Gaelic Leaguer* (Cork: CUP, 2000).

Conor McNamara, 'A Shopkeepers' League or a Tenants' League? The Town Tenants Movement in the West of Ireland, 1914–1918', *Studia Hibernica*, 36 (2009–10), pp. 135–60.

—, '"The Most Shoneen Town in Ireland", Galway in 1916', *History Ireland*, 19:1 (2011), pp. 34–7.

—, 'Liam Mellows and the Irish Revolution', *History Ireland* (19:4), 2011, pp. 36–7.

—, 'The Most Bitter Struggle of them all: The Clanricarde Estate and Legislative Reform in Ireland', *Journal of the Galway Archaeological and Historical Society*, 67 (2015), pp. 184–201.

—, 'It is the deed that counts ... Liam Mellows' "True Story of the Galway Insurrection"', in Marie Mannion (ed.), *Centenary Reflections on the 1916 Rebellion, Galway County Perspectives* (Galway: Galway County Council, 2016), pp. 132–50.

—, 'The War of Independence in Connacht'; 'War of Independence in Galway', , *Atlas of the Irish Revolution* (Cork: Cork University Press, 2017), pp. 600–7; 614–18.

Liam Mellows, *Notes from Mountjoy Jail* (London: Irish Communist Group, 1925).

Patrick Melvin, *Estates and Landed Society in Galway* (Dublin: Edmund Burke, 2010).

Miriam Moffitt, *Soupers and Jumpers: The Protestant Missions in Connemara, 1848–1937* (Dublin: Four Courts Press, 2008), pp. 159–73.

—, *Clanricarde's Planters and Land Agitation in East Galway, 1886–1916, Maynooth Studies in Local History* (Dublin: Four Courts Press, 2011).

—, 'Protestant Tenant Farmers and the Land League in North Connacht', in Conor McNamara, Carla King (eds) *The West of Ireland: New Perspectives on the Nineteenth Century* (Dublin: History Press, 2011).

Richard Mulcahy, 'The Irish Volunteer Convention, 26 October, 1917', *Capuchin Annual* (1967), pp. 400–10.

—, 'Conscription and the General Headquarters Staff', *Capuchin Annual* (1968), pp. 383–6.

David Murphy, *The Irish Brigades, 1685–2006* (Dublin: Four Courts Press, 2007).

Cormac Ó Comhraí, *Sa Bhearna Bhaoil: Gaillimh 1913–1923* (Gaillimh: Cló Iar-Chonnacht, 2016).

—, K.H. O'Malley (eds), *The Men Will Talk To Me, Galway Interviews by Ernie O'Malley* (Dublin: Mercier, 2015).

Séamas Ó Conghaile, *An Leacht Nár Tógadh* (Baile Átha Cliath: Coiscéim, 1982).

Batt O'Connor, *With Michael Collins in the Fight for Irish Independence* (London: Peter Davies, 1929).

Peadar O'Donnell, *There Will Be Another Day* (Dublin: Dolmen Press, 1963).

Martin O'Donoghue, 'The "humdrum little town"? Tuam at Easter 1916', in Marie Mannion (ed.) *Centenary Reflections on the 1916 Rising: Galway County Perspectives* (Galway: Galway County Council, 2016), pp. 181–96.

Ella O'Dwyer, *The Rising of the Moon, The Language of Power* (London: Pluto Press, 2003).

Tomás Ó Fiaich, 'The Irish Bishops and the Conscription Issue, 1918', *The Capuchin Annual* (1968), pp. 351–68.

Colm Ó Gaora, *Mise* (Baile Átha Cliath: Oifig an tSoláthair, 1944).

Mícheál Ó hAodha, Ruán O'Donnell (eds) *On the Run, The Story of an Irish Freedom Fighter, A Translation of Colm Ó Gaora's Mise* (Cork: Mercier, 2011).

Seán Ó Luing, 'The German Plot, 1918', *Capuchin Annual* (1968), pp. 377–81.

Ernie O'Malley, *On Another Man's Wound* (London: Anvil Press, 1936).

—, *Army Without Banners, Adventures of an Irish Volunteer* (Boston: Four Square, 1937).

William O'Malley, *Glancing Back: 70 Years' Experiences and Reminiscences of a Pressman, Sportsman and Member of Parliament* (London: Wright, 1933).

Rosaleen O'Neill, 'Modern Languages', in Thomas Boylan, Tadhg Foley (eds), *From Queen's College to National University: Essays on the Academic History of QCG/UCG/NUI, Galway* (Dublin: Four Courts Press, 1999), pp. 360–83.

T.P. O'Neill, 'Political Life: 1870–1921', in Michael Hurley (ed.), *Irish Anglicanism 1869–1969, Essays on the Role of Anglicanism in Irish Life* (Dublin: Allen Figgis, 1970).

Seán Ó Tuairisg, *An Mine: Sléacht agus Ár i gCois Fharraige* (Gaillimh: Cló Iar-Chonnacht, 2017).

Paul Ricoeur, *Memory, History, Forgetting* (Chicago: UCP, 2004).

Lennox Robinson (ed.) *Lady Gregory's Journals, 1916–1930* (New York: Macmillan, 1947).

Bridget Ruane, 'Memories of my Early Years in Cahercrin, Craughwell', *Beginnings Magazine* (Galway: Presentation College Athenry, 1982).

George Rude, *The Crowd in History: A Study of Popular Disturbance in France and England, 1730–1848* (New York: Serif, 1964).

Erhard Rumpf, A.C. Hepburn, *Nationalism and Socialism in Twentieth Century Ireland* (Liverpool: LUP, 1977).

Desmond Ryan, *Seán Treacy and the 3rd Tipperary Brigade* (Tralee: The Kerryman, 1945).

Joshua A. Sanborn, 'Unsettling the Empire: Violent Migrations and Social Disaster in Russia During World War I', *The Journal of Modern History*, 77:2 (June 2005), pp. 290–324.

Amartya Sen, *Identity and Violence: The Illusion of Identity* (London: Allen Lane, 2006).

Burton E. Stevenson, *The Charm of Ireland* (New York: Dodd, Meade & Co, 1913).

Paul Taylor, *Heroes or Traitors?: Experiences of Southern Irish Soldiers Returning from the Great War 1919–1939* (Liverpool: LUP, 2012).

William Irwin Thompson, *The Imagination of an Insurrection, Dublin Easter 1916* (Oxford: OUP, 1967).

Charles Tilly, *The Rebellious Century, 1830–1930* (London: J.M. Dent, 1975).

Charles Townshend, *The British Campaign in Ireland, 1919–21, The Development of Political and Military Policies* (Oxford: OUP, 1975).

—, 'The Irish Republican Army and the Development of Guerrilla Warfare, 1916–21', *English Historical Review*, xciv (1979), pp. 318–45.

—, *Political Violence in Ireland: Government and Resistance Since 1948* (Oxford: OUP, 1983).

Pauric Travers, 'The Priests in Politics: The Case of Conscription', in Oliver MacDonagh, T.W. Mandle, Travers, (eds), *Irish Nationalism and Culture, 1750–1950* (London, 1983), pp. 161–81.

Jackie Ui Chionna, *He Was Galway, Mártín Mór McDonogh* (Dublin: Four Courts Press, 2016).

Tony Varley, 'Agrarian Crime and Social Control: Sinn Féin and the Land Question in the West of Ireland in 1920', *Whose Law and Order? Aspects of Crime and Social Control in Ireland* (Belfast: Sociological Association of Ireland, 1998).

—, 'A Region of Sturdy Smallholders? Western Nationalists and Agrarian Politics during the First World War', *Journal of the Galway Archaeological and Historical Society*, 55 (2003), pp. 127–50.

—, 'Irish Land Reform and the West between the Wars', *Journal of the Galway Archaeological and Historical Society*, 56 (2004), pp. 213–32.

—, 'Tom Kenny and the Agrarian Dimension of the Galway Rising', *Farming & Country Life, 1916* (Galway, 2016), pp. 23–8.

—, 'The Eclipsing of a Radical Agrarian Nationalist: Tom Kenny and the 1916 Rising in County Galway', in Marie Mannion (ed.) *Centenary Reflections on the 1916 Rising, Galway County Perspectives* (Galway, 2016), pp. 92–113.

Mary Anne Vaughan, 'Finding Constable Whelan: An Incident From 1916', *Ossory, Laois and Leinster*, 4 (2010), pp. 231–5.

Brian M. Walker, *Parliamentary Election Results in Ireland, 1801–1922* (Dublin: RIA, 1978).

Michael Wheatley, *Nationalism and the Irish Party: Provincial Ireland, 1910–1916* (Oxford: OUP, 2005).

Cumann na mBan, County Galway Dimensions (Galway: Galway County Council, 2016).

'No Reduction, No Rent, The Story of Woodford and the Archbishop of Dublin on the Plan of Campaign', *The Pall Mall Gazette Extra*, 30 December 1886.

Newspapers

Connacht Tribune
Freeman's Journal
East Galway Democrat
Galway Express
Irish Independent
Irish Times
Tuam Herald
An t–Óglach

Parliamentary Papers

Returns Showing How Farms from which Tenants Were Evicted on Certain Specified Estates Since the 1st May 1879 were Occupied at the Time of the Inquiry of the Evicted Tenants Commission; and on the 1st Day of May 1903, H.C., 1903 [Cd. 173], lvii, p. 505.

Tenth report of the Royal Commission Appointed to Inquire Into and Report Upon the Operation of the Acts Dealing with Congestion in Ireland: Evidence and Documents: Appendix to the Tenth Report: Minutes of Evidence Taken in Counties Galway and Roscommon, 18th September to 4th October 1907, H.C., 1908 (Cd. 4007), xvii, p. 5.

Bill to Facilitate the Provision of Land for Certain Evicted Tenants in Ireland, and for Other Purposes Connected Therewith, and to Make Provision with Respect to the Tenure of Office by the Estates Commissioners; Amendment by Commission, H.C. 1907 (HC. 258), ii, p. 129.

Eleventh Report of the Royal Commission Appointed to Inquire Into and Report Upon the Operation of the Acts Dealing with Congestion in Ireland; Digest of Evidence, 1908, H.C., 1908 (Cd. 4089), xlii, p. 587.

Report and Tables Showing the Number, Ages, Conjugal Conditions, and Destinations of the Emigrants from Each County and Province in Ireland During the Year 1910; Also the Occupations of the Emigrants, and the

Number of Emigrants Who Left Each Port in Each Month of the Year, H.C., 1911 (Cd. 5607).

Census Returns for Ireland, 1911, Showing Area, Houses, and Population; Also the Ages, Civil or Conjugal Condition, Occupations, Birthplaces, Religions, and Education of the People Province of Connaught, County of Galway, H.C., *1913* (Cd. 6052, 6052-I, 6052-II, 6052-III, 6052-IV, 6052-V), cxvii, p.1.

Criminal and Judicial Statistics for Ireland, 1912, xvi, H.C., 1913 (Cd. 6916), lxxvi, p. 659.

Report on Recruiting in Ireland (Cd. 8168), H.C. 1916.

Agricultural Statistics of Ireland; With Detailed Report for 1914, vii., H.C., 1916 (Cd. 8266), p. 621.

Report and Tables Relating to Irish Migratory Agricultural and Other Labourers for 1915, p. 4, H.C., 1916 (Cd. 8386), xxxii, p. 815.

Agricultural Statistics, With Detailed Report, For Ireland, p. 9., H.C., 1916, (Cd. 8266), xxxii, p. 621.

Irish Land Acts, 1903–09: Report of the Estates Commissioners for the Year from 1st April, 1917, to 31st March, 1918, and for the Period from 1st November, 1903, to 31st March, 1918, with appendix, p. iv, H.C., 1919 (Cmd. 29), xxiv, p. 137.

Irish Land Acts, 1903–09: Report of the Estates Commissioners for the year from 1st April, 1917, to 31st March, 1918, and for the period from 1st November, 1903, to 31st March, 1918, with appendix, p. 28, H.C. 1919 (Cmd. 29), xxiv, p. 137.

Archival Manuscripts

Hardiman Library, NUI Galway
Letterfrack/Leenane, Landing of arms at (POL2, NUIGA).
Loughnane Brothers (Pol 4/7, NUIGA).
UCG College Annual, 1917.

UCD Archives
Patrick Moylett Memoir (P78, UCDA).
'Jack Feehan', Notebooks of Ernie O'Malley (P17b, 113, UCDA).
'Jack Comer', Notebooks of Ernie O'Malley (P17b, 136, UCDA).
Papers of Margaret and Father Tom Burke, Castlegar (P30/34, UCDA).

National Library of Ireland
Clonbrock Papers (MS 35,781; MS 35,782; MS 35, 784, NLI).

Geraldine Plunkett Dillon, Untitled manuscript, Geraldine Plunkett Papers (MS 33,731, NLI).

Handwritten manuscript by Francis Hynes (MS 15,289, NLI).

Irish National Volunteers: Order book, 1914–1916, Maurice Moore Papers (MS 9,703, NLI).

Unpaginated manuscript, Pádraig Ó Fathaigh Papers (MS 21,288, NLI).

Typescript Notes by Pádraig Ó Fathaigh (MS 21,289, NLI).

Liam Mellows to Joseph McGarrity, 9 January 1920, McGarrity Papers (MS 17,628/8, NLI).

Correspondence of Lady Mahon, 1925–8, Mahon Papers (MS 47,903/4, NLI).

Papers of the Galway Branch of the IUA, Mahon Papers (MS 47,874/2, NLI).

Correspondence of the Galway Branch of the IUA, Mahon Papers (MS 47,874/17, NLI).

Liam Mellows, New York, to Ms Herbert, dated 10 February 1919, (Uncatalogued material, NLI).

Bureau of Military History

Bureau of Military History Witness Statements.

Larry Lardiner, 'History of the Irish Volunteers in Galway' (BMH CD 151.3).

Military Service Pension Board Records

Military Service Pension Board Pension Awards and Applications.

Easter Week 1916 County Galway (A/21/4/A).

Easter Week 1916 County Galway (A/21/4/B).

IRA Nominal Rolls (RO/1-611).

Cumann na mBan Nominal Rolls (CMB/1-165).

West Yorkshire Archive Service

Clanricarde Papers, Harewood Archives, West Yorkshire Archive Service, Leeds.

Galway County Council Archives

Statement of DI Heard at Inquest into death of Constable Patrick Whelan (GS 15/01, GCCA).

Minute Book of the Galway County Council (GC1/02, GCCA).

Minute book, Galway branch Sinn Féin (GS13/01, GCCA).

Irish Volunteer, Galway Corp, Minute Book, 27 July – 5 October 1914 (GS01/02, GCCA).

National Archives Ireland
Joseph Kilbride to Chief Secretary regarding Rebellion in Galway (CSORP, 5611/7872, NA).
Damage to Property Compensation Act 1923; Registration of Claims (2D/62/60-69, NA).

National Archives, Kew
General Administration of the Army in Ireland (WO 35, TNA).
Hostile Acts or Outrages, HQ 5th Division (WO 35/93A/2, TNA).
HQ 5th Division, Location of Troops (WO 35/93A/2, TNA).
Courts Martial of Civilians (ACT-BRO, WO 35/121, TNA).
Military Courts of Inquiry (WO 35).
Irish Grants Committee (CO 762, TNA).
County Inspectors RIC Monthly Confidential Reports (CO 904, TNA).
Dublin Castle Special Branch Personality Files (CO/904, TNA).

House of Commons Hansard Archives
Hansard 5 (Commons), The Parliamentary Debates (Fifth Series), 1909–42.

RCB Library
Register of Births, Kilmacduagh, 1874–1967.
Register of Births, St Nicholas Parish, Galway.
Ballymacward Vestry Book, 1891–1940.

Private Collections
Jack Comer Papers (courtesy of Una Kavanagh, Moycullen).
Cleary Family Papers (courtesy of Sean Cleary, Athenry).
Corporal Stephen Diviney Papers (courtesy of Éamonn Gilligan Snr, Craughwell).

Index